Joseph B Walker
804 E. 3rd St.
Bloomington,
Indiana

RELIGION AND HEALTH

THE MACMILLAN COMPANY
NEW YORK · BOSTON · CHICAGO · DALLAS
ATLANTA · SAN FRANCISCO

MACMILLAN AND CO., LIMITED
LONDON · BOMBAY · CALCUTTA · MADRAS
MELBOURNE

THE MACMILLAN COMPANY
OF CANADA, LIMITED
TORONTO

RELIGION AND HEALTH

By

SEWARD HILTNER

NEW YORK

THE MACMILLAN COMPANY

1947

To

HELEN JOHANSEN HILTNER

"She openeth her mouth with wisdom,
  And in her tongue is the law of kindness.

"The heart of her husband doth safely trust in her,
  And findeth no lack of gain."

Proverbs 31:26, 11.

INTRODUCTION

This book attempts to survey religion's relationship to health. During one of my summer vacations in college years I was a surveyor—or rather I held the rod and plumb-bob while the engineer sighted them through his transit. Every now and then I asked for a chance to look through the instrument myself. Fortunately for the road we were laying out, the engineer did not take my observations alone as authoritative, but he seemed to understand that my rod-holding would be more efficient if I had an occasional view through the transit.

Twenty years ago there were few writings about religion's relationship to health which were both scientifically sound and theologically literate. Now there are many. But this very number may be confusing, since most of them quite naturally deal only with certain parts of the field. Occasionally one wants to look through the transit himself. This is what I have tried to do, and I hope the eye-piece has been properly focused for others.

Throughout religious history there have been intimate connections between health and religion. In primitive days the religious leaders were also the guardians of health. Christian institutions have always played a major rôle in the care of the sick. But from the latter part of the Middle Ages until quite recently religion and health grew further apart. This division reached its climax in the nineteenth century. By that time most medical workers had a materialistic philosophy of health, and religious workers generally kept their religion away from their health. For example, they so "spiritualized" the healing ministry of Jesus that one got the impression of Christianity only as a vague kind of "motivating influence," so far as health was concerned.

When science began to turn its search-light on mental and emotional symptoms, the gap between religion and health at first became greater. Psychiatrists and psychologists, studying many of the same data religion observed, drew different conclusions. "Psychologizing" religious reality out of existence was not infrequent.

But then the picture began to change. The physiologists studied emotion in a new way, and began to learn of the intimate connections between the body and attitudes. The psychologists and psychiatrists saw complexes rooted out, but patients got well only when positive and constructive interests also entered the situation. Preventive medicine came into being, and the preventive mental hygiene movement was born. Instead of asking merely why people got sick in body, mind or spirit, the scientists began to wonder why so many did not.

Meanwhile religion was itself discovering some things. Ministers began to use the new insights of science in their understanding of persons they were trying to help. Some physicians, like Richard C. Cabot, envisioned a new kind of religious ministry to the sick. The religious education movement incorporated some of the scientific findings into its work and philosophy. Prayer came to be thought of vitally and constructively in connection with health. Clinical training for the clergy was started.

During the past twenty years these constructive movements have made progress. The idea of health as related to the whole personality has been increasingly accepted. For a time the contributions seemed to be largely in one direction, the application of health insights to religious work. Within the past five years, however, the situation has changed. What religion does for health, concretely and specifically, is now also beginning to receive the attention it deserves. The religious approach has increasingly been put to work by the bedside, in the study, the home, the prayer room, and its findings are emerging with a new authority.

Not all the aspects of the relationship of health to religion are considered in this volume, but the fields chosen cover a wide area. Among the important subjects deliberately omitted are: religion and public health; theology and health; methods of research and of education; descriptions of specific projects; and basic theoretical material.

So far as possible, the attempt has been made to emphasize what is generally agreed on by careful students of the field. More different points of view, conflicts and misunderstandings exist than this treatment might suggest. I have not tried to avoid differences, but have endeavored to lay a foundation at the points where a foundation actually exists—after which controversy may be productive. Even so, it can scarcely be suggested that everyone will agree with everything.

I am far from being an "expert" at first-hand on all the subjects considered. Yet my efforts to see the field as a whole have so impressed me with the importance of trying to do this that I have not hesitated, with help and counsel from others, to write on some subjects where my personal knowledge is not large. The reader will find part of the clue in the foot-notes, which are inversely proportional to experience.

I want to express deep appreciation to those who have aided me by reading and commenting on part or all of the book, whose names are listed in a later section. Their suggestions have been of great value.

I want also to express appreciation to the Commission on Religion and Health of the Federal Council of Churches, which encouraged me to go ahead with preparation of the volume.

It is my work as Executive Secretary of the Commission that has brought me in touch with the many aspects of religion's relationship to health.

Finally, I want to thank those who have helped with typing and editing of the manuscript: Gladys E. Pratt, Frances C. Rogers, Helen G. Yergin, Janet Y. Rogers and my wife, Helen Johansen Hiltner.

SEWARD HILTNER

New York City
July, 1942

CONTENTS

CONTENTS

RELIGION AND HEALTH

CHAPTER I

WHAT MENTAL HYGIENE TEACHES THE CHURCH

The Mental Hygiene Movement. Early in the nineteen hundreds a young Yale graduate went to work on Wall Street. He was somewhat addicted to periods of elation followed by feelings of depression but never thought of himself as having any particular mental difficulties. Yet before he quite knew what was happening, he found himself locked up as a patient in one of the mental hospitals of Connecticut.

Soon he began, like the prodigal son, to "come to himself." So far as he could see, no one had done much to help him along toward recovery. But he was getting better.

As he looked about him, he found many of the patients intelligent, cultured and educated. Very few of them were the "raving maniacs" he had assumed were committed to "insane asylums." He soon became convinced that they were sick and not just crazy.

Some of them got better, and some became worse, but no one seemed to know why. Beers was shocked at the conditions for care and treatment of patients, but even more by the realization of the man-power that was going to waste. It was fortunate that the main question he asked was: What can be done outside the hospital to prevent these disorders from arising in the first place? [1]

When Clifford Beers was discharged, he had a new purpose

in life, what Adolf Meyer soon appropriately called "mental hygiene." His sincerity and persistence, and the fact that he had some solid facts to support him, finally won him a hearing from several prominent physicians, psychiatrists, clergymen and laymen. In 1908 the Connecticut Society for Mental Hygiene was born, and a few months later the National Committee for Mental Hygiene was organized, with Beers as secretary, a post which he retained until recently. Many other states and cities soon organized local mental hygiene groups, so that today there are twenty-six societies functioning in the states and forty in counties and cities.

Those who have guided the movement to date have in large part been psychiatrists—physicians who specialize in the study and treatment of mental difficulties—and these leaders have been among the best physicians in the country. Thomas W. Salmon, Clarence M. Hincks, Arthur H. Ruggles—these are but a few of the great medical names which adorn the roster of the mental hygiene movement.[2]

It was natural that the movement should be led at first almost entirely by psychiatrists—except for Beers—and that it should concentrate on improvement of conditions for the treatment of mental illness. Conditions were so bad in most mental hospitals that something had to be done about them. Although the mental hygiene movement wanted to concentrate on work out in the community which would prevent people from getting to mental hospitals at all, it had obviously to attack the most urgent problem first. The National Committee must have felt at first a little like the early researchers on malaria—wanting to find whatever it was that spread malaria so people would not get it at all, but having an obvious duty to give quinine treatments to persons who had already contracted the disease.

The fascinating and readable story of the mental hygiene

movement can be read more completely in such volumes as
A Mind That Found Itself[1] or *The Mental Hygiene Movement.*[2]

Largely as a result of this movement, there are few states today
whose mental hospitals are not very different places from what
they were in 1908. Clean and hygienic living conditions, adequate privacy, competent psychiatric and medical attention,
trained nursing, occupational therapy—these and many other
services are part of the treatment of any good state mental hospital today. It must be added, however, that a large number of
hospitals are still deficient at one or more of these points.

But a prime purpose of the movement was prevention. Once
steps had been taken to improve the care and treatment of those
already sick, it was possible to study means of detecting such
illnesses in their earliest stages. This gave rise to the "guidance
clinic" movement, at first for children and later for adults as
well. For it was soon found that a trained eye could often detect
in children signs—or "symptoms" as the physicians call them—
in behavior and conduct suggesting the presence of difficulties
and conflicts beneath the surface which, if unchecked and un-
solved, might later emerge as mental illness or delinquency.
These signs, the mental hygienists soon learned, were not only
overt anti-social conduct—that is, the kind which irritates parents or teachers—but often excessive shyness, seclusiveness, dependence on other people, or day-dreaming.

Clinics were set up, at first on an experimental basis; then as
the value of this method was proved, on a more permanent
foundation. They were affiliated with general hospitals, with
mental hospitals, with schools, with juvenile courts, with community welfare departments, with whatever community agency
seemed most appropriate. In the earliest days they often had to
be set up "on their own" until their value was proved. Children

who for some reason were not getting along well at school, at home or at play, were brought to the clinics by parents, by teachers, by physicians, by social workers, or by clergymen. Here was a boy of nine who had spent three years in the first grade but had not yet learned to read. His teacher thought he was "just dumb" but decided to try the clinic. It was found that his intelligence was considerably above the average, that his difficulty grew out of his natural resentment at the way he was treated by his dominating and even cruel father who refused to accept the fact that his son was not the brightest boy in school. Once this was discovered, the situation was mended with remarkable speed.

As the guidance clinic movement progressed, it became concerned with improving "the social adjustment of children for the sake of this social adjustment itself." [3] That is, it very soon outgrew the idea that it needed to justify its existence solely on the basis of the ills which it might prevent. This change from the necessary negative to the even more pertinent positive has not been recognized sufficiently as yet by the public.

Such clinics today have several trained workers on their staffs. At the head is the psychiatrist, who is a physician duly licensed to practice medicine and who has chosen disorders of the mind and mental deviations as his medical specialty. It might be said that in the clinic he is in charge of finding out what is wrong with "the whole person," and of all treatment. Then there is the psychologist, whose particular job is psychometrics, or the measurement of anything which can be measured about the personality. He uses tests to measure intelligence, aptitudes, interests, vocational abilities and the like. Although there are limitations on the value of tests, the psychologist knows these well and works within them. The social worker is the third member of the team. It is his job to go into the home, the school, the playground and the church to study the living human relationships which have governed the life of the child. There is of course a general physician to check thoroughly the physical condition of the child.

There are several hundred such clinics in the United States today, not all of them, of course, doing the same quality of work nor with equally adequate staffs. Many of them deal with the problems of adults as well as with those of children. In addition, almost every first-class general hospital now has a "psychiatric" or "neuropsychiatric" department which ministers to ambulatory (persons who need not be put to bed) patients whose troubles or illnesses are of mental or psychic origin.

In addition to these regular clinics set up under the inspiration of the mental hygiene movement, many similar "detector" (because they try to detect difficulties before these become too serious) and treatment services have been established. "Visiting teachers" are social workers who are also trained in educational and child psychology. They are attached to a school or a school system, and work with children referred to them by teachers. They also try to educate teachers to be more "mentally hygienic" in their teaching and to recognize the signs of difficulty so that problems can be ironed out in their early stages.[4] The tremendous value of visiting teachers has been amply demonstrated even in rural areas.[5]

"Visiting nurses" are in part a result of the mental hygiene movement. They are trained nurses who, if they have recently attended the schools of public health nursing, have also studied social work. Attached to hospitals, visiting nurse societies or community welfare departments, they go into homes on call to give nursing assistance. If their training has given them the insight, and if they have time, they may be able to look at the situation as a whole as well as give ordinary nursing assistance.

Where the nurse cannot be of help herself in a family situation, she may refer the person or family to other agencies than her own. Potentially at least, she is an important factor in the mental hygiene movement.

Social and community welfare agencies in general have been much influenced by the mental hygiene movement, and one standard by which their competence may be judged is the relative degree of attention they have paid to mental hygiene. Their workers should become aware that troubles are not always what they seem, or not *entirely* what they seem. If they deal with a person whose trouble is poverty, it is often nothing but poverty in origin; and the problem can be solved only through the economic channel, by securing a job or at least adequate financial assistance pending a job placement. But as likely as not, the poverty may be due to unemployment, and the inability to get a job may be due in part—but only in part—to defective eyes, or to a spirit of defeatism brought on by a nagging wife, or to a dreamy outlook which can do little except look back on "the good old days." It is increasingly true that the activities of trained social workers are being oriented to the mental hygiene point of view, which is at least an indirect result of the mental hygiene movement.

Indeed, few people in America have been uninfluenced by the mental hygiene movement, whether they realize it or not, whether they are professional people or laymen. Physicians in general practice are paying increasing attention to the "patient as a person" rather than to a lung named Larkin or a stomach named Stein, with person attached.[6] Considerable progress has been made along this line in the schools.[7] The work of the National Committee for Mental Hygiene in orienting the program of teachers' colleges to mental hygiene is outstanding.

Judges and other court officials are beginning to pay some

attention to mental hygiene, although legal procedures are so slow to change that one seldom sees real mental hygiene in operation except in juvenile courts. Most of our courts still permit the senseless and barbarous practice of having psychiatrists appear as "expert witnesses" *for* the defense or *for* the prosecution. Should they not be independent witnesses, there to give the truth as they see it, not acting for or against either side? The recognition of mental hygiene by law and the courts is still in its infancy.

To skip over many other important aspects of our social life which have been influenced by the mental hygiene movement, what has it done for and to the church? In the first place, it has taught ministers that mental hospitals are really hospitals for the treatment of mental illnesses and difficulties, and not "insane asylums" in which to put people who have "forever lost their reason." Ministers have in turn been able to help many a family to understand that commitment of one of its members to a mental hospital is not a psychological death sentence but a necessary step leading in the direction of improved health and strength of the whole personality. Many ministers do not yet know this, and that is unfortunate. It is important that ministers and others in the church learn to know what a mental hospital is and to change their older "unreasonable" attitudes toward it.[8]

Many ministers have also learned from the mental hygiene movement that there are resources available in their communities which may help people whose difficulties are not so deep-seated as to make them need care in a hospital.[9] It has helped to open their eyes to the value of mental hygiene and psychiatric clinics, to family welfare agencies, to visiting teachers and visiting nurses, to school psychologists and psychiatrists, to character-building groups such as the Boy and Girl Scouts, the Boys Clubs of America and others, to recreational facilities and workers, and to many other aspects of modern constructive "social welfare." Some of these activities—the Boy Scouts for example—have been more or less incorporated into the program of the local church. But ministers have learned that not all of them should be so affiliated, and that it is in no sense a failure on the part of the minister or of the church to "refer" people to these various agencies for proper care and assistance.

The mental hygiene movement has begun at least to teach both ministers and church school teachers that religious education programs cannot produce strong Christian character or "spiritual health" without paying some attention to mental health.[10] It may be merely the high spirits of childhood which makes Jimmy Bold, aged eleven, throw spitballs in Sunday school; but the chances are that Jimmy is rather angry about something down underneath of which he is not quite aware himself. But in any case, he will have some discipline applied to him because the "symptoms" are disturbing to other people. His condition is much more fortunate, therefore, than that of Edward Meek who always knows his lesson but who sits with his head down, never speaks unless spoken to, goes to and from the church by himself. A teacher may think him a model pupil, and so he is, if model pupils are those who do not irritate the teacher and who gratify her "ego" by making her think that her teaching of facts has been so good that it sinks in. But with his unsocial, shy, and dreamy symptoms, he may be on the road to serious mental illness unless something is done to "socialize" him. He may absorb all the facts in the world about religion, or indeed seem to have all the proper attitudes toward religion and toward ethical conduct, and yet be a better candidate for a mental hospital than for the Kingdom of Heaven. As this kind of situation is being increasingly recognized for what it is, church schools are becoming healthier, both spiritually and mentally. Character, after all, is a matter of living and not merely of knowledge. It is of little value if it is only a façade or false front. It has to reach down to the lowest depths of personality and up to the greatest heights if it is to give that steadfastness which we believe character may be.

Among the other ways in which mental hygiene as a movement has influenced the church, several will be suggested in later chapters. It has had a significant influence, for example, on pastoral counseling, on sermons, on church social work, and even on church administration. This influence should be even greater in the future.

Mental Hygiene as Knowledge. Mental hygiene is not only a movement, as we have discussed it above. It is also a content of knowledge, as we shall discuss it here. And as we shall see later, it is also a point of view toward human problems and difficulties.

The need for human beings to grow and make adjustments in the face of living is as old as human history. But because psychiatrists were the first modern contributors to the content—or knowledge—of mental hygiene, it has generally but erroneously been thought that the content of mental hygiene was made up entirely of psychiatry.

This is not true, as has been increasingly demonstrated in the mental hygiene movement by the growing importance attributed to the mental hygiene work of psychologists, social workers, ministers, teachers, nurses, physicians and others. Actually the content of mental hygiene has come from many kinds of studies, among them psychology, social work, general medicine, physiology, sociology, anthropology, philosophy and theology. Psychiatrists deserve the major share of the credit for the newer principles, but mental hygiene is not merely "practical psychiatry."

Hygiene is the study and practice of those conditions which

make for "health and efficiency" of the body. Mental hygiene is by analogy the study and practice of those conditions which make for "health and efficiency" of the mind. In so far as mental hygiene is a content, therefore, it studies the conditions which tend to produce mental health.

Some of the conditions which make for mental health in our society have already been suggested in the illustrations of children becoming socialized or learning to express their resentments. Perhaps some broader principles may be stated.

It is fairly obvious, in the first place, that a person's mental health will be improved either by the removal of those difficulties, within or without, which have made it poor, or by the development of some kind of resistance within to help him face the difficulties. That is, mental health depends upon the environment, upon insight, and upon what we call for lack of a better name "strength of character."

The environment may be outside or inside the person. To speak of the outside environment, one's mental health is considerably influenced by such factors as his economic and social status. Thus, one brought up under marginal economic conditions may have his whole outlook so restricted by this that his mental health will be considerably affected. Conversely, one brought up with every economic advantage will tend to have great difficulty if his economic advantages are suddenly decreased. The influence of the external environment is so plain that it needs only to be mentioned.

The "internal environment" is also important. Such factors as one's size, physical efficiency and muscular coordination have a significant though not always conscious influence upon his outlook. More subtle but equally noteworthy is the taking into oneself of the cultural environment as well as the physical environment. Anthropologists have shown that there are persons who would be considered mentally healthy in one group, representing a certain culture or way of life, yet who would be considered very sick or out of place in another.[11] Most of us, for instance, would be "deviates," or people out of place, in a tribe of cannibals, to use an extreme example. For the basic demands which the culture or society makes on the individual do not remain outside him where they started but are taken in and accepted by him as part of himself. The situation becomes even more complicated in a culture like our own, where the demands of society are themselves often in conflict, and therefore the individual gets within himself a picture of a social environment which frequently makes impossible demands upon him because its claims contradict each other.

A person who is mentally sick can be improved, generally speaking, if the environment can be improved. One who has had no real love offered him by his external environment and no sense of security by his internal environment, can ordinarily be helped if real love in some measure can be given him. Even more important, if the external environment has been mentally healthy, what is taken in by the individual will probably be healthy mentally. Real preventive mental hygiene will have been given—even though no one has thought it out in those terms.

Dr. Bernard Glueck is reported to have said, "Man is a creator of his environment but he is also a creator of it to a much greater extent than he is willing to admit. The human being carries within himself, within the constitution of his own nature and tendencies, those elements which make possible the trouble itself as well as its cure." [12]

Mental health depends also upon insight and "strength of character." No environment can or should be of the type which fails to make demands of the person in terms of adjustment and readjustment. Growing up in any environment is a process of facing and overcoming difficulties. Either these difficulties must not be so great as to overcome the person, or the inner resistance must be sufficiently developed to stand in the face of them.

We used to think that "will power" was the secret of this inner resistance. Our environment said, for example, that we should not be hostile to our parents, no matter what they did to us. This we accepted in our internal environment and hence as a part of what we thought of as "ourselves." If we felt hostile feelings arising, we kept telling ourselves that these were so wrong that the desire of our "self" would alone push out our feelings of resentment. We now know that this is not true. Man can not lift himself by his own bootstraps.

What then is really the heart of this inner resistance, if it is not will power? The element of it which mental hygiene has done most to demonstrate is "insight." In the instance mentioned above, if there is a hostility toward one's parents which is trying to express itself, we assume that this has had causes and did not "just grow." Mental hygiene has shown not only that a refusal to face the inner hostility adds fuel to its subterranean flames, but that some understanding or comprehension of how it developed and what function it now serves is often in itself enough to make the trouble disappear. Thus insight is not only getting the "gunpowder" out in the open so that it will explode harmlessly, but developing a method of looking at the causes of personal difficulties in such a way that one develops new sources of psychological resistance.

It is not enough to have "insight" in a merely intellectual sense. Insight must be emotional and volitional as well—that is, it must result in feelings and actions. The whole "pattern of character" of the person must be transformed in favor of giving him increased ability to meet the difficulties which he will be called upon to face. Perhaps "strength of character" may give the wrong suggestion; for what we want is a character which is related to the reality of the difficulties which the person actually faces.

In the broadest sense, therefore, much of the content of mental hygiene is very old. And much of what has been taught is today proving sound. Yet some of the new knowledge demands significant changes in our thinking; and it is natural that the content of mental hygiene should be thought of especially in connection with those elements which have tended to change traditional ways of looking at things.

What are some of these newer elements which modern mental hygiene has emphasized? We can mention but a few of the more important, and do little more than mention them. One concerns the development by the child of emotional independence from his home. The ill effects upon a child of a home where there is constant conflict are too well known to need comment. But they may at times be less harmful than those of a home in which a cloying and absorbing kind of affection (which is no affection at all) ties a child so rigidly that he never really achieves emotional independence. One psychiatrist spoke of "idealistic but infected homes," where parents have what seem to be high ideals but which are in reality devices for setting up the most exploitative kind of relationship with their children.[13] Children should have an increasing independence from their parents throughout their entire period of growth, so that by the time they reach adult stature they may establish adult relationships with their parents. If this process is impeded, one is likely to find either continued dependence or a complete reaction against dependence which indicates that emotional dependence still exists. This should not be understood to mean that parents and children should have no emotional ties; that is absurd. But it does mean that the ties change character so radically that the adult relationship is "independence" compared with the complete "dependence" upon his parents with which the child started life.

This suggests to the church, of course, that it must be discriminating in its judgment of the beauty of parent-child relationships. The parent is no ogre, as some have erroneously concluded after reading certain popular psychological works. But it is not infrequently to the church that an exploitative parent will look for approval of his conduct on some such ground as that he is ill and that his child must therefore continue to live with him and remain unmarried. The church can understand also that adolescents who do some deed which looks as if they hated their parents are probably expressing something which should have been expressed long before, and that with insight into why they did it they may soon be on far better terms with their parents than ever. To condemn them for the outbreak is to condemn them for their move in the direction of health.

Another "specific" of mental hygiene relates to the method for dealing with fears, anxieties and hostilities. It has been said that fear and anger in the young child are much the same thing, but that fear occurs when the object is bigger than the child, and anger when it is smaller. We do know that in adult life some fear and anger are necessary, fear in the face of really fearsome things, anger in the face of genuine injustice. In terms of character traits we might call the desirable development of fear "reasonable caution," and of anger "sensitivity to true unfairness." Mental hygiene has stated unequivocally that neither fear nor anger are in themselves evil, and that it is no virtue to refuse to recognize their existence in oneself.

It has long been recognized that expression of fear or anger without control was perhaps man's most dangerous enemy, but before mental hygiene there was no general recognition of the fact that the surest way to let fear and anger be expressed in inappropriate ways was to bottle them up and deny their existence. So true is this still that most adults cannot recall the resentment or anxiety they sometimes felt as children toward their parents. This does not mean that one should be a kind of introspective Diogenes of anxiety or anger, looking within for every small sign of emotion so that it may be expressed. But it does mean that these emotions, when unrecognized and undealt with, can wreak havoc in a person's life without his even being aware of their existence.

This suggests that the church should recognize that fear may cast out love if love does not cast out fear. In a practical sense, it means the church must not condemn anger out of hand, but teach more about the social and spiritual expression and control of anger. Anxiety, for example, must not be praised on the ground that if a mother really loves her son she will have anxiety about his welfare; of course she will be concerned about him, but anxiety is irrational fear which impedes and blocks one's health and efficiency. The church should know, too, that no words or formulae can change anger or fear into love, or indeed control them in any effective sense. Only personal relationships can do that when they are of the sort which touch the emotional centers of gravity.

In the process of teaching children how to bring their emotions under regulation, the larger problem is to learn how to do this in a constructive rather than a repressive manner. Mental hygienists point out that the infant is a "little savage." He is neither moral nor social as yet. To treat emotional responses in a child as moral issues, meeting them with threats, shame, punishment or other "reactions," is to put something else above "the fundamental needs of the child." [14] Much remains to be learned along this line, but Lawrence K. Frank suggests one essential, "The child needs reassurance and reinforcement in meeting the strange, unknown, and apparently threatening experiences that confront him, and if we will accept the child's view that a situation is terrifying, even if we see that it is not, we can avoid the usual mistakes. Nothing is so helpful as learning some effective method of dealing with a fear-producing situation." [15] Children are not merely candidates for adulthood; but they will reach a mature adulthood only if the emotions of childhood have been dealt with constructively, which implies something quite different from the casual "good and bad" distinctions. This principle has implications for the mental health of children in wartime.

Mental hygiene also suggests something about the nature of security. Security, the church has said, does not consist in the abundance of the things which one possesses. Mental hygiene adds that neither does it consist in the abundance of the love that one professes, or that is professed on one's behalf. Oversolicitude is not genuine affection, and cannot buy true love. Love can only be received by giving it, and not by bribing it. Here is a real reinforcement of what the church has taught, but with an emphasis the church has sometimes avoided on the ground that it is negative teaching. If it is negative to see through hypocrisy, so be it.

Mental hygiene teaches something, too, about guilt, sin, and forgiveness. The recognition that one has fallen short is the beginning of salvation, the church has said. This idea is reinforced and clarified by mental hygiene. Unless a man wants to be helped, to be improved, no one can help him. But one may feel guilty not concerning what he should feel guilty about, but about something else. This is a form of self-deception, and one which is perhaps as much in evidence within the church as without. Mental hygiene leaves plenty of room for morals, but little for moralism.

Of course mental hygiene principles and content suggest much more to the church, but these samples may be suggestive.

The Mental Hygiene Point of View. The essence of the mental hygiene point of view is less difficult to grasp than to state. It is that human behavior and conduct spring from real causes and that within limits these can and should be understood in the interest of the greater health of the individual and of society. It might be called the technology of human conduct. It is not the science, for that is found in psychology, psychiatry, and the other studies which provide the knowledge which mental hygiene uses. It is not the morals and ethics, for those deal with certain premises or presuppositions which in some measure mental hygiene can neither approve nor disapprove. There is some difference of opinion as to how far a more positive philosophy of human conduct may be identified with mental hygiene. For example, could there be a mental hygiene apart from democratic axioms about the worth of the individual? As individuals we all believe that life without these would not be very worthwhile; but are "we" speaking as mental hygienists or as philosophers, or both, when we make this judgment? It seems probable that mental hygiene in the future will increasingly have a basic philosophy, and that therefore it will operate more frankly in the realm of values and ethics. Here there need be no conflict with the church if we realize that mental hygiene tends to make minimum statements, leaving it to institutions like the church to make more broadly positive statements.

If one believes that human conduct has specific causes, he cannot then be content to say merely, "Johnny is like that," and believe that he has explained anything about Johnny. He wants to know what there is in Johnny and his relationship to his environment which may help in understanding this particular behavior. Increasing experience suggests that some of the real causes can always be found, and that they provide the lever with which to lift Johnny out of the morass in which he may be.

Neither can the mental hygienist profess to *explain* specific conduct on the basis of God's will. A mother whose son became delinquent, who felt she had always done everything possible for him, would be consoling herself rather than getting at the truth if she should say, "It is God's will that he should do this." In a very profound sense the will of God is concerned with all man's acts, but not in this superficial way.

The mental hygiene point of view cannot commend the attitude of "I felt like doing it; so I did it." This, too, assumes a short-circuited principle of explanation. To believe that one's feelings alone constitute the only necessary rules for guidance of conduct is a distinct reversion to the unsocial condition of the infant.

All of these points of view war with that of mental hygiene. For they assume that human conduct has no antecedents which can be seen and disclosed; and therefore that when there is difficulty one seeks to excuse it or describe it away rather than to understand it. To mental hygiene understanding is at least partial control; and without some control there can be no mental hygiene.

The question which mental hygiene asks of all behavior and conduct is, "What does it mean to this person and to his social relationships?" Under this lies the assumption that, however bizarre or perverse or stupid it may seem to us or to society in general, it has some meaning to the individual. We want to understand what this is. We want to understand it more than we want to judge or evaluate it. Judgment and valuation are necessary, and that is where ethics and religion come in. But to evaluate before we have some understanding of the meaning is like a physician's prescribing for a fever alone—which may be caused by a thousand different things each of which has a different cause and therefore requires a different treatment.

The basic conviction of the mental hygiene point of view involves faith or deep confidence, buttressed by a good deal of evidence. It is that conduct can be understood, and therein lies the hope of mental health. Each new situation or person involves a test of that faith; but to deal with ourselves and our fellows without it is to commit the sins we are too blind to see.

Summary. Thus far mental hygiene has given most of its attention to therapy and early detection of disorders. In the future it will certainly become more preventive. Such preventive activity is basically educational. It therefore behooves the church to pay special attention to this aspect of mental hygiene, since the church's own work is so largely educational in the same sense.

The church has learned much from the mental hygiene movement, the constantly evolving principles of mental hygiene, and the mental hygiene point of view. It can learn much more, and practice a great deal more. It might be wise to re-emphasize the fact that mental hygiene does not teach the church merely to do more or even better personal counseling. That is advisable, but it is only the beginning. The mental hygiene functions of the church in the early detection of disorders are more important for it than therapy; and those relating to prevention and education are still more necessary and urgent.

These two are great potential allies; but unless they are real allies, they may in the future become competitors. They should not and need not compete with each other. Mental hygiene has suggested new insights which may change some misinterpretations which have been made of Christianity; but it has reinforced and given new weight to many of the basic truths. The process of interaction should continue to be constructive and fruitful.[16]

CHAPTER II

SOME CONTRIBUTIONS OF RELIGION TO MENTAL HEALTH

Mental hygiene teaches something to religion and the church. But religion and the church make contributions to mental health whose full significance is not always realized. "There is no integration which compares with that which comes from religious faith or a religious goal," says Dr. Earl D. Bond.[1] "I am convinced that the Christian religion is one of the most valuable and potent influences that we possess for producing that harmony and peace of mind . . . needed to bring health and power to a large proportion of nervous patients," reports Dr. J. A. Hadfield.[2]

Fortunately we are not wholly dependent upon the personal testimony of scientists for our conviction that religion does have a constructive influence for health in the widest and deepest sense. Such quotations as these, which could be multiplied, perform the service, however, of indicating how we may look for the kind of contribution which religion in practice makes to health.

A Word of Theory. It is tempting to equate mental hygiene with science, and to suggest how (in this particular field of health) religion basically makes contributions to science. It would be easy to show that mental hygiene, a product of science, in its new aspects at least, has certain limitations imposed upon it, and that religion overcomes those limitations. It would tend to fortify our confidence in religion to show that to some extent its approach to reality is different from that of science, though it may be even more valid. It is tempting, in short, to discuss the basic philosophic and theological issues involved in the relation of religion to science, in the light of our special concern with mental health and hygiene.

The fact that our approach will be more practical is no reflection upon the relevance of these basic issues. But such discussion involves a rather different scope from that contained in the rest of the book; and it becomes increasingly difficult for us to understand how discussion of that sort can be significant without some prior attention to the kind of essentially practical wisdom which is being considered here.

Further, mental hygiene is not to be equated with science. It is more nearly akin to technology than to science; but it includes certain assumptions which are more closely related to religion than they are to science. In following this course we are not assuming an attitude of theological or philosophical positivism. We do not intend to suggest, in the basic sense, a particular theology or philosophy, though we shall inevitably deal with certain ideas and practices which seem to be basic to all Christianity.

In approaching the contributions which religion makes to mental health in a practical sense, we must accept two points as preliminaries. The first is that religion is not interested merely in health. Theologians would say that health, even considered in the modern sense as relating to body, mind and spirit, is not the same as salvation because health is "temporal" or in time, and salvation is "eternal" or beyond time. As George A. Buttrick puts it in reference to prayer, for example, "The integration wrought by prayer goes far beyond health of body and 'mind'—

as it must to be convincing, for all men must die."[3] Assertions of this kind are true in the basic sense in which they are intended. It is also true that Kagawa in the slums of Tokyo spent his physical health, perhaps to the advancement of his spiritual health—yet that which he enhanced can hardly be completely circumscribed under the idea of health. Christianity says there are other things than health which man should seek. But it does not say that one should seek ill-health.

It may be worth while to indicate that the notion of "mental health," which carries the idea to most people better than does the broader and more accurate "health," is a misleading notion. Modern medicine and related clinical studies have shown that the old idea of mere "physical health," which we usually term "health," has less meaning than we once thought.[4] The first, and still dominant, tendency was to suggest the new implications by talking of "mental health" in addition to "health" or "physical health." This was helpful, but it tended to connote that it is chiefly the brain which is involved, or that mental and spiritual well-being are distinct from each other. The more recent, and more accurate, trend is to refer to "health" as including the whole personality, or as we inadequately try to describe it, health of body, mind and spirit.

An eminent physician writes, for example, "Man is a unity of mind and body, and medicine must consider this unity. Physiology, chemistry, and biology cannot alone or together explain all the intricacies of illness. The disturbances of mind and body cannot be dealt with separately; they form two phases of a single problem. To insure health for the individual, the mind as well as the body must carry out its natural functions freely and efficiently."[5]

This is a practical statement and a very important one; and we shall do well to consider the contributions religion makes to health in this sense, rather than in the restricted sense of "physical health" as if this were independent of what we call our mind and what we call our spirit.

Healthy and Unhealthy Religious Interpretation. The second introductory point we must make is that not all interpretations (and living out) of religion, or of Christianity, are healthy, in the sense of health of the whole personality. We have not spoken of "healthful" or "unhealthful" religion. This is because use of the latter words would imply a discussion of the relative soundness of something before the individual got hold of it (or before it got hold of him). It is certainly true that healthful and unhealthful religions exist. We believe that a religion glorifying the state as a substitute for the Christian God is possessed of, to say the least, unhealthful tendencies. We believe that a group which, wittingly or not, emphasizes but one aspect of the nature of God to the exclusion of all others is unhealthful, as for instance sentimental groups which say that because God forgives, he never judges. Yet our concern will not basically be with the healthfulness or unhealthfulness of religions; that has been well written about in other places.[6]

What we must also recognize is that a Christianity sound in ideas can be so interpreted by an individual that its total influence upon his personality may be progressive or regressive, healthy or unhealthy.[7] This fact has always been recognized by the church in some measure. As early as Cyprian's time, and probably earlier, we find church leaders counseling against those who went out to seek martyrdom. Heinrich Suso, the great mystic of the Middle Ages, was refused canonization because he had "punished" himself too much and too severely. Thus the basic impulse to sacrifice for the sake of the Christian cause was recognized as sound, but the church had to be sure it was "for the Christian cause" and not for something else of which even the individual might be unaware. Catholic theology in particular has paid a good deal of attention to such matters.

But in recent years we have been aided to more basic standards for judging whether or not an individual is interpreting his religion soundly. A few suggestions about the criteria for distinguishing healthy from unhealthy religion are in order at this point.[8] We suggest six criteria.

A healthy interpretation of religion must be related to the whole personality. To put it one way, it cannot profess to deal only with the soul or spirit and neglect the mind and body. There are still people who believe that because Christianity deals with the eternal and the hereafter it has no relevance to the state of things today. There are literalists who are concerned with salvation of the "soul" to the neglect of the individual's total welfare, which includes neglect of what is, from our point of view, his spiritual welfare. Much moralistic interpretation of religion belongs in this class. One might of course point out kinds of religion which emphasize the body out of proportion to the mind and spirit, and even some which emphasize the mind out of proportion to the body and spirit. But the danger of confusing the soul with the personality is more common in Christianity. That indicates both its high state and its great danger. The thing that we are forced to call the total personality is that to which our interpretation of religion must be related.

Religion must grow up intellectually and emotionally along with other aspects of the personality. This is not done by interpreting religion after the Alice in Wonderland fashion, believing seven impossible things before breakfast. If religion sometimes means dealing with the impossible, it is never *because* it is impossible. The great lawyer, Clarence Darrow, used to make annual trips to the Chicago Theological Seminary to discuss religion with the students. With his keen mind, he would nevertheless spend these sessions explaining why he did not believe in a religion that none of his hearers had believed in since their earliest childhood. An interpretation of religion which insists on remaining at a childhood level can only be rejected. There is no more point in "disbelieving" in a childish conception of God than there would be in disbelieving in what such concepts as "earth" or "art" meant to one as a child. There is no point in disbelieving in the existence of one's father merely because the early belief in the father's omnipotence has changed with the growth of the personality. Religious ideas and feelings must grow up.

Emotional interpretations of religion must be non-substantive. Religion, for example, which replaces the need for earthly friends by supplying heavenly friends may be more healthy than no religion at all, but it is still rather far down the scale. Religion brings something which nothing else can bring; it is not a substitute for something else. It is not even a substitute for relaxation, for work, for clear thinking, for making autonomous decisions, or for suffering. It is not an automatic solver of problems. In the basic sense it does aid in the solution of problems, but not as a substitute for hard work, clear thought or courageous decision. It strengthens the resources with which problems may be solved, though it may at times heighten the urgency of the problems.

Religion must be interpreted in a non-compulsive manner. There are some types of individual attitudes which are often incorrectly praised as fine religious outlooks. One of these is submissiveness, which is essentially a strategy of trying to get what we want by making the other fellow sorry for us. Mental hygiene has told us enough about the dangers of the model child to indicate where the danger lies. Power-getting through the institutions of religion is also sometimes, though not so frequently, mistaken for a sound religious outlook. There is the church worker who expresses his craving to lead or to boss only in church activities because there he does not expect to meet with the open rejection of his ambition which he would find elsewhere unless it were curbed by social interests.

More subtle than either of these compulsive ways in which religion may be used is trying to coerce others into loving us. Love and security are fundamental needs. The only proper way in which to get them is first to give them, as they are first given us in childhood. If the child is not given them, he will—indeed he must—try somehow to get them. Parents who have themselves been frustrated in receiving affection and basic psychological and spiritual security may not be able to receive spontaneous affection from their children because they cannot give it; and they may use coercive methods without any awareness of what they are doing. They may bribe, threaten, appeal to pity or to duty—and all of these techniques may be bound up with religion. Where religion is interpreted in this way, the soundest of Christian ideas will be badly warped. The compulsive element lies in the fact that, although the strategy is self-defeating, under the circumstances it seems impossible to do anything else. This is the spiritual vicious circle at work, and it scarcely makes for a healthy interpretation of religion.

Religion must be interpreted in an outgoing manner. It must have a social as well as a divine object. "Emotional atheists" are usually people who feel so defensive about themselves, who have so little real regard or affection for what they feel themselves to be, that they cannot possibly have regard or reverence for anything outside themselves. Love and regard (which are akin to reverence in the high Christian sense) are not quantities; and in their deepest respects are not to be compared with energy concepts. For one cannot love others (or God) more as he loves (or has regard for) himself less. Without some self-affirmation there can be little affirmation of others or of God which is not spurious.[9] Religion is sometimes interpreted in such highly individualistic terms that it has no real social reference. To call religion "what man does with his solitariness," as A. N. Whitehead does, is one thing which in a deep sense is true.[10] To say that religion has no social reference is quite another, as is the common attempt to separate a mythical "individual" from a "social" gospel. Religion will furnish no technical answers to questions of social organization, politics, and the like; but it will have reference to change in social organization as much as it will to the basic concerns for the status of others represented in all welfare movements. Religion must be interpreted in an outgoing manner.

There are other ways of approaching the standards by which healthy and unhealthy interpretations of religion may be judged. Those which are exploitative are unhealthy. Those which condemn the sinner as well as the sin are unhealthy; those which insist that the sinner is always more and greater than the sin are healthy. Those which are sentimental are unhealthy; as are those which are purely rationalistic or voluntaristic. Religion is not all idea, not all will. Those religions which make the personality equivalent to consciousness are unhealthy; those which see the whole personality as something both greater and deeper are not. Those which refuse to face the potentialities for evil in men as well as in man are unhealthy; but so are those which refuse to recognize the potentialities for creation and for good.

These criteria are not purely those of mental hygiene, nor yet of religion. They represent the infusion of mental hygiene discoveries into the pattern of critical Christian thinking. Without first accepting some basic Christian notions, it would be difficult to accept them all. It is beyond our scope to go much into their background; yet their character is sufficiently self-authenticating for us to recognize the validity of most of them even as they are stated. The fact that mental hygiene reinforces most of them indicates only the increased necessity for religion and mental hygiene to work co-operatively together.

It is useless, however, to consider the contributions which religion makes to health without this prior attention to the relative healthiness or unhealthiness of the interpretations of religion. Religious ideas themselves are important; and various criteria, including those of healthfulness or unhealthfulness, may be used to evaluate them. One idea is not as good as another. But there has rarely been any danger of forgetting that fact, while there is a constant danger of forgetting the importance of the emotional interpretation. Hence this introduction.

Contributions of Religion to (Mental) Health. If we suppose that a person has a healthy emotional interpretation of religion, in what ways specifically does his religious life support and enhance the health of his whole personality? Though it is valuable to put our question in this way, we should not forget that none of us have "perfect" interpretations of religion. What we do is to share certain insights into the nature of reality and our relationship to it. We are speaking, then, as much of religious outlooks and practices that may be used for improving health as of simple examination of the influence of fine religious insights that are already present.

Religion can help us to integrate our lives around the reality in the universe which is both rational and meaningful—the only worshipful reality. We have already hinted that a lack of reverence or regard for what we mean when we say "God" is a kind of blocking of natural trends toward socialization, and that it is caused by a feeling of lack of psychological safety and security within ourselves, however unconscious this feeling may be. If a person is tied up in knots inside himself, will power will not get him out. But if religion can give him a vision of something in the universe that he can actually trust, whose counterpart is within him, he is on the road to finding himself. In such a person's background we usually find that he has not been able to trust—that his mother, for example, sometimes slapped him and sometimes gave him a stick of candy when he disobeyed instead of being consistent about his emotional education. How can such a person be other than tied up in knots? Of course he may take religion and tie it up inside himself along with everything else. But if he gets any vision of that meaningful reality which does protect and bring safety and security, it may help him so that he will look for the evidences of security and affection that exist all about him and even in himself.

In the second place, religion may help to get a person away from egocentricity, infantilism, and the avoidance of responsibility. We know today that most stages in the development of the emotional life are accompanied by more pain than we later remember. Once the transition is made—for example, from the gang period to adolescence—the rewards of growth and new responsibility normally outweigh the pains. But in some persons the pains are so great as to retard the progress, and in none of us is the process entirely smooth or complete. And it is so easy to relapse into infantilism or avoidance of responsibility about some things that are especially important. Here religion may enter. Suppose that one's particular infantilism is to ridicule the prevalence of great social needs, to feel at least that paying attention to them is none of one's own business. And suppose that such a person somehow gets a vision that the brotherhood of man is the other side of the coin of the fatherhood of God? His social conscience can no longer be so dull or so dulled.

If we had a text, it would be this story from Luke: [11] "When a foul spirit goes out of a man, it roams through deserts in search of rest, and when it finds none, it says, 'I will go back to my house that I left.' And it goes and finds it unoccupied, cleaned and in order. Then it goes and gets seven other spirits more wicked than itself, and they go in and live there, and in the end the man is worse off than he was before." The search for health cannot be merely negative. Mental hygiene cannot be merely a process of chasing out evil spirits. For if the devils are chased out and nothing constructive takes their place, the person may indeed be worse off than before. Never take away a man's crutch unless you can say, "Take up thy bed and walk." And religion can say this, metaphorically speaking. Healthy religion ought to furnish the constructive occupant of the house. The evil spirits must be driven out, to use the ancient language, but that is only half the story. Health in our usage is not merely negative—it is also positive; but it cannot be truly positive unless the perspective and the insights of religion are a part of it.

There are two ways to reach a goal. The first is by keeping one's eyes fixed on the goal and ignoring the obstacles. This should be known as the cracked-shin method. The other is by keeping one's eyes on the obstacles and failing to look at the goal. We may call this the wander-in-circles method. Neither is adequate in itself. The great contribution of mental hygiene to religion is the pointing out of the real nature of the obstacles; the great contribution of religion to mental hygiene is the vision of the goal.

Healthy religion makes a person less dependent upon mere cultural standards, upon keeping up unconsciously with the Joneses. We live in a culture in which a man's worth is too often judged by his skill in competition, and especially in economic competition. The spiritual danger arises at the point where a man has no other standard of judgment of his own worth than that which this cultural pattern, as one example, can give him. We know of the suicides that followed the beginnings of the depression in 1929. Though there were individual factors involved, we could see in the lives of such persons the confusion of their success in competition with their very selves. They had no concept of themselves except that which they accepted from their culture; hence they had no resources when the crisis came. We are not implying that personal worth should be independent of what one does, but that one should have standards in reaching an estimate of one's personal worth which go deeper than that of keeping up with the Joneses. If religion gives anything at all, it is this. What but this can give the magnificent courage to our brother religionists and others who are being persecuted in many lands? This is what we mean by the religious statement that every man is a child of God. There is something in the nature of the universe that in itself gives life meaning and value. We call recognition of this freedom, but it is not merely freedom of the will. We would do better to call it freedom of the whole personality.

We thought once that "human nature" was what we saw in people around us and in ourselves, that is, that our culture was the only possible expression of inherent "human nature." Those sciences which have contributed to mental hygiene, and in this case anthropology in particular, have shown us how false this is. Through the comparative study of different cultures, we have seen that inherent human nature is a great deal more flexible than anyone fully realized even a half-century ago.[12] Such conclusions suggest an additional reason why religion is not simply something to reinforce the prohibitions or commands laid upon the individual by the prevailing environment. Underlying assumptions become more necessary than ever. Science can make clear to us what the prevailing assumptions are, and that these are not the only possible ones; but only religion can furnish the kind of assumptions needed to transform the unsatisfactory elements in our own culture. Religion can speak of what life ought to be as well as pass judgment on what it is.

We know, too, that religion may actually have a marked influence upon the processes of healing. With mental and spiritual symptoms this scarcely needs proof. But there is also some evidence that religion has an influence upon bodily symptoms and processes. This basic matter is considered at some length in a later chapter.[13]

Worship is a religious method that helps to develop healthy persons, though this is of course not the only aim of worship. Worship ought to and does mean many things; but prominent among them is the sense that an individual thereby becomes one of a community on the level of aspiration. He bows before that which he reverences, not so much to honor it as because it is natural to do so, and he thereby gets a sense of "communion" with all mankind. All high religions believe that this community is not artificial or merely sociological, but that it goes deep into the nature of reality. Worship is, then, a discovery in some measure of the reality of that community. It makes a great difference what one worships. We know now why the early Christians could not worship the symbols of the Roman Empire. For only in religions of the quality of Christianity and Judaism do we find a God who is truly worshipful. Worship itself is a natural activity of man, one of the motivating forces toward which is the desire for fellowship and communion; but it makes a great difference what one worships. For religion cannot be satisfied with reverence of that which is not worshipful, and cannot be interested merely in an integration of personality around ideals that are temporarily successful or efficient but that in the long run are destructive. The integration that brings real health must in the long run be one that corresponds with the nature of the highest reality of which we are aware.

Still another contribution that religion can make to health is in developing what has been called "tension capacity." Children want what they want when they want it. As adults we have to learn that the fulfilment of some needs or wishes must be postponed or even renounced. Thus we must learn to live in situations that would ordinarily produce tension without being tense. This is an inner achievement. No one else can do it for us. This emphasis on self-discipline (which does not mean bowing the head in defeat) rather than discipline from outside is an essential part of all healthy religion. Such religion can help us attain it.

Finally, religion appreciates and helps us to face what may be called the irreducible mystery of life. Fortunately life is not all a mystery; and religion performs a poor service to health if it tries, as has often been done, to create a mystery where none exists, or to seek allegiance by claiming a special hold on mystery. But when all that is said, much of life and experience is still a mystery. One may ignore or deny the mystery, which is blind. Or one may think only of the day when it may be past, which is romantic. Or one may work as the scientist does to make the mystery intelligible at specific points, which is praiseworthy, of course, so far as it goes. But some mystery still remains. Religion first of all faces this mystery as such. At its best, the mystery is never reverenced. We do not worship God because we have no idea of what He is. But the mystery is there.

In the ordinary experiences of life we know that problems must be faced as problems, not evaded or ignored. If one is to have health of spirit as well as of body and mind, one must apply the same principle in this cosmic realm. Emerson said of the great historian, Gibbon, "That man Gibbon had no shrine." A man with no consciousness of the mystery within his existence is ignoring or evading a problem. The proper attitude is, of course, not to magnify the mystery nor to worship it, but to face it as such.

To make a bit clearer the ways in which religion may make contributions to health, we shall give more attention to one of these contributions than has been possible for the others. We select prayer, among the eight or ten religious factors mentioned here, for further consideration, all too brief though our treatment will be.

Prayer and Health. "The power of prayer in the realm of health has hardly yet been tapped," writes George A. Buttrick.[14] In a deep sense, this may be considered the most basic contribution of religion to health, however little we may know about it as yet. For prayer is in fact the deepest well-spring of religion.

In essence prayer is the deliberate recognition of God, or the "practice of the presence of God." The simplicity and reality of prayer have been captured in these words of John W. Suter, Jr.: "If I pause while writing these words and keep very still for a few moments, letting a peaceful frame of mind possess me, making myself aware of the Divine Spirit which pulses through the universe, whose name is Love—that act is prayer. I say no words aloud and it can almost be said that I think no thoughts. I simply 'feel a situation' and invite a mood. Perhaps I shut my eyes while doing this. Perhaps I let them rest on the tree outside my study window, whose leaves dance in the sunlight. Or I might look at a picture on the opposite wall, where tall pines frame a much-loved garden. The only thing that really matters is the one thing which all these acts have in common and which makes all of them prayer: the deliberate putting of myself into a state where my awareness of the Presence of God becomes intensified.

Before I made the pause, while I was still pounding the keys of the typewriter, God was just as much present with me as He was when I stopped and paid attention to Him; for one does not change God by thinking about Him. What one changes by thinking about Him is not God, but the situation. What happens is deliberate recognition." [15]

Before considering specifically how prayer may contribute to health, let us consider an analogy which is, in a sense, more than analogy. Psychoanalysis, that extremely useful tool of emotional surgery when in expert hands, has found that its task is to help bring the elements or patterns of the personality (many of them hidden or obscured) to a level of consciousness where there is a chance of dealing with them in line with the most basic purposes of the whole personality. This statement is not a definition of psychoanalysis or of its aim, but is one important descriptive statement among others that could be made. The process is not, therefore, merely analysis in the usual sense; for helping to put the pieces together, to see the pattern that actually exists, becomes fully as important as finding what the pieces are. It is not only, or indeed mainly, a matter of intellectual recognition or awareness that is involved. Sometimes the patient will not "know" something yet will "register" it somewhere. And at other times he will "know" something and yet not really feel what it means.

Without pushing the parallel very far (for this would do injustice both to prayer and to psychoanalysis), is it not possible that at least a few moments' reflection on it may help us to comprehend what prayer should mean, at least in relation to health? Prayer is a "slant toward health," to use Suter's phrase. It has definite limits adequately suggested in all the good books on prayer. It is not a substitute for life itself. Consider our analogy again. Important though it is, writes Karen Horney, psychoanalysis should not be overrated. "Life itself is the most effective help for our development. The hardships that life forces upon us—a necessity to leave one's country, organic illness, periods of solitude—and also its gifts—a good friendship, even a mere contact with a truly good and valuable human being, co-operative work in groups—all such factors can help us to reach our full potential." [16] So it is with prayer. Its function is its own.

Omitting for a moment the usual connotations of prayer, suppose we think of a practice in mental hygiene somewhat as follows. Before retiring at night our hygienist gives himself several minutes of solitude as complete as his living arrangements permit. Relaxed, he allows his thought to wander, more or less systematically, over the events and feelings of the day that is past. At one point he has a recurrence of his feeling of happiness at having completed a long task. At another he feels a twinge of guilt because of his behavior in an interview, which seems irrational as he now looks back upon it. Now it suddenly comes over him that he gave no thought all day to the agony of millions across the world, not that he was callous but just busy.

As a hygienist he is not concerned to balance the scales, as two successes against two failures. He hopes for a new insight as to why this and that; so that he may be a strengthened man as he steps into the old routine on the morrow. If he is suffering any great stress, he should know that the methods he is following are not enough; he will probably need counsel. But on the assumption that stress is not great, what he is doing is an important act of mental and emotional hygiene; and, if carried out with honesty, will help to bring the result he wants.

Now back to prayer. No one to whom the God of Christ is a reality can go through such a process without linking it up with God. Of course the god may be a small god and the process a superstition. God may be used, too, as a giant bank clerk merely to draw balances for the day. But suppose the process contains awareness of the Christian God from beginning to end. Then we have the beginning of the process of prayer, or a beginning of the "lower levels of prayer," as this is sometimes called. Whether any but the saints ever get far beyond these "lower levels" not even the Gallup poll can say.

How does prayer influence health? We have already suggested one part of the answer—the process itself helps to make real the insights which renew life though with stabs of pain. As we shall see in subsequent chapters, our attitudes are of fundamental importance in reference to the health of our whole personality. Since insights refer to attitudes moving in the direction of truth, what brings insights helps health.

Prayer may also bring us relaxation. This has been more cultivated by the Eastern than the Western religions; but all healthy religion has some comprehension of it. By relaxation we mean the ability to go to bed at night, to relax our muscles, to forget the cares of the day and the morrow, and to go to sleep. We mean the absence of an anxiety that drives the whole person to continuous physical and psychic tension. We mean the ability to alternate work and release in such a way as both to use and to safeguard the "muscles of the mind and spirit" as well as of the body.

Some exceedingly useful material is available on relaxation from the physical point of view, and the physical aspect is important.[17] But it is not all. Cultivation of the power of spiritual receptivity by some such process as the "lower levels of prayer" is as important as learning to recognize and control our muscle groups. Prayer ought to imply relaxation of the spirit which, if real, has an immediate influence on our physical tensions. This is not to say that relaxation is the only aim of prayer; prayer will frequently make us recognize, or be aware of, tensions we have avoided, or even at times produce them. But its long-run

effect is relaxation in the deepest sense of the term; for even
when it produces tensions, real prayer brings the conviction of
the strength to deal with them.

Prayer's real power to help bring health has suffered from
two things, a lack of concrete scientific observation, and over-
statement of what we now know. We are beginning to make
some progress with the former. *How to Find Health through
Prayer* is the title of a recent book which typifies our dilemma
in reference to the latter. Prayer is one factor in finding health
—a more important one than most doctors realize, we believe,
but not so all-embracing as enthusiasts think—but if we exag-
gerate its scope, or what we know of its scope, we put what
intelligent use of it now exists in jeopardy.

Suter writes, "A cold in the head may grow, through several
stages, into pneumonia. Or it may quickly clear up. What will
happen depends on a whole complex of interrelated factors,
among which is the mental and spiritual attitude of the person
who has a cold; and that mental and spiritual attitude in turn
depends upon several factors, among which is the person's religion, and on whether that religion is in good working order.
For religion is lived. It is life lived as in the presence of God;
deeds performed with reference to God, and in His direction;
thoughts thought with reference to God; attitudes offered to
Him.

Religion is, in the realm of the spirit, in the realm of
moods and motives, like athletics in the realm of the body. In
other words, we may properly speak of religious aptitudes, religious skills, religious knack, religious improvement from year
to year. A man's religion is wrought. In the course of his life
he has a religious career (good or bad), just as he might have
an athletic career. And in so far as his religion is in good working
order, he has a slant toward health of body and health of
mind." [18]

We have not even mentioned the usual practical questions about prayer: words or thoughts, regular or irregular, prepared or not, petitionary or not, and the rest. Nor have we referred to the deeper levels of prayer, nor to the distinctively Christian theory of prayer. All that has been done is to suggest some of the main ways in which prayer is related to health, without fully developing any of these directions.

This discussion of prayer, in turn, has offered a hint as to how any of the contributions which religion makes to health could be developed. None of these contributions operates automatically or magically. To be effective, they must follow criteria such as those suggested early in this chapter. When they do, they give a "slant toward health."

Conclusion. We have been able only to suggest some of the contributions which religion can and does make to health. We believe that these contributions are among the most significant, though not the only, functions of religion. In so far as religion helps persons to face realities, and especially realities which are actually or potentially evil, and provides strength or wisdom or courage to deal with them—it leads toward health as well as toward Christian character. Not all religion, not all Christianity, and not all interpretations of sound Christian ideas accomplish this; and one of our first steps in attempting to make the Christian contribution to mental health larger is to recognize this fact. Armed with some comprehension of what kinds of religious interpretations and practices tend to make for health and which do not, we are in a position to consider both the general and the specific contributions of religion to health.

We have dealt here only with rather general contributions. Discussion of specific contributions is continued in various aspects in each of the following chapters. But the modern conception of health is such that it is almost self-evident that sound religion makes an important contribution to it.

CHAPTER III

THE CHRISTIAN WITNESS OF HEALTH AND HEALING

Jesus sent out his disciples "to preach, and to have power to heal sicknesses and to cast out demons." [1] The Christian church has never doubted its obligation to perform both commissions, but the story of what it has done about healing is much less well known than what it has done about preaching.

To Jesus healing was a manifestation of God's redeeming love —it was revelation. "He did not heal in order to commend himself or to overcome opposition or prejudice, for some of his miracles resulted in stirring up opposition and he knew they would so result. He did not heal to attract a crowd, for he sometimes said to those whom he healed, 'See thou tell no man.' . . . He does not seem even to be concerned to make use of the evangelistic opportunity to preach to those he healed. His ministry of healing was not just done casually, as if secondary and unimportant. He put forth both physical and spiritual energy to heal men. He refused to perform works of healing as signs. He is not described anywhere in the Synoptic Gospels as using his cures as texts for his sermons." [2] This profound statement by the Christian Medical Association of India places the proper perspective upon the Christian ministry of healing.

Almost from the beginning of its history, the Christian church had much to do with caring for the sick. After the structure of the Roman state began to crumble, it was the church or some of its organizations which "largely took over the functions of poor relief and of care for the orphaned, the aged, and the sick." [3] After the rise of the monastic movement, it was they in large part who performed these functions on behalf of the Christian community. Special orders and brotherhoods developed to look after social service responsibilities, including, and sometimes specializing in, care of the sick. The first special order of which we have record was founded in Siena in the late ninth century.[4] Two centuries later it had become customary for many parish churches and cathedrals, as well as monastic institutions, to have their own hospitals.[5] This must have been unusually costly and wasteful, however; for by the thirteenth century the special monastic institutions had superseded the parish churches and cathedrals as the maintainers of hospital and other social services. A majority of all monasteries at this time had hospitals, and some even gave a kind of medical training. Most of them cared for the poor and the orphaned as well as for the sick. Not all the hospitals were general, however. "Thousands of them" were for the special care of lepers, since leprosy was common in the Middle Ages.[6]

The Crusades influenced the development of Christian hospitals. Organizations, formed to protect the pilgrims, developed into bodies to care for the sick and afflicted. The best known of these orders were the Knights Templars and the Knights of St. John of Jerusalem, the latter specializing in care of the sick, later becoming known as the Hospitallers. Some of the institutions, founded then, are at least known about even today. Bernard of Menthon, for example, archdeacon of Aosta, founded two hospices for the comfort of travelers in the Alpine passes, which became known as the Great St. Bernard and the Little St. Bernard.[7]

Not all care of the sick was in the hands of the churches and monasteries. Society was organized feudally, and the lords of the manor assumed a good deal of responsibility for the sick as well as for the poor and orphaned, especially in the earlier years of feudalism. In the later years, when cities were beginning to threaten the feudal pattern of life, the large communities began to take increased responsibility for the care of the sick and unfortunate. But there is no doubt that the contribution of the church in all those years was enormous.

One of the darker pages in connection with the treatment of the sick is related to the mentally ill or "insane." Although Jesus does not seem to have made categorical distinctions between the sick and the mentally sick, the church followed the pattern of its day, and did very little for the relief of this group of unfortunates. They were usually driven out of towns; and with the development of cities, only the very "worst" patients were confined in the foul holes that passed for mental hospitals. The church seems not to have had this problem on its conscience; for the same pattern in considerable measure was followed in Puritan New England during the Colonial period and even later.[8]

Medicine was at a standstill or worse during the Middle Ages, considering the Greek physicians as its authorities and doing little or nothing along the lines of empirical investigation. Such new ideas as were developed seem to have come largely from Arabian physicians; but these did not lead in the west to any spirit of first-hand investigation. So intent were the Middle Ages upon following authority laid out in all its details that it was news when the nun Hildegard of Bingen wrote about some elementary botanical observations she had made.

Although there were some signs of first-hand investigation in medicine during the late Middle Ages, it was really not until the

Renaissance and Reformation were in full bloom that "scientific medicine" began to emerge. The churches have frequently been accused, not only of not aiding in this process, but of actually hindering it. Their preoccupation with ancient authority during the Middle Ages, and their misunderstanding of empirical method in later years, are blamed for much of the delay. Opposition to dissection of the human body, for example, on the ground that it was sacred, is said to have held back the first-hand study of anatomy and physiology. There is some truth in such statements, and the church has need to repent here as elsewhere. But there is another side to the story, not only the care of the sick but the concern that the best care possible be brought to men everywhere.

By the beginning of the nineteenth century, the main elements of scientific method had been established in reference to the medical studies, though it is often said that modern medicine did not take great strides until the middle of the century. It was to take another century before it should become clear that medical science was not necessarily linked with a particular philosophy. To some extent the whole nineteenth-century conflict between science and religion involved the medical sciences, and it is only in recent years that that conflict has been considered well on the road to co-operative resolution and solution.

If it seems strange, therefore, that the medical missionary movement did not begin until the nineteenth century, that is not to be accounted for wholly because the general foreign missionary movement was not in full swing until that time, but also because the main principles of scientific method in medicine had not been established until then. In looking back on those days, it is rather remarkable how soon medical followed other missions, and how soon they followed the development of a medicine which could be authoritative on the basis of its method.

Early Medical Missions. The immediate cause of the medical missionary movement was the spirit of Christian compassion for the sufferings of those without medical care. "The suffering of the people in non-Christian lands made such an appeal to missionaries that they began to do what they could themselves to relieve the sick, and called for medical missionaries to come to their aid." [9]

In 1793 John Thomas, a British ship's surgeon, returned from a visit to India where he had been overcome with the suffering of the people there. He joined the English Baptist Missionary Society, and went out as a colleague of William Carey.[10] During the earliest years in India there was not very rapid progress. The great name in Indian medical missions is John Scudder, who went there in 1819, all of whose seven sons became missionaries.[11]

In China the first western medicine was introduced by a British ship's surgeon, Alexander Pearson, who brought vaccination to one of the coastal cities. Another East India Company surgeon, Thomas R. Colledge, opened the first western hospital in China in 1827, the Macao Ophthalmic Hospital. But the real founder of medical missionary effort in China was an American, Peter Parker, sent out by the American Board of Commissioners for Foreign Missions. In 1835 he founded the Medical Missionary Hospital in Canton, which later became Canton Hospital, now a part of Lingnan University.

Parker and Colledge joined forces to found the Medical Missionary Society in China in 1838. They had expansive plans for this enterprise which, while they did not work it out as projected, did succeed in making the home countries conscious of the need in a way that later brought results.[12]

There were only three medical missionaries in China before 1841, but by 1852 there were thirteen.[13] By 1887 over one hundred and fifty medical missionaries had worked in China.[14] Owing to the lateness of women in getting into medical work, and to the necessity to segregate work for men from work for women in the Oriental countries, medical work for women could not be started until after 1850. The first woman physician, Lucinda Coombs, went to China in 1873.[15]

Medical missionary work therefore followed other types of missionary work very rapidly. The American Board did not enter China until 1830; yet Parker established his hospital in 1835. The same situation was duplicated on most other mission fields.

What did the early missionaries find? "Medical missionaries, like other westerners, were kept apart in a secluded area at first, and later remained in compounds, quite aloof, often wholly apart, from the main stream of Chinese life. The newly arrived doctors made little effort to understand the old Chinese practice, or to analyse and use the age-old drugs. Thus, they failed to capture the imagination of the masses." [16]

What is said here of China was true in some degree in all mission areas. The earliest missionaries had little appreciation for the cultures which confronted them, and this seems to have been as true of the physicians as of others. They did not see what later missionaries have been able to see, the basically sound elements even in Oriental medicine, though they might go hand in hand with much rubbish. Edward H. Hume has described the Chinese situation thus: "The thought life of the Chinese is the resultant of millenniums of conflict with the forces of nature and of struggle against human foes, external and internal. It has grown out of adaptation and adjustment, rather than out of analytic inquiry with a view to control and transformation. It would be a mistake to describe it in terms of defeatism and despair. Rather, it is an attitude towards the universe which thinks of all life, human, animal, vegetable, as part of a totality, in which the vital process moves on; while danger, disease, disaster, death, are as normal a part of the universe as health and happiness. The dark and light patches of existence stand side by side, often inextricably interwoven. To accept this and live accordingly, is wisdom; to struggle impatiently, to chafe and strike out in resistance, is simply to misunderstand the nature of the cosmic process." [17] Small wonder that the early physician missionaries sometimes peddled a pill they found hard to sell.

There is no doubt that in the earliest days medical missions were sometimes used as a "bait to trap the unwary." Yet it did not take long before the missionaries themselves saw a deeper reason for their existence than being ancillary to a ministry of preaching. A priceless story comes to us from the Ecumenical Missionary Conference of 1900. "If the Good Samaritan had sat down by the side of the wounded man who fell among thieves, and spoken to him of his sins, and preached the Law and the Prophets to him, our matchless parable would never have been written, and the lawyer would have been as uncertain as ever as to who was his neighbor. But when the Samaritan bound up the wounds, and poured over the bandages oil and wine, the best antiseptic dressing in his power, and then made an ambulance of his ass, and took the injured man to the nearest inn, and made provision for his nourishment and nursing until his return, he became a true medical missionary, and gave to our Savior a luminous illustration of His own Golden Rule." [18]

This attitude goes back a good deal further than is generally realized. As Hume puts it, "The modern medical missionary has come to think of his work not as a means to evangelism, but as a form of witness, an expression of the very deepest of religious impulses. He believes that the entire staff should demonstrate the spirit of Christian love." [19] Albert Schweitzer avoided these pitfalls without refusing to interpret in words as well as in deeds. "As I did not make the smallest attempt to foist any theological views upon them, they soon laid aside all mistrust of me and rejoiced, as did I also on my side, that we were united in the piety of obedience to Jesus, and in the will to simple Christian activity. Not many months after my arrival I was invited to take part in the preaching, and thus was released from the promise I had given in Paris, 'd'être muet comme une carpe.' " [20] Paul Harrison puts it more positively, "Nobody in Arabia needs to be saved from his Mohammedanism any more than men in New York need to be saved from their Greek Stoicism. They need to be saved from their fears and their hates and their pride and their sin." [21]

Early medical missions had no notion that religion and health had very much kinship on scientific grounds. They worked therefore with a kind of handicap which would be impossible for the modern physicians, trained not only in the intricate technicalities of man's body but also having some vision of how man's psyche is related to that body. The early workers were as well trained in the medicine of their day as the physicians who remained at home, but they confronted tremendous problems with reference to giving even the simplest medical treatment to those to whom they ministered. They had problems of organization—getting a place in which to work, tools with which to work, the education of aides, and "public relations," or getting the confidence of nationals. They had to sell their variety of science to those who seemed to operate their lives on the basis of sympathetic magic and witchcraft, or who were thoroughly satisfied with the national system that prevailed in their own land and that depended on an extensive *materia medica*. Nothing in the training of these missionary doctors had prepared

them to expect to find things of value in what seemed superficially to be "superstitions." Even when the wisest of them began
to find hitherto unknown medicinal properties in native drugs,
for example, this principle was not extended to the field of the
psyche. In recent years much more scholarly attention has been
devoted to Oriental medicine, as in Hume's *The Chinese Way
in Medicine*.[22]

The Ecumenical Missionary Conference of 1900 illustrates this
lack of understanding of national medicine. "Medical missions
break the power and destroy the prestige of the medicine-men
and witch-doctors. They teach the true nature of disease and
death, and their independence of the malignant spirits which
are supposed to be their cause. They urge the use of the means
which God has given to men to cure the one and ward off the
other. The *modus medendi* of drugs can often be understood by
the simplest heathen. They can see and partially understand a
surgical operation. When they have once grasped the idea that
their witch-doctors are a fraud, they disbelieve in the demons
which they had invoked. . . . Thus, through beneficence to the
body, the doctor undermines the quackery which has so long
crushed the soul, and unveils the face of a merciful God, who
seeks to save body and soul together from suffering and sin." [23]
This is all quite true but for its lack of understanding of the
meaning of national culture and national medicine.

Religion and Health in Medical Missions. In every one of the
districts to which medical missionaries went, the kinship between religion and health, psyche and soma, the body and the
soul—was taken for granted by the people. Both because of the
obviously detrimental effect of some native religion on human
interrelationships, and the equally bad effect of some native
medicine on physical health—it was natural at first that the
doctors should pay little attention to this kinship. They had too

hard a time getting people to submit to a surgical operation, instead of merely wearing a witch-doctor's charm, to think much along these lines.

It is interesting that the fostering of religion's relationship to health in most of the mission lands has traditionally been in the hands of specialists. The voodoo priest-doctor is, after all, a specialist, as is the Buddhist priest. Besides, they are specialists on "full-time service"! Oriental medicine has changed in this respect through the centuries. For example, the ancient Chinese character for medicine was originally in three parts. In the upper left corner it had a quiver with arrows; in the upper right, a hand grasping a spear; and below, the symbol for sorcerer or wizard. The whole character meant "the use by the priest of potent weapons to kill or expel the demons of disease." [24] Later, the sorcerer symbol was replaced by the symbol for wine, indicating that the practice was no longer confined to priests. Medicine had become a profession as exemplified in the language itself.

If the earliest medical missionaries had had in their armamentarium the knowledge that we possess today concerning psychosomatic interrelationships, it is almost beyond the power of imagination to conceive of what they might have accomplished. The fact is that all medicine, including medicine on the mission field, has been slow to wake up to these connections; and many physicians at home and abroad still class all emphasis on psychological factors as some form of "superstition." [25]

Today the Christian opportunity for medical missions is unparalleled, and that opportunity will be fully accepted only when health's relationship to religion is fully recognized and utilized. Because of the linkage of religion with health from time immemorial in every country of Asia and Africa, the ground is already broken for a more vital and realistic connection between the two when Christianity comes with its message and its work. The national, whether Asiatic or African, has no difficulty in understanding when the Christian leader, even in an area new to Christianity, speaks of the healing ministry of Jesus or of religious ministry to the sick. He may have what the missionary thinks is a superstitious idea of the connections; but if the latter honestly knows and believes there is a connection in a deeper sense than the national realizes—a new day has dawned both for medical and other missions.

Early medical missions were on the defensive about religion's relation to health. If the doctor had to sweat blood convincing a prospective patient that an amulet would not help him while a scalpel would, he was inclined to discount far too much the influence of any psychic or psychological factors as mere superstition, rather than utilizing them and guiding them into more constructive channels. This must have seemed curious to many of the nationals. They knew Jesus had healed the sick without the paraphernalia of modern medicine, which must have been its distinguishing feature to them; yet the followers of Jesus not only would have nothing to do with their means of healing, but discounted all such methods as having any demonstrable efficacy. It is true the missionaries urged prayer, but they seemed to think of prayer as ineffective in the national's sense—certainly they were uninterested in what prayer did for health from the point of view of the Oriental.

It is noteworthy that only within the past few years has any mention been made at missionary conferences and meetings, even at medical meetings, of religion's relation to health. Nothing was said at the great Edinburgh meeting of 1910 or even at the Jerusalem meeting of 1928. Not until the meeting at Madras in 1939 did this subject receive serious consideration on the agenda of a large missionary gathering. Yet there is real reason to feel gratification that this subject has been introduced, and well introduced, into missionary thinking. The soundness, and protection of scientific method and discovery, of the current trend is well indicated in the Madras statement, which read in part: "In the relationship of religion and health lies an imperative call for pioneering. The scope of the hospital's ministry will be enlarged by using specially trained members of the staff to inquire as to the economic, social, mental and religious background of every patient, so that both bodily and spiritual ministration may be provided in ways adapted to the special needs of the individual, both while in the hospital and after leaving it. The hospital would thus become a center where search could be made for ways in which spiritual ministry might aid in bringing full health to patients. We have scarcely crossed the threshold of such a quest as this. We need fuller understanding of the interrelationship of body, mind and spirit. We need continued study and development of the contribution that faith and prayer and religious practice can make to the maintenance of mental and physical health and to the cure of disease. We ask the churches and hospitals to undertake together in selected centers continued inquiry in this significant field." [26]

Even at Madras, in the face of a consideration which was so obviously true to the concern of the scientific method, that of having all humility before what is still unknown, some had a certain timidity. In general, they were those who had had experience with the peripheral Christian healing groups which had paid little attention to medicine and had made exaggerated claims for the methods of the "spirit" rather than those of "science." The way in which this distinction has been misused has given an especial warning to all who would be both Christian and scientific in their approach to this field.

If the high call to religion and health work on the mission

field is to be accepted, what is it that is most needed? We may get insight into this by examining the basic kinds of difficulties which have to date hindered such work. The first has already been referred to, that conception of medical missions as a "bait to trap unwary souls." That notion has disappeared almost entirely. Furthermore, every intelligent student of the missionary movement must realize how much medical missions are needed throughout the world. For example, Henry P. Van Dusen has pointed out that, even at the center of the great Dutch East Indies empire, near Batavia, "the only agency which reaches out in humanitarian help to the millions 'beyond the city limits' is the ministry of health and healing of the Christian Church." [27]

The former Chinese Ambassador, Hu Shih, recently paid this tribute to missions, "As an unreconstructed heathen, I wish to pay my respects to all the Christian missionary workers, Protestant or Catholic, who have aided China during these years of China's war of resistance to aggression. Throughout these years many of the missions have lost their property and have suffered casualties in personnel. Their women workers have been sent away and have suffered great indignities, physical hardships and misery because of wartime troubles. But as far as I know, no missionary worker has deserted his post whether he be a member of the Mission for Lepers or a medical missionary or a teacher in a mission school. Their missions have become centers of refuge for thousands, and in some cases for tens of thousands, of Chinese civilian sufferers, particularly women, children and the aged. It is this spirit of service, this devotion to work, this sympathy for the cause of China's independence and freedom that has won for them the warm admiration, high respect and love of the Chinese people. And I sincerely believe that it is not proselyting, but this truly religious spirit of service that will continue to win the sympathy and support of the entire Chinese nation for the Christian missions in all the years to come." [28]

The second difficulty in the way of a sound and effective religion and health movement on the mission field has been that very few, if any, physicians and other health workers have been trained to develop the religion and health relationship on a professional basis. We must be agreed that "all who take part in the ministry of health and healing should have the best possible professional qualifications for the work they are called upon to do." [29] Comparison of the studies, for example, of Harold Balme in 1919 and Snell in 1934 or Hume in 1938 in China, will indicate how well the medical training and skill of missionary physicians compares with that of those on the home front, and how well it has kept pace with the trends in medicine. This is important, and the way physicians who are home on furlough take up graduate study furnishes an example to physicians at home.

It is also recognized that all workers on the mission field, including medical workers and their aides, should have "adequate training" for religious work. What we see now is that these two types of training should not be held in water-tight compartments. Religion should certainly be the basic, moving force behind the medical work of the physician on the mission field. But if his religion has no intimate connection at a professional level with his medical work, then our greatest opportunity for co-ordination of religion and health is lost.

The missionary doctor, therefore, has a real need, not alone for personal religion, important though that is, but also for training in religion as related professionally to his medical work. Similarly, the nurse needs training in the professional connections of religion with her work, as well as personal religion.[30] We take it for granted that these and other health workers have adequate training in medicine, nursing, etc.

This lays a new obligation upon the religious and educational missionary workers. No longer can they think of the work of physicians and nurses as being wholly unrelated to the spiritual realm. They face a new obligation to learn how their own work is intimately related to that of the health workers. This cannot be done without some training, and it is obviously to such training that the Madras conference was looking when it made the statement which has been quoted.

There is, then, a great opportunity in the medical mission field to demonstrate what the effective relationship of religion and health may be, but comparatively little use has been made of it. Instead, the religious services of the hospital have, far too often, been like a routine chapel exercise in some school where it has not been recognized that the worship service is at the very heart of the enterprise. Each member of the hospital staff may well be trained to understand his position as a religious ministrant. Each day these ministrants—doctors, nurses, orderlies, technicians, and others—may meet for a season of communion in worship, to fortify themselves, as they approach the patients through the day, in ward or dispensary, for a service as full of meaning for the patient's well-being, for his healing and health, as any scientific therapy can possibly be.

There is urgent need that those who go to the mission field as medical workers be trained for and be commissioned for the spiritual ministry they are to render. They do not go out as doctors or nurses who shall also be religious workers. They go, instead, as trained spiritual ministrants, taking the healing of psyche and body as their mission. In St. Luke's Hospital in New York City, over the altar in the chapel that faces the main entrance, are inscribed the words, "Corpus sanare—Animam salvare." This double ministry requires a more searching and prolonged training than has yet been provided for the medical workers of most Protestant missionary societies.

What is most needed is, therefore, as the Madras report suggested, the undertaking in a few selected centers of a new kind of religion and health co-ordination. Prior to this must come some training for religious and medical workers in the professional connections between religion and health. As other chapters of this volume point out, such facilities for training have increasingly been made available; and some missionaries have availed themselves of these opportunities, and have begun to put these relationships into practice on the mission field.

Church and hospital must be related even more integrally on the mission field than at home.[31] In 1936 a group of Chinese Christian leaders pointed to the following facts as the main causes of "incomplete relatedness of church and hospital." [32] First, the churches tend to think of the hospitals as profitable ventures, that is, as ventures that make a profit. Second, church members tend to think that an individual's or church's connection with the hospital furnishes a way to personal or financial advancement. Third, the churches tend to test results in terms only of church membership. Fourth, church and hospital fail to discover each other. Fifth, there is too little concrete collaboration. It is interesting that several of the church bodies in China have recently created National Medical Committees to facilitate church-hospital relationships. These have been very successful thus far, and are a necessary preliminary to more effective relationship of religion to health.

"The ministry of medicine affords tangible and unsurpassable expression of the inner meaning of Christianity. It brings a challenge to the church to furnish special religious workers who have been trained to understand the social and economic back-

ground of every patient, who can discover relevant ways of bringing him a vital religious message. Such an approach is an
essential part of therapeutic procedure, as well as sound religious
ministration." [33] The question is not whether the health worker
will leave all the speaking to the religious worker, as Schweitzer's
Paris advisers apparently suggested, or even in the way the Laymen's Inquiry understood the matter when it recommended,
"The spoken word may have its appropriate place in the hospital.
It is not possible always to dissociate bodily from spiritual
requirements; the wise physician, responsive to the unspoken
needs of his patients, is often able through intimate conversation
to enlarge and enrich the professional service he has given, and
to convey hope and assurance to troubled minds." [34] He is not
a wise physician unless he does this; but we err in thinking of it
in terms of the "spoken word." It is rather a matter of understanding the forces, physiological, psychological and spiritual,
which operate as a unity. Perhaps the medical missionary is, as
Harrison suggests, "an extra-legible edition of the Gospel." [35]
Actions speak louder than words; but our concern is not with
words but with meanings.

There are in all missionary lands today approximately 1100
missionary physicians and 2300 missionary nurses. Nine hundred
of the 1100 doctors are Protestant, and 1200 of the nurses. Two
hundred physicians and 1100 nurses are Roman Catholic. Of the
900 Protestant physicians, about 350, or nearly 40%, are from the
United States and Canada. Of the 1200 Protestant nurses, about
400, or 33%, are from North America. Although the war has
forced some from their posts, most of these are still carrying on
their work. These are impressive totals.[36]

More than thirty of the mission bodies in the United States
and Canada which send out medical missionaries have formed
the Christian Medical Council for Overseas Work, which acts as

the medical division of the Foreign Missions Conference of North America. This indispensable organization is aiding the churches to make their medical service count most by working in co-operation and in co-ordination.

National medicine is improving in mission lands, and governments are taking a more active hand, especially in China. There are signs that missionary health workers will aid in these endeavors, thus improving the entire health coverage of the nation with the special skills they possess. This co-operation is highly desirable.

Medical missionary workers are thinking seriously of the religion and health call extended to them from Madras in 1939. In 1940 the Christian Medical Association of India, Burma and Ceylon heard a paper on "The Relationship of Religion and Health" presented by a well qualified minister and published it in their journal.[37] In some ways the mission lands may be ahead of us!

Many obligations face the missionary health worker. For one thing, Hume points out, "With the coming in of synthetic drugs and the rapid extension of treatment by injection, there is scarcely a town in China where drug vendors do not ply their trade." [38] They have secured a hold on the popular imagination which may be a hindrance to the physician's work. This reminds us of the story of Claude Bernard, sometimes called the founder of modern medicine, who, when working as a young man in a pharmacist's shop, was so shocked to discover that the cure-all drug, "theriac," could be made out of anything and everything that he left the business and eventually studied medicine.[39]

The health workers also face nationalistic differences which existed long before the war. Hume speaks of three schools of medical thought in the minds of nationals: Japanese, German and British-American.[40] These seem to be not unlike sects in clamoring for attention. The missionary has a sectarian problem not only in religion but also in medicine.

Then there is the psychoneurosis and mental disease problem. India has only about twenty mental hospitals, none under church auspices. An editorial from an Indian medical magazine says it is false to think that the slower pace of life in the Orient creates fewer neurotic disturbances. It says, referring to psychoneurosis, "If by this term we include hysteria and neurasthenia it may be argued that psychoneurosis is much more common in the East than in the West." [41] In trying to suggest what may be done about it, the editorial says further, "Most of the patients are up against some difficulty or are failing to face up to life. They need a greater faith. It is no good merely to tell a man not to be anxious. He needs new faith, new trust in a higher being." [42] The medical missionary has an obvious advantage and obligation at this point.

There are other problems, of which war is now the most apparent. But the whole medical missionary enterprise is today without question one of the most noteworthy achievements of the Christian church. If one could cite figures to show the help, and even life, it has given, it would seem well-nigh incredible that so much could be done by so few. One must sum it up much as E. M. Dodd does: "After all that has been said about the healing work of Christian doctors and missions; after we have followed the pioneer across deserts, through forests and over mountains; after we have watched the life-giving work of the hospitals; after we have seen the toiling search for the deadly germ, and then the application of this knowledge to prevent suffering and tragedy; after we have met the fine young men and women who are developing into responsible workers for their own lands; after all this, we can imagine no higher tribute to the work of Christian doctors and nurses than that of a simple

Korean woman patient who said, 'If the Jesus doctrine makes folks treat others as you have treated me, I want to follow the Jesus way.' " [43]

What Medical Missions Teach Those at Home. The Protestant Reformers were much concerned over the matter of "Christian vocation." As has frequently been pointed out, "the priesthood of all believers" did not mean that every man was his own priest, but rather that under certain circumstances, any man could be another's priest. Being called to the ministry of the church was not necessarily a higher calling in the sight of God, therefore, than being called to work for Christ through other professional ways. Robert L. Calhoun has suggested that the most lamentable aspects of secularization in the modern world have come about through loss of the sense of Christian vocation.[44] Is it not possible, or even likely, that if this sense of vocation is to be regained and revitalized, it may begin most significantly in our conception of the true "vocation" of workers for health and healing? The health worker—physician, nurse, or social worker—on the mission field undoubtedly has some real sense of Christian vocation. Under the stimulus of the Christian and the scientific movements for health and religion, this sense of vocation and conviction of its reality should be strengthened and deepened. And is it not possible also that we may have here the beginnings of a new sense of "being called" by all Christians who work to heal the body as well as the mind and spirit? Cannot the medical missionary movement, through a sound but cautious beginning in the field of religion and its professional relationship to health, offer us a new beginning for a sense of Christian vocation on the part of all Christian physicians, nurses and social workers—whether they be in lands across the seas, on the prairies of Wyoming or in the streets of New York?

In the Dutch East Indies, all physicians and nurses have been regularly "commissioned" for their work at a service of worship. Herein lies a symbol of the reality of Christian vocation in the various health professions, one that might well be adopted in other parts of the mission field. It may not be too much to hope that eventually some kind of symbolic recognition (whether of this or some other type makes little difference) may indicate through an outward sign the inner spiritual grace which obviously ought to motivate and guide the activity of every Christian health worker.

The first thing medical missions need, therefore, from the point of view of religion and health, is an even stronger conviction than they and their supporters now have that their service is integral and central within the ongoing life and work of the Christian church. This implies that they are badly needed, and how badly it is almost impossible to imagine if one has not seen at first hand some of the emaciated bodies and bedraggled souls which have been made healthy and radiant across the world through the influence of Christian medical missions. If they are needed within five miles of Batavia, the center of what has been called the most human empire in the world, the need for them across wholly untouched regions of the earth is so great as to be no longer questioned.

It is not unlikely that in the future government hospitals in many of the native lands which now depend largely on missions for medical service will increasingly provide basic health services for their populations; though in the judgment of all expert students of the subject this will be a long time ahead in most lands. But unless the world is lost in chaos, this will come as it has increasingly come in our own country. What, then, may be the function of medical missions? At this point we must look at what has happened in our own country, with the increased secularization of hospitals and other health services, even those which are under Protestant auspices, at the failure of many such hospitals to adapt themselves to the changing social scene so that they continue to make a supplementary or distinctively Christian contribution rather than being competitors, striving to maintain their institutional status against the advancing wealth and power of government-supported institutions.

In this country the tide at last has turned. Increasing attention is being paid by Protestant hospitals to their distinctive function, and there is every reason to believe that in them the Christian concern for health and healing will be a co-operative, albeit a more distinctive, contribution in the immediate future than it has been in the recent past. This should offer some suggestions to medical missions. They need not go through a period in which they will simply be fighting defensively for their existence as institutions if they profit from the mistakes which the Protestant institutions for health and healing have made in this country. If a few of them start now, as there are real signs that they are doing, to keep their distinctively Christian contribution at the forefront of their task, at a professional as well as at a personal level, then there needs to be no period in which they merely fight to save the institutions. Their distinctively Christian contribution would then be so apparent, and indeed so much in line with modern science, that no matter how social conditions improve, so far as provisions for health and healing care are concerned, they will still continue to make the most vital and lasting contribution possible in terms of following out Christ's command to heal the sick.

If medical missions, along with the entire missionary enterprise, are not ready to move ahead after the war, the eventual health—physical, mental and spiritual—of missions may be endangered or lost. What we now know about the relation of religion to health is a tremendous tool in the hands of the medical missionary movement which should help it to meet whatever changed conditions may result from the unparalleled incursions of war. Jesus still commands the Christian church to heal the sick. A new message of modern science about the ways in which religion is related to health may come out from the home lands to the mission field. Coming from the mission field to the home lands should be an increasing consciousness of the way in which all health work should be under the vocation of God, so that here, as abroad, it is not the minister who prays and the doctor who heals, but the minister and doctor who, hand in hand, summon the healing power of God for the sake of the broken bodies and spirits of mankind.

CHAPTER IV

THE RELATION OF CHRISTIANITY TO THE MAINTENANCE OF HEALTH AND THE CURE OF ILLNESS

I. SCIENTIFIC BACKGROUND

Most people believe in a vague way that religion may have a curative influence upon illnesses. But if we are asked how, what, when or where, we are likely to hedge, or to respond with some story of a cure brought about presumably by prayer *after all else had failed*. We do not want to become fanatics, and we think the groups which seem concerned to apply religion only to curing illness are wrong and misguided. We believe in medicine in connection with all illnesses of whatever kind. But our vague ideas about the relation of religion to illness sometimes become almost as "magical" as those of some of the borderline groups. As we shall see, sometimes religion can help after other things have failed; but that is an exceedingly minor part of its function in connection with illness.

We are more ignorant of the influence of "psychic" factors upon illness and health than we need to be. "Psychic" may seem a queer word suggesting séances and table-tilting in the dark. But it is derived directly from the Greek word "psyche," which referred to the personality as mind, soul or spirit. In spite of the connotations which it unfortunately has today, there seems no better word which we may use to describe the mind-soul-spirit.

The Greek word for the body that went along with "psyche" was "soma," and these two words are being used increasingly today to indicate the two main ways in which we look at the personality in health and illness.

Philosophers since time began have argued about the relationship between mind and body. In its proper place, that discussion is still in order; and the ultimate philosophical answer will probably never be given by science. But in a practical sense, science and especially medical science has taught us a very great deal in recent years. One of the reasons why modern science prefers to talk of "psychosomatic" interrelationships instead of mind-body interrelationships is that it wants to suggest that it is not dealing with the ultimate philosophical truths but rather with the ways in which body and mind-spirit are interrelated in specific ways and instances. For this reason we follow the scientists in the use of words; for our concern here is basically with some of the specific ways in which *psyche* and *soma* are interrelated, even though we realize that in other connections religion is concerned with the ultimate philosophical issues.

Psychic Factors in Somatic Illness. Modern medicine is rapidly coming to the conclusion that whether an illness is physical *or* psychic is the wrong question, and that the real question is, *"To what extent* physical and *to what extent* psychic." [1] "There is no such thing as a purely psychic illness or a purely physical one, but only a *living event* taking place in a living organism which is itself alive only by virtue of the fact that in it psychic and somatic are united in a unity." [2]

In another chapter the practical differences between "mental" and "physical" illnesses are discussed, but here we are concerned mainly with those illnesses usually thought of as "bodily" disorders. And we find physicians saying that psychic as well as somatic factors are involved in them. [3]

Let us look at some specific illustrations to see what is meant by this. George W. Gray writes [4] of "a young woman who was disturbed because of an affliction of the fourth finger of her left hand. Its tip looked like chalk. It felt cold, numb, asleep. The condition, commonly called 'white finger,' is a disorder of circulation known to medical men as Raynaud's disease. The cause is a prolonged constriction of muscles surrounding certain small blood vessels. Usually Raynaud's disease symmetrically affects the body's extremities, the toes of both feet or the fingers of both hands; but in this instance the trouble was sharply localized. There was only one white finger, and the fact that it was the ring finger seemed to point to an emotional involvement of some kind. Eventually the patient told of a crucial experience in her personal life which showed, only too clearly, that such indeed was the case. It seems that a few months previously she was the happy fiancée of a young man. But there had been a misunderstanding, a quarrel developed, and in a moment of rage she took off her engagement ring and 'threw it at him.' That night she became aware of a curious tingling in her ring finger. She rubbed the finger awake. Later the sensation returned. Finally exercise and rubbing were of no avail. The circulatory disorder grew more pronounced and alarming and at last caused ulcerations which drove her to the doctor."

There is no doubt that Raynaud's disease is a "real somatic" or organic disorder in the sense that during its course conditions occur which can be observed somatically or organically. Some physicians would point out that it is a "functional" disorder rather than a "true organic" disease, which is true in the sense that easily discernible psychic factors are involved in its causation. But whether any such thing as "organic" disease exists without *some* psychic factors being involved is another question.

This case is selected here because the involvement of the psychic factors is rather obvious.

Certainly the difficulty with this finger could not be called an imaginary illness. Its immediate causation was a prolonged constriction of muscles in a restricted area around small blood vessels. But there is another kind or level of causation which has to be considered, namely, what causes the muscles to become constricted? The careful work that had presumably to be done by the physician in this case before he was able to assert that the cause was to be found in the area of the young woman's relationship to her young man would be too long to recount here. We should avoid jumping to conclusions, though we must of necessity use illustrations which are simple. But the physician in this case saw a fairly obvious connection between the conflict in the young woman's *whole personality* and her finger disorder. The conflict was such as to suggest that the symptoms had localized themselves in the finger. We shall consider later just what is involved in such conflicts.

Walter B. Cannon quotes a case from Emerson, in which "a man of twenty years had a quarrel with his fiancée. She, pretending to commit suicide, had in his presence swallowed some pills and fallen down screaming. The man departed hastily. Within a week he was suffering from swelling of the neck and nervousness. When he appeared at the hospital four months later he had lost weight, he presented a large goitre over which a definite thrill could be felt, and his basal metabolism was up 24 per cent above the normal level." [5]

These cases illustrate—or would illustrate if we had and gave all the data—how psychic factors may affect somatic factors and the result be illness which has organic involvement. It would be even simpler to show how some illnesses which seem to have only psychic symptoms are really produced by somatic factors.

However, a reminiscence about the way one's most recent head-ache or upset stomach influenced his outlook will dispel the need for that demonstration.

Not all modern physicians have accepted the psychosomatic approach in medicine. Says one concerning the current situation, "There are those who attempt to find an organic condition to account for every psychic state; there are those who see only the psychic aspect and overlook the somatic; and finally those who see organic as well as psychic pathology from a psychosomatic point of view." [6] The first group must be shown by other physicians that they are one-sided, and leading physicians are now in process of doing this. The second group includes not many physicians but a great many laymen who believe that there are religious or other substitutes for medicine. It is a part of our duty to show them that they are one-sided. The third point of view is that taken by most physicians who have examined the problem at all carefully and is the one which we accept from these investigators.

It would be very easy indeed to pile up illustrations showing that psychic states influence somatic conditions. But except for those persons who are so blind that they will not see, this would be superfluous. For once it is recognized that these interrelation-ships may exist, the question is *to what extent*. A well-known physician writes, "The literature is still confused by contribu-tions which serve merely to indicate what we have always known, that somatic symptoms may have psychic etiology [causes] and vice versa." [7] If we assume this is true, and we must accept the physicians' conclusion, our problem then is with the *how* and the *how much*.

It is precisely at this specific point of *to what extent* psychic and somatic influences are at work in illnesses that modern medicine has been contributing to our understanding. The most obvious practical conclusion we must draw is that the importance of having the physician at the center of the treatment of illness is increased, and that anything which would put mere generalities (in the psychic as well as in the somatic field) before specifics would be to use something less than the full scope of modern medical knowledge.

No amount of knowledge, therefore, about the general way in which psychic processes may be related to somatic disturbances can be substituted for knowledge of specific situations. Some of the general knowledge is valuable, especially from our religious point of view, however, provided we get it not from arm-chair philosophizing but from conclusions drawn out of specific clinical observation.

How Conflicts May Help to Produce Illnesses. One general conclusion of great importance is in reference to the nature of the "conflicts" in the personality which may produce somatic illnesses. The studies seem to show that economic hardship, deaths in the family, business reverses and the like are not in *themselves* the psychic *causes* of illnesses. Of course malnutrition, brought on by poverty, may produce illness directly; but the kind of open, conscious worry which economic hardship, for example, tends to bring about does not produce illness psychically. Let us clarify this by reference to the business man who is confronted with the possibility of his business' going to pieces. He has a normal worry about this, normal because the situation demands that he think of what can be done to save the business, and what will happen to himself and his family if he cannot think of anything. Emotion will be generated in the course of his worry, and it may furnish useful energy which may be directed toward the solution of the difficult personal and social situation which he faces. If it does not seem possible to save his business in the light of the concrete situation, this emotional energy should definitely be of help in getting a new job, or establishing another business, or otherwise making a satisfactory adjustment.

Suppose, however, that this man's worry turns to anxiety, that is, to a state of chronic inability to dwell on anything except the "situation," to a state of continuous muscular tension and the like. The state of worry is then "frozen into" his whole personality, and is what the psychiatrists call *anxiety*. Study of such cases always reveals that this frozen state is brought about not alone by the present crisis (in this case the financial and business threat), but also by emotional factors relating to the man's basic attitude toward himself. Another way of saying this is that the conflicts lie in the unconscious realm, or that the man associates his "self" with the success of his business. If the business goes, he goes; his own self-respect is at stake, and without that no man can live unchanged.

A physician writes of such a case. "An apparently normal business man developed an obstruction in his sigmoid during an emotional crisis where he had to sacrifice either his principles or his position. Opaque enema showed a complete block and the patient only escaped laparotomy because his physician was wise enough to repeat the examination several times." [8] There are many ways in which such a conflict might legitimately be described. Here the physician implies that it was between "principles" and "position." It might be more relevant to say that it was between one attitude of the patient toward himself and an opposite unconscious attitude. The basic condition in any case was one of anxiety, and such anxiety would not have been possible unless there were certain unconscious driving forces pulling in different directions. Whether or not these unconscious forces are instinctual has little to do with the matter. It is certain that they are operative within the personality. How anxiety arises and becomes ingrained within the whole character pattern will be discussed in chapter seven.

Investigation shows that the kinds of factors which help to produce illnesses include most of the "divisive" emotions which we know, producing conflicts about whose elements the person is unaware or only partially aware. A conscious feeling of guilt, therefore, about some act which one has just committed will not tend to produce illness; but if this guilt is rooted in the character pattern, and that which originally produced the guilt disappears into the unconscious realm, the basic difficulty may show itself in illness. It is obvious that the other divisive emotions, or rather ways of talking about emotions, such as anger, rage, jealousy or fear may operate in similar ways.

How far these conflicts may take the person is evidenced in well-authenticated stories from clinical records. The psyche seems able to operate in connection with any organ or organ-system, though the way in which and the extent to which this is done is better known in reference to some systems than to others. The gastro-intestinal system was one of the first to which attention was directed, one physician as early as 1845 calling attention to the frequency with which gastro-intestinal disturbances occurred during the course of psychic disturbances.[9] Much is now known about the psychic factors in this organ system. In reference to stomach ulcer, for example, one investigator says the ulcer itself "is only the last manifestation of the disease." [10] It is "the result of a central process which is either psychically caused or at least psychically conditioned, leading to anatomical alterations only as a result of anatomical preconditions of the stomach . . ." [10]

It was interesting to note a few months ago the press reports of a considerable increase in stomach ulcer in Great Britain since the war began. Since the reports quote British medical journals, they may be presumed to suggest at least a trend. If it were true that ulcer could be produced by immediate fear-producing situations such as being bombed, an increase in the number of ulcers might be a negative comment on British morale. The press reports quoted British military physicians as denying that psychological factors have anything to do with the situation. Though we can but guess at the facts, we can see how morale might be injured if people believed that fear was an element in producing ulcers—*without realizing what kind of fear was involved or the time process necessary.* Vague and hair-splitting though some of these distinctions may seem at first glance, they assume increasing significance as we understand their implications. For with what we know of peptic ulcer, we can say that even a considerable increase in its incidence would not be a negative comment on the morale of the British people.

The influence of psychological factors in the development of ulcer is different, for example, from the situation in which a pregnant woman had a miscarriage as a result of shock induced by the news (proved false within an hour) that her husband had drowned. In the case of ulcer, we are probably not dealing with something which is directly "caused" by certain attitudes and emotions, but which is influenced indirectly by these attitudes and emotions. The distinctions are important.

The endocrines are closely related to psychic influences though the extravagant and irresponsible claims which have been made on this score should be ignored. One illustration, however, will suffice, that of exophthalmic goitre. One psychiatrist has pointed out that the symptoms of this disorder are precisely similar to those of fear, which suggests that the disorder is "a self-protective mechanism." [11] Everyone knows that the state of the thyroid gland is influenced by the amount of iodine it has; but there is considerable proof that it is also closely related to states of fear and anxiety. We recall that it is no longer a question of either-or, but of how much. Another physician reports, "A very famous surgeon sent a young woman who was suffering with toxic thyroid to him with the request that he get rid of some of her fears so she could be operated on, her pulse being so rapid that surgery could not be considered. The psychiatrist analyzed the girl and at the end of three months sent her back to the surgeon minus fears and minus her goitre. The famous surgeon bewailed the loss of his patient but expressed happiness over the outcome of the case." [12] The endocrines are in delicate balance, and a change in the function of one throws the whole system out of kilter. Future investigation will indicate more about the extent to which specific psychic factors influence the whole endocrine system as well as parts of it.

Considerable work has been done on the extent to which psychic factors influence skin disturbances. Eruptions on the skin have been produced by suggestion under hypnosis, indicating that such symptoms may be of direct psychic origin.[13] Two of the greatest dermatologists of the day write, "The larger our experience and the more careful our search, the more we are inclined to believe that in . . . [certain types of skin disorders] which . . . seem far removed from the psychologic considerations, the tension make-up, the personality defect, the conflict and anxiety, the repression and the complex have their place as causal influences, to be sought out and rectified side by side with, and sometimes even before, the correction of the more apparent physical dysfunctions." [14]

Numerous other organ systems could be cited. In the respiratory system it is noticed, for example, in reference to asthma, that "even in those who are extremely sensitive to allergens, it is noticed that the asthma attacks regularly occur in reactions to situations which seem to threaten the patient with loss of love of some person upon whom he is emotionally dependent." [15]

Even cases of accident frequently show psychic influence of which the person himself is unaware or at least is unaware of until after the accident. Gray cites a man who had injured his back. He had been a "mother's boy" before his marriage, and was not reconciled to what he felt was indifference on the part of his wife. He said after the accident, "She'll have to take care of me now. I guess it serves her right." [16]

The chronic fatigue and irritation which some people have may indeed be physical, but "the fact should be borne in mind that changes in muscle tonus are among the most frequent mechanisms of psychic expression." [17] Thus general "neurasthenia" or chronic fatigue and irritability are not related so much to the nerves, somatically speaking, as to the muscles and body fluids; but they have psychic connections in the personality of the individual.

An interesting example of how important it is to be specific in this field is demonstrated in a series of observations by three scientists.[18] They "tested the effects of emotion (the thought of an impending operation) on the basic metabolic rate in three groups of operative patients (twelve general patients, twelve hyperthyroid patients previously given the iodine treatment, and six hyperthyroid patients who had had no iodine). All were told one day that an operation was impending the next day. The emotion of anxiety produced little effect in the first two groups, but the third group showed a marked increase in the metabolic rate." If we said, therefore, that bodily changes measured in terms of metabolism were *always* to be found in patients who were facing an operation, we should be wrong; we should be wrong also if we said this was true of all thyroid patients. But if evidence in this particular case is adequate (and that is for the scientists to decide), hyperthyroid patients without iodine treatment have a marked change in their metabolic rate, caused by the emotion induced through thought of an impending operation! How cautious must the layman as well as the physician be about making generalizations.

Thus the scientists go forward with specific investigation. One of the problems in which they are naturally most interested is whether there is any correlation between certain factors in personality and the tendency to have certain types of illnesses. Little is really known about this as yet, and the scientists are properly cautious in making generalizations. The hypothesis that the personality, illustrated by the aggressive and rushing person who unwittingly longs for care and protection, is more prone to develop a stomach ulcer than are other types, may eventually be proved to have validity. But it is not yet an accepted scientific fact. Similarly the hypothesis, that the person who is excessively gentle and submissive, who unwittingly desires to express the chronic rage lying underneath, is more likely to have high blood pressure than others, is worthy of further investigation. Dunbar believes, "There are indications that, in cases of somatic disorder where the psychic component is of determinative significance, this factor is of a specific nature for each disease entity thus far investigated." [19]

Pending further investigation, great caution should be exercised at the point of linking specific personality factors with types of illnesses. Some religious writers have laid themselves open to severe criticism here. Glenn Clark, for example, writes that he proposes "to find out what form of wrong thinking may be the cause of each particular illness so that each patient may concentrate upon removing that one specific cause." [20] In discussing specific illnesses, he then proceeds not only to go beyond science, which is permissible in terms of hypothesis, but actually runs counter to some of the cautiously expressed but significant scientific findings which we have attempted to summarize.

Emotion and Illnesses. Physiologically, as Walter B. Cannon points out, "The bodily changes in emotional excitement may be considered as anticipatory of many of these dangers." [21] The dangers he refers to are, for example, the tendency of the temperature to rise and "imperil the integrity of the brain," of having too little sugar in the blood thus leading to possible coma, etc. Emotion attempts to preserve "homeostasis," constant conditions in the body fluids. "The forces of the organism are put upon a war footing. But if there is no war to be waged, if the emotion has its natural mobilizing effect on the viscera when there is nothing to be done, obviously the very system which functions to preserve constancy of conditions within us is then employed to upset that constancy. It is not surprising, therefore, that fear and worry and hate can lead to harmful and profoundly disturbing consequences." [21]

Gray makes an excellent summary along this line, showing how these basic factors, to which Cannon refers, tend to produce anxiety, which lies so close to the source of psychic influence on somatic illness. "The plight of modern man lies in this: that the nature of his conflicts has changed, but his neuro-chemical mechanism for protection has not. The man who has just lost his fortune in a bank failure is terrified but he cannot give release to his emotion in any physical way. His fear is just as reasonable as was the fear of a caveman confronted by a wild beast. The caveman was served by swift and elaborate adjustment which instantly took place in his body. Whether he turned and ran or stood and fought he needed the stronger heart beat, the change in blood distribution, the additional red corpuscles, the extra sugar and all the rest. But these adjustments are superfluous to the victim of bankruptcy. They prepare him for action which does not take place. They glut his system with substances which he does not need, and leave him with a prolonged constriction of secretion which further aggravates the perversion of function. The end effect is an internal conflict. Such conflicts tend to be suppressed, but the fact that they are unconscious does not mean that they are innocuous. Quite the opposite. The poisoning effect of a source of anxiety seems to increase in inverse ratio to the victim's awareness of its identity. Often the experience responsible for the emotional upset is so buried that it cannot be recalled without assistance." [22] Indeed, the experience is often so deeply ingrained as a part of the character pattern itself that the "whole person" must be changed. But it is to be noted "that it is not concrete worries, but unconscious conflicts that produce somatic symptoms." [23] Parts of these are to be found in the "culture" in which the person lives and has lived, which have become internalized to form in part the content of his conscience, at least that part which he accepts without question.

We should beware of confusing cause with process in looking at the psychic influences upon illness. Among non-medical people who have become interested in this field, there is sometimes a tendency to say, for example, "he developed a stomach ulcer because he wanted attention." This is very inaccurate and misleading. It is inaccurate because "he" refers to only part of the person in this sentence, the part that is now unsatisfied. There is only a compromise solution in the personality, not a real reconciliation of conflicting desires and claims. Further, the cause and effect is not direct. The temporary acceptance of a compromise solution of the conflicting desires may set processes in motion which eventually lead to gastric ulcer; but the person is not only unaware of the "logic" of these processes, but of the real elements in the conflict. With a person in such a state, he might be given all the love and attention in the world and still the process would continue, because he would be incapable of receiving them until a personality reorganization was begun. Caution then should be observed about identifying process with cause.

"Voodoo" Death and "Miraculous" Cures. These psychic influences upon somatic conditions may operate in almost any degree, depending upon the depth of the person's emotional need. Of the lesser degrees enough has been said. But it is not unusual for the experienced clinician to find in the course of his career at least one or two patients who die without having in the organ-systems sufficient derangement to account in themselves for the deaths. An experienced pathologist of one of our best and largest hospitals cited recently the death of a middle-aged woman patient in which the autopsy failed to show adequate organic factors to account for death.[24] Sometimes, of course, the psychic influences disturb the somatic state so much that death ensues from somatic causes, but these other situations are of no less interest. There are not many of them which have had thoroughly good medical examination before and after death, nor is a personality report always available. But there seem to be enough to indicate that even death is possible from psychic influences, working either indirectly through somatic disintegration or more directly.[25]

On the other side are the "miraculous" cures for which the Lourdes shrine has become so well known and in which so many of the healing cults place their confidence. Much remains to be investigated about these sudden cures. It is hardly necessary to state that most of the reported cures are not deep or permanent. Of what use is it to do as one patient did who had been to a psychiatrist about the tic in his right arm which made him move it up and down constantly to cover his eyes? He returned the following week to the psychiatrist and reported himself cured, in proof holding out his right arm steadily, when suddenly he noticed that his left arm was making rapid up-and-down movements!

But there are cases on record (very few, however, that are adequately attested) in which a serious and unmistakable organic disorder showed tremendous improvement in a very short time.[26] This is a complicated subject, and one which can only be touched on here. From what has been said above, it must be obvious that if psychic influences can help to produce illness they can also help to produce health—different kinds of psychic influences being involved in either case. What seems to make a few cures "miraculous" is, therefore, not the presence of unmistakably psychic influence but the apparent rapidity of the somatic healing. The complete cure of serious tubercular lesions, for example, within two or three days is not generally accepted as a fact by physicians; but if it were discovered to be a fact, albeit a very rare one, it would not seem to disturb sound medicine or to make any particular change in the "psychosomatic" approach to medicine. If such great rapidity, on the other hand, should not be found and authenticated, that too would make little difference. The great value of discovering and genuinely authenticating such cases would be one of education and publicity, dramatically calling attention to the operative power of psychic influences.

There is one psychological hypothesis which has been offered in connection with "miraculous" cures, and which operates conversely on deaths "without adequate organic cause." There are other explanations given, but only this tentative one seems to stand up under the limited scientific scrutiny which has thus far been given the subject. To consider the deaths first, it is not correct to say that "the person wished to die and so he died." If we intended that to be on a non-metaphorical level, we should be implying that the person took a gun and shot himself. He did not die through "will-power," even though he may have said he "wanted" to die and then died. Somehow the frustration and conflict had gone so deep that no solution seemed possible; yet the person could not consciously take his own life. To see just what the conflict was would be to examine each individual case.

With the "miraculous" cures, the hypothesis also begins with the statement that will-power cannot do it, that a conscious desire to live or to get well may have little to do with cure. If it is possible for a person to have a psychic conflict which is of such a nature that something, some time, might solve it instantaneously, and if this conflict were the main factor in producing a somatic illness, is it possible that such situations would account for cures which seem to be more rapid than the extremes which ordinary clinical experience would indicate? This would seem possible, if it is not *too* fast. Whether this can be substantiated or not will remain for the scientists to determine. But it is interesting that the best authenticated cases of real "miraculous" cure seem to be those in which the patients have consciously given up hope of living or getting well.

Blanton suggests that the people who are susceptible to these "miraculous" cures are those who "have reached the limit of their emotional and physical capacities to adjust to the demands of their illness. For some reason inherent in their own psychological functioning they cannot any longer accept life and yet they cannot quite accept death." [27] The psychic change which occurs in such a patient Blanton calls "surrender." It is important to consider what is surrendered, which Blanton believes to be the "will to die." Thus he implies that in such cases there is a process in operation which will lead to death; that by psychological change this process is reversed; and that as a result of this reversal the forces of healing within the body are liberated and come into operation.

But it is of the greatest importance to realize that, whatever is found out about these sudden cures, no marked change will be made in the psychosomatic approach which has been discussed here. It would, so to speak, be expanded at one end, but the central structure would remain untouched.

The Meaning of Health. This section has thus far considered illness rather than health, because it is in the deviation from the "normal," however normality be considered, that we get our best introductory knowledge about the normal. Science frequently flounders when dealing with the "normal," unless it be dealing with the average. Such definitions of health as "efficient and happy living" do not seem to help us much. But practically, the physician *as scientist* is well justified in starting his thinking about health in terms of the *absence* of something that would indicate illness. This is especially true when psychic factors are considered. If the physician happens to be thinking of feet, and notices that his patient's extremities are not flat, he may conclude tentatively that the man's feet are "healthy" (provided also he does not have athlete's foot, etc.). Even more important, if he examines the patient and finds that he does not have psychically conditioned goitre, or does not exhibit any anxious neurotic behavior, he may conclude for the moment that his patient—in the absence of psychic as well as somatic disturbances—is healthy. The physician is, of course, more than a scientist. He is interested in helping his patient, and there is an art as well as a science of medicine.

Increasingly physicians are interested in *"positive health"* as well as in *"absence of illness."* Exactly how far the physician may find it within his province to define health in positive terms is a matter on which there is at present disagreement. Some suggest that a physician who has repaired a man's broken leg has aided him to *health*—whether the cured patient walks around the corner to rob a bank or to save a child from an approaching automobile. Others would broaden the meaning of "health" to include judgments of social and ethical value, and would contend that the man who robbed the bank was *ipso facto* still unhealthy. For the present at least, the question seems to be largely one of definition of terms. It would seem unwise to broaden "health" to include all ethical values; for this takes it too far from ordinary usage. To confine it to "absence of" illness, however, does injustice to the facts.

Some physicians concerned with health as a positive state have used such terms as "emotional well-being," "happiness," and the like to suggest certain aspects of it. One physician says, "Illness is a deviation from health or from a state in which all natural activities and functions are performed freely and efficiently without pain or discomfort." [28] Perhaps that is as far as science can go at present, though it can say that there are positive aspects of health which it can recognize but not completely define. The physician as "artist" will undoubtedly go further.

Some physicians are speaking of health in a positive sense in such terms as "not merely helping the person to get well, but helping to make him 'weller.' " Considered from the point of view of the progressive physician, this concept has real meaning. One large hospital reports a survey it has made over a period of several years with several hundred persons in "normal" health, who permitted themselves to be guided in matters relating to health by the physicians.[29] The physicians made careful examination at stated intervals of at least the following factors: heredity, endocrines, infections, nutrition, body mechanics, various organ systems, and personality and personal relationships. They report tentatively several conclusions of real interest. Most important, people who were not "ill" in some particular respect could nevertheless be guided by the physician's knowledge to become much better in that respect. This seems almost self-evident, as in the case of improved posture; but few persons have given a thought to positive health in terms of following a physician's suggestions along such lines. Many people take exercises, for example, to improve their posture; but few get advice (or diagnosis) from the person best equipped to give it to them about the particular direction in which they should move in order to improve their health. The physicians found also that the knowledge about health which these people had (most of them were intelligent and well educated) was abysmally low, and that the sources of getting such knowledge as they had were poor. Physicians will undoubtedly move into this field more in the near future, and laymen should be ready to meet them at least half-way. The knowledge which the laymen had about disease was greater (though not much more accurate) than the knowledge they had of health. This situation is bound to change, unless the quacks and cultists expand.

It is useful, incidentally, to make a distinction between "illness" and "disease." G. Canby Robinson suggests that we use "disease" to refer to the process that goes on, especially in the body, and that we use "illness" to refer to the patient's experience.[30] He says, "Disease is only one element of illness, and is not the only cause of disturbances of the activities and functions of the body. There is in fact no fixed relationship between disease and illness. Disease does not necessarily cause illness and illness may exist without disease, as I have defined these words."[31] These seem to be useful distinctions which, on the whole, have been followed in this discussion.

Summary. The scientific evidence shows that the time has passed when it is necessary to "prove" that psychic influences are operative in producing physiological conditions, but that we are just on the threshold of knowing to what extent each influence operates in particular cases and types of cases. Thus the scientific contribution is, as we might expect, in the direction of the specific. Following what are sometimes called the general principles of the Hippocratic method, medicine has taken the first step of examining its material; then the second step of going over the material in search of general principles, which are then set up as hypotheses; and it is now at the third step, checking the hypotheses against the material. Most of us are too much engaged in making hypothetical statements without getting them first from the material, or checking them afterward with the material. It is doubtful if even the most rarified philosophical discussion of the future on the body-mind problem can ignore the specific scientific findings, as they are available today and as they will be available with greater certainty in a few years. But these findings do not determine *all* the philosophical issues, any more than they determine the activities of the man whose broken leg has healed.

It should be emphasized that a great many specific sciences have made contributions to this scientific knowledge which has been summarized so briefly here. Physicians and medical investigators have been in the van; but they have been aided by physiologists, psychologists, pathologists, physical-chemists, social workers, sociologists, and many others. Some debt is due also to religious workers, though this has seldom been acknowledged until recently, because a few religious workers have so exploited the psychic factors as to negate anything the physicians did or might do. But too few religious workers have thus far been in the forefront of such investigations by scientific method.[32]

CHAPTER V

THE RELATION OF CHRISTIANITY TO THE MAINTENANCE OF HEALTH AND THE CURE OF ILLNESS

II. Religious Implications

General Implications. The importance of the newer approach of "psychosomatic" medicine for religion can scarcely be overestimated. Perhaps most significant, it leaves the way open for religion to have an integral relationship with health. In the days when somatic conditions and psychic states were thought to have little direct connection with each other, it was easy to assert that only quacks were concerned with the direct relation of religion to health, or to hold religion in a purely "spiritual" compartment and the processes of health and illness in a purely "physical" one. Science has now made that impossible. If religion has anything to do with one's psyche, and it is scarcely religious unless it has, then it is inevitably connected with health or illness, for better or for worse.

Christianity has always believed that "as a man thinketh in his heart, so is he." [1] We are now seeing that it is equally important how he "thinketh in his muscles and blood vessels." For how he thinketh in his heart has a very great influence upon how he thinketh in his muscles.

This is not to give *carte blanche* to all religion nor to all interpretations of Christianity, group or individual, as enhancers of health. But it does point to the soundness of most of the basic Christian affirmations. The central significance of love and fellowship are illuminated in a new way when we see how a suppressed longing for love may influence the development of gastric ulcer. The importance of letting faith drive out fear and anger is illuminated by our vision of how repressed hostility may help to produce high blood pressure or of how repressed fear may help to produce exophthalmic goitre. The central meaning of sin in the Christian tradition as alienation from God, but sin for which God is ever ready to offer forgiveness, is sound; for sometimes illnesses which have been plaguing a man for years can be improved or cured in a relatively short time if the psychic root can be reached. That grace is needed is demonstrated anew by the fact that one cannot pull himself out of illness by his own bootstraps. "In quietness and confidence shall be our strength" is a reality which brings healing, provided it reaches into the depths of the psyche and therefore into the muscles and blood vessels.

These comments suggest the many new connections made possible to religion and health by the modern approach in medicine. It seems necessary to add, however, that not all interpretations of Christianity emphasize what we shall probably have to name "healthy" interpretations such as this, either as to intellectual or emotional content. Fundamentalists may interpret many true ideas so literally as to make a mockery of their deeper content and may hang to them with an intensity which never allows any state but that of "tension" to exist in the emotions and in the spirit. Ritualists are legalists of a more relaxed nature, but they run the constant danger of "compulsiveness." "Modernists" run the danger of being more interested in an idea because it is new than because it is true, and of glossing over the potentialities for personal and social illness which are resident in human

beings. "Neo-Orthodox" theologians run the danger of philistin-
ism, stating the worst so that they are able to "look unmoved
upon the sufferings of others"—as some one has facetiously defined the philosophic function. "Emotionalists" run the danger
of never permitting relaxation and of confusing the depth of
emotional appreciation with more or less irrelevant symptoms.

But for our purposes the more important dangers of interpreting Christianity in relation to health lie in individual emotional interpretations. Like the physicians' contribution to the
problem of body-mind relationships, this is less significant for
its contribution to philosophy than for what it teaches about specific people. It suggests more about a doctrine of men than
about a doctrine of man.

Two men, for instance, may hold the same intellectual doctrine, and yet in one man this may be interpreted so as to contribute to health, and in the other so as to contribute to illness.
Take, for example, two men who were entirely in agreement
about the need to overcome fear and anger with love. Both men
were well educated, theologically literate; and both had done
well with their vocations and their families. Both were pleasant
persons and seemed to get along well with other people. One
of the men, however, was so effusively sweet to his wife that we
were justified in wondering if the feeling was wholly love. The
man developed a fairly serious cardiovascular disorder at an age
much earlier than would have been expected. The other man was
neither "sweet" nor sour to his wife and brought disagreements
and basic clashes of temperament out into the open even when
it hurt. His blood pressure had scarcely changed in ten years.
The first man was attempting a short-circuited kind of emotional
interpretation of overcoming rage with love. Hostility cannot
be overcome once and for all; neither can it be overcome if it
remains unrecognized. By always attempting to "love," the

shadow was confused with the substance, the symptom with the cause. This leads us back to thinking "in the heart," which the second man did and the first did not. The fact remains that it was the emotional interpretation of a basically true doctrine which made all the difference in the world.

This should settle the question as to whether all religion or all interpretations of Christianity contribute to health. They do not, and the distinctions are not merely in terms of ideas, ritual, or ethics—they relate to the total personality, including the so-called unconscious factors. So many attempts which have been made to "prove" the beneficial influence of religion upon health have been one-sided; that is, they have taken *good* forms of religion and shown how these have helped to produce good results in terms of health (usually "miraculous" cures of some kind). It is indispensable to recognize that some forms of religion are generally detrimental to health and, even more important, that some emotional interpretations, even of Christianity, are inimical to it. As a matter of fact, the beneficent influence under proper conditions is so great and obvious that it is high time we stopped "defending" it. When the influence is not beneficial, we should seek the causes. But we must first confess this fact.

This is, of course, no charter of intolerance. It is just the opposite. If Mrs. Juggins has just been through a trifling operation, and has used it to get all the attention she possibly could, we are well justified in questioning in our own minds whether the sweetly sentimental book of meditations which she reports pulled her through really did what she believes.[2] So would the physicians question her report that "Gulliver's pills" staved off the operation for twenty years. There is no less reason for objective observation, and critical diagnosis, about religious influences than about others. In believing that Mrs. Juggins received less help from her religious reading than she thinks, indeed in believing that it merely reinforced certain neurotic prejudices, we have no intolerance for Mrs. Juggins. We are substituting the principle of understanding for the principle of gullibility. Not all who call upon the name of the Lord shall enter into the Kingdom.

What kinds of interpretation of Christianity do not make for health? There are many justifiable ways of looking at this matter, and every wise religious leader has his own, whether he is articulate about it or not. One approach to this question has been discussed in chapter two. It may be summarized in this way: a religion which makes for health is based in content upon the best of the Christian tradition; it respects the autonomy of the personality; it is related to the whole of the personality and not merely to the soul or spirit; it is non-substantive and non-compulsive; it is outgoing; and it is related to the emotional well-springs of life.

Chapter two has also suggested specific ways in which this kind of religious interpretation makes for health. About those there can be little question. If health is not a static norm, but a condition which is capable of improvement in any one, then a religion which brings a positive and affirmative interpretation to life, even in the face of greatest difficulty, is bound to make for improved health. All the evidence of psychosomatic medicine suggests that anything which is done to make conflicts conscious, to face them and solve them is a contribution to the improvement of health, whether the person is judged ill or not. In so far as it is a part of the function of religion to perform these tasks, it certainly makes for increased health. In so far as religion affirms life, especially in the face of difficulty, it makes for health. Just when this is being done or not being done is a problem for judgment in specific instances.

This psychosomatic approach in medicine has other implications for religion. Perhaps most important is this: if ministry to the *psyche* is intimately related to ministry to the *soma*, the religious worker has a real place on the team which works with those who are ill. His ministrations can no longer be self-sufficient, having little or no relation to the "health" of the patient. They can no longer go unexamined by the other members of the team; for if they are the wrong measures, or are done badly, the work done by others may be worthless.

Progressive scientists and physicians are concerned with making physicians "psyche-conscious," using psychiatrists only for the most technical and difficult aspects of the work. This is well and good; and there is no suggestion that religious workers should become third-rate, or even first-rate, psychiatrists. But the great problem in connection with so many who are ill or who have "normal problems of growth" (where there are significant psychic complications) is to make real contact with them. Very frequently a religious worker will make such a contact possible, when a psychiatrist or physician would have a difficult time.[3]

Scientific workers sometimes suggest that religious workers necessarily deal only with symptoms. They may, for example, it is contended, repeat affirmations (e.g., "God takes care of me") to people who need to make affirmations (life *is* worth living), but with no attempt to help the people understand why they have not of themselves been able to make affirmations. This charge is sometimes justified; and where it is true, it is merely another illustration of the fact that religious workers, like any others, must not fail to make adequate (spiritual) diagnoses before they give prescriptions. But there is nothing in the nature of religious ministry which commands it to carry but one pill-box in its kit. Religious ministry should become as specific as medical ministry.

In summary, psychosomatic medicine does not prove the truth

of religion. It has nothing more to say about things of that sort than has any science. But it suggests a great deal about how religion may be interpreted, for good or ill, by individuals. It suggests that the first step in the therapeutic use of religious resources is a clinical one, recognizing the harm done by neurotic interpretations, and the potential good accomplished by sound interpretations. It suggests certain approaches to criteria for distinguishing healthy from unhealthy interpretations. Potentially, it places the trained religious worker side by side with the physician, psychiatrist, and others, in the cure of illness as well as in the maintenance and improvement of health. It indicates more strongly than the older medicine how important it is for religious resources to be used only hand in hand with medical resources, and exposes the fallacy of trying to do "religious healing" apart from such co-operation. In short, it permits religion to have an integral relationship with health.

The Healing Ministry of Jesus. The interest which Jesus had in health and healing is obvious from even a casual reading of the four gospels. The healings which Jesus performed may have been included in some of the accounts in order to show how great he was or what special power he possessed, but to us they demonstrate how essentially his ministry was related to the whole of man. If a paralytic could not have been cured of his paralysis, doubtless Jesus would have been concerned that his mind and spirit be "made whole"; but his effort was to change the entire man if possible.

We now know that healings, such as are described in the gospels, are not impossible or inexplicable. Even though our understanding of the processes involved is still in its infancy, we have some dependable clues on the basis of which investigation may bring us further wisdom. From the theological point of view we may still refer to "miracles of healing." But we rejoice that the "miracles" no longer have a "hands off" sign on them so far as credibility or understanding is concerned.

So long as our belief in the *fact* of the healing miracles of Jesus went counter to our reason, it was natural that our insight into their meaning and value should be defensive and one-sided. This usually resulted in emphasis on matters which were characteristic of the age in which Jesus of Nazareth lived but which were not essential to the actual processes of healing. We are told little in the gospels about the superficial techniques which Jesus used in healing, only such things as that he spoke some words or touched with his hand. This type of technique was in use by many healers in Jesus' day and has little to do with the actual healing processes. The point is that so far as the superficial techniques were concerned Jesus used those of his day and generation.

Considerably more important is Jesus' deeper method or technique. He sought for faith—a living conviction in the possibility of healing—and when he found it he let it work. Knowing it was present at least potentially in all who came to him for help, he did not create it, though he may have seemed to do so to those who were aided. Someone has said that he "demanded an act of faith." The person had to recognize the presence and power of the healing forces, and then perform an act of recognition of them. What is important is the interpersonal relationships, the deep-reaching quality of the faith engendered, and the active response of the whole personality to its recognition of the possibility of healing.

Justification for some queer practices in healing has been sought by literalists in the methods of Jesus. Because he used only "spiritual" means and not drugs or surgery, they use only "spiritual" means and eschew drugs or surgery. Or because he seems to have had no failures recorded against him, their faith is weak if any failures are written up against them. He apparently healed every type of disorder indiscriminately; they must do likewise. He made no diagnosis in our sense of the word; therefore they will make none. Such misconceptions arise from literalism or lack of historical perspective, and from absence of insight into the basic methods of Jesus' healing ministry.

More significant are the mistaken conclusions often asserted about Jesus' use of "suggestion therapy." He did not analyze, attempt to deal with specific causes, or even let the person discover the healing forces for himself, they say. He did it all by suggestion; so will they. As a matter of fact, it seems likely that Jesus did analyze, seek specific causes (though not in our modern medical sense), and help the person to discover the healing forces himself. Three questions confront us: what suggestion therapy is, what is its value, and whether it was what Jesus used.

If "suggestion" be considered in its usual connotations, it implies that someone is putting something over on somebody else. It may be for his good, but the whole person does not necessarily accept it. This is well illustrated by the inclusion of hypnotism under the suggestion category. Hypnotism may bring remarkable results temporarily, even in the field of healing; but because it does not include genuine assimilation of all that is involved, it is of little value as a therapeutic method. If one wishes to stretch the meaning of suggestion to include all attempts to aid another in achieving insight, naturally the significance of suggestion would be radically changed. But in that case all psychotherapy would be suggestion, and that would be meaningless.

In the former sense suggestion therapy is of doubtful value. It may easily exploit for ill as well as for good. Even when its aims are the best, it may preclude assimilation and acceptance of those things, good and evil, upon which depends one's lasting health. It works only under two conditions, assuming the worthwhileness of its aims: that it become through the learning process a real part of the habit-patterns; and that it be in line with the basic integration of the personality, and not a concealer of problems. In the "insight" sense, it means that it must be accompanied by a growing insight, and not be illusory or escapist. If one has expanded the meaning of "suggestion" to include active and benevolent goodwill for people, praying for them, and the like, then the value of suggestion definitely becomes much enhanced.

It is doubtful if the former "mechanical" definition of suggestion has much if anything to do with Jesus' healing ministry. His calm and absolutely assured conviction that the healing forces were prepared to operate was certainly communicated to those who were healed. But this is not suggestion in our sense. Theologically speaking, Jesus was the means of mediating grace to these sufferers.

The equation of Jesus' methods of healing with "suggestion" in any ordinary sense is, therefore, not only false but misleading and dangerous. For if this is assumed, analysis, diagnosis, and insight may be thrown out the window by those who seek to find in the ministry and life of Jesus light for their own. At any rate, any view which says that Jesus' healing methods were only "suggestion"—whether the view laud or condemn suggestion— is in fact incorrect. The last word on suggestion has not been spoken, and some elements implied in it will probably be increasingly seen as valuable—such as the need for people to affirm, not anything and everything, but that which they ought to affirm. But there are other elements in "suggestion" today.

Jesus' concern for healing and for health can hardly be understood without an attempt on our part to span the intervening years and to have some better understanding of the culture in which he lived. Failure to do this will lead us to unfortunate extremes. The Greek and Aramaic words for "healing," "health," "being whole," and "salvation" are the same or very similar. To say that health is salvation would be wrong. But to indicate that there was in Jesus' mind a close connection between all these things would be almost self-evident. We add certain meanings to each of these words; if we do not push these additions too far but concentrate on the element which all have in common, we may have a better idea as to one of Jesus' central concerns.

"Spiritual Healing" Groups. Pastoral work with the sick has always been a function of the church. Medical missionary work is a great achievement of the last century. Both these are discussed in other chapters. But the interest of the church, it came to be realized, could not soundly rest on what science seemed to disprove. Thus it was that during the nineteenth century, and indeed for a considerable time before, the "respectable" forces of religion had little interest in healing in its relation to religion because science had apparently closed the door. Modern psychosomatic medicine has shown that that door was shut much too tightly; and the possibilities of rapprochement with scientific forces are very different today from what they were, for example, in 1870 or in 1900.

Christian Science was by no means the first movement with Christian backgrounds to make large claims for the place of religion in healing, though it has certainly been the most successful. This group is questioned today on two grounds: its philosophic and theological bases, which are not discussed here; and its attempt to have "religious" workers do all healing by "religious" methods without co-operation with the manifold scientific workers led by the physician. A corollary of this is the lack of differential diagnosis or treatment. Most of the "healing groups" may be criticized on the same score, though of course some of them are worse, from the medical point of view, than Christian Science.

It is sometimes said that if the church had been awake to its opportunities in relation to health and healing in the nineteenth century, Christian Science and other religious healing groups would not have come into being. In a literal sense this is probably not true. For if the church had been awakened it would have had to put forth its convictions almost completely against the science of the day, and the cleavage between religion and science would have been much more severe than it was. Had the church possessed proof, gained by the same scientific methods which have resulted in the modern psychosomatic approach in medicine, it could have stood its ground on the proof. But true though it is that the church has awakened to this interest only in comparatively recent years, it should not be "blamed" for letting healing cults arise. Furthermore, any interest which the church should have in these questions cannot now be a "short-circuited" concern, which is the pattern for all peripheral groups in varying degrees. The church must be content to work more in the direction of specifics and less in the direction of such general affirmations as have characterized even Christian Science among the healing bodies.

A frequent question is whether Christian Science and similar groups are likely to modify the anti-medical aspects of their beliefs sufficiently to work with other Christian groups in matters related to health and healing. Since in a few places Christian Science forces have been co-operating actively with other Christian bodies on matters other than health and healing for some years, we take it for granted that that trend will continue.

If this rapprochement is to occur, it is certain that relaxation of the proscription of medicine will be the central practical change.

One hears increasingly of Christian Scientists who have visited physicians. Some of these do not seem to have left the church. One may be fairly certain that others, and probably in increasing numbers, will continue to use physicians and the other resources of modern medicine. The question then becomes: what will the Christian Science leaders do about such people? Will the membership be closed? Will the defection be overlooked? Or will there be development leading to a new statement and a new creed?

New creeds always come last, and there is not likely to be an exception here. It is possible that even though large numbers should use medical resources, the church would remain adamant, and this seems to be the prevailing conviction among students of the movement. But a new factor has been introduced into the total situation by the psychosomatic approach in medicine. The medical materialism which Christian Science fought may still be with us in places, but it has no support from scientific findings. It is possible, and indeed not unlikely, that changes both in medicine and in Christian Science may make a working relationship possible within a quarter of a century. It seems likely in any case that such a working relationship with medicine will precede a working relationship with other churches on matters of health and healing. But this analysis is mere speculation.

Is the interest on the part of the church which is obviously being recommended through this volume to be mainly in the direction of health or mainly in the direction of healing? It is easy to say that it should be both, but not very helpful. On the whole, the interest should be with health and better health. But in so far as religious resources (through religious workers, prayer, meditation, and the religious influence of physicians, nurses and others) can be brought to bear upon patients who are "ill" as well as "diseased," the church should strive to have this done well. It cannot be done without more knowledge to come out of research carried on by religious workers in collaboration with others; and when this knowledge does come, it is unlikely that it will make any dramatic statements about Christianity *always* doing this or that. It will come as specific knowledge: what kind of religious worker best helps what kind of patient, what kind of prayer helps what kind of patient, and when. Religion, and especially religious workers, must become more "person-minded." [4]

What should the church do in reference to the "healing groups"? Some of these are sincere but one-sided. Others are quacks unconsciously; and a good many are quacks consciously. There are a few which only need a more adequate apprehension of the meaning of theology to be significant contributors to the whole Christian enterprise; and a very few which are fairly sound from the health point of view and from the Christian point of view at the same time. The course is clear with reference to the two last. But the quacks and the one-sided present other problems. The right to practice the healing arts is limited by law in most states to those qualified to practice medicine, but almost everywhere exemptions are practiced with reference to religionists in order to preserve the freedom of religion. This lays a special obligation upon the Christian forces to consider the harm being done by religious groups. Active opposition may occasionally be in order; but adequate examination and investigation of the work being done by groups which are suspectedly quacks, and dissemination of this information widely, would in itself do much to rid the country of some of the worst offenders. With such groups as Christian Science, rapprochement may be possible in less time than most people think. Certainly the most important need at the moment is for the Christian churches unitedly to sponsor discreet investigations of the healing work, good or bad, now being carried on under supposedly Christian auspices.

What Spiritual Healing Is. One theological assumption has been suggested in previous sections but it remains to be stated directly. It would seem so obviously true as to require no proof. This is that any distinction made between "religious healing" or "spiritual healing" and other healing is only a practical difference so far as method is concerned. That is, healing influences which are permitted to operate through the method of prayer, for example, are not necessarily more "religious" or more "spiritual" than those set in motion by the surgeon's knife or the psychiatrist's analysis. For all healing comes from the *vis medicatrix naturae,* or the *vis medicatrix Dei,* the healing power of nature or of God, depending upon whether we are making an empirical or a religious statement. It is legitimate to make a practical distinction between the surgeon's knife, on the one hand, and prayer, on the other, and even to call the beneficent influence of one "spiritual healing," so long as it is recognized that one is not basically more "spiritual" or "religious" than the other. For both may be looked on in the broader sense as channels of the *vis medicatrix Dei,* which is another way of saying that the healing influences are ready to operate if the conditions are set up to permit them to work. In some situations the surgeon's knife must cut out offending tissue in order to release the forces of healing; in other cases the personality analysis is the central need; and in still other cases the conscious recognition of the power of these healing influences is most needed. In the majority of cases, something of all three may be helpful. We know more about when the surgeon's knife (or drug, or a new diet) is needed than we know about the others. We know more about when personality analysis is needed than we do about when prayer is needed; but we are learning new things about both. And we find increasingly that the three, applied intelligently, benefit the whole person more than any single one without the others.

Perhaps the central matter in what we distinguish practically as "spiritual healing" relates to consciousness in a special sense, to the degree of awareness of the beneficent influences which are ready to operate in a healing direction if they can be released —that is, it relates to affirmation of things which can really be affirmed on the basis of all sound religious experience and which do not conflict with the findings of science. It involves something which has not usually been recognized by those interested in "spiritual healing," a special relation between conscious awareness and the unconscious driving forces of human life. Real spiritual healing is not symptomatic. It does not deal with making affirmations about how wonderful God is to look after us as he does (cf. *Susan and God*) when at the same time these affirmations are used as a cloak shrouding recognition of basic problems (and sins) within us which remain unexamined. Real spiritual healing brings forgiveness for guilt about things concerning which one ought to feel guilty, after the real guiltiness has been recognized. It brings personality reorganization after the powerful elements of disorganization have been investigated. It brings peace after the causes of "internal warfare" have been subjected to scrutiny and have been accepted as "emotional facts." It brings love after one's capacities for hostility have been seen and diagnosed. It brings security after one's anxieties have been understood and faced.

This does not mean that the process is mainly an intellectual one; for it is not. The kind of analysis which we might give of the situation, with some verbal precision required on account of the need to communicate what we mean, is not the basic factor in the situation. It makes comparatively little difference whether the person is capable of carrying out conscious and deliberate analysis of the type we have been doing; but it makes a great difference whether the "conscious" acceptance of one's "unconscious self" is basically honest emotionally, or whether it is merely an intellectual smoke-screen. Generally, intellectual knowledge of what happens in such processes should help, provided it is sound knowledge. But possession of the knowledge does not necessarily bring the forces into operation. The psychiatrists make a similar point in their reference to the difference between "intellectual" and "emotional" insight. All of these phrases are inadequate to explain the reality, but they do offer suggestions.

Healing Functions of the Church. We are now ready to consider the healing functions which the church has and ought to have. The work for health of Christian physicians, nurses, social workers, and others must be accepted as "spiritual healing" in as basic a sense as is the work of ministers and other "religious" workers. Let us assume what has been discussed in another chapter, that no consideration of the church in relation to health and healing can overlook such work. The more conscious such workers can be of the "Christian vocation" in which they operate, and of the specific ways in which they may utilize distinctively Christian resources in their ministry, the more our medicine, social work, nursing, and the like will be effective. This does not mean that the surgeon should stop in the middle of an operation to pray, when delay would be dangerous, but rather that he should have his prayer beforehand, and it should be such a prayer as will guide and steady his hand, not excite him or make him falter.

It should be clearly understood that these other Christian workers for health have certain "professional" responsibilities and that their linking of their professional skill with their religious faith should not mean taking over the rôle of the "professional" religious worker. It may be appropriate for the surgeon sometimes to pray with a patient, just as it may be appropriate for him to discuss the patient's fears and worries. But he is probably no specialist in knowing when this should be done; at least, if he is, it is not necessarily related to his skill as a surgeon. The same is true of the psychiatrist, though this point is not quite so obvious. To expect a psychiatrist to stop in the middle of a consultation and offer a spiritual homily is sheer misunderstanding of the function of psychotherapy. There should and will be occasions in the practice of every Christian psychiatrist when some efforts will be made to link the patient's basically sound Christian affirmations to the resources needed for the solution of the current difficulty, or for the understanding of a past difficulty. For psychotherapy is not, as many believe, merely analysis; it is also a synthetic process. For although the psychiatrist helps to synthesize what is sound, he often cannot, in the nature of the case, introduce elements that are not already present. To some extent the religious worker (professionally speaking) can introduce such new elements; though actually he probably introduces really "new" ones considerably less often than he thinks. But the forms (prayers, religious homily, Biblical quotations) should not be confused with the essentially Christian service which the Christian physician, psychiatrist or social worker may perform.

When this is said, it remains true that the professional religious worker and the religious layman, who pretend to none of the professional skills like medicine or nursing, have a vital and distinctive function to perform in relation to healing. That this function must be considered with a care equal to that which the physician gives to the problem has been asserted many times. Therefore much more attention must be given to the training of religious workers for ministry to the sick. This should mean more really significant chaplaincy work. It should also mean more significant ministry to the sick (and the less well) on the part of ministers generally. Far more good work is being done by ministers than is ordinarily recognized; but unfortunately far more bad work is being done than is customarily admitted. This whole question is considered in detail in a later chapter.

Shall there be healing specialists within the church? Of course there will be our Christian physicians, psychiatrists, social workers, nurses, as well as ministers and chaplains. There will also be, we hope, an increasing number of the lay visitors of churches who are trained in the field of personal ministry. But shall there also be professional specialists in "spiritual healing"? The church has said no, and there is probably a wisdom in that conclusion which is deeper than the reasons often given for it. To have professional religious workers, such as trained chaplains, who collaborate with other healers, is one thing. To have specialists in the sense in which many religious healing groups have them is quite another. In the nature of the case these specialists cannot (and would not if they could) be members of a team. They can be specialists in their sense only by presenting their resources for healing *as opposed to* other resources. Further development should take place in bringing the distinctive resources of religion to bear for purposes of healing; but specialists in the isolationist sense can have no place in the total interest of Christianity in health and healing. Lest this dogmatic statement be misunderstood, it is emphasized again that pastors or others, especially trained for ministry to the sick, are much to be desired. How active their co-operation with other health workers is to be, in particular cases, will depend on many factors. There will certainly be occasions of emergency when "spiritual first aid" should be administered even though active co-operation with other workers is not possible for the moment. The kind of specialist in whom we do not believe is quite different. He is the one for whom working alone is a creed. Such an isolationist will do harm whether his creed grows out of ignorance or conviction. But if it is only out of ignorance, there is hope.

The religious worker concerned with co-operation in connection with healing has been at a disadvantage because his work has seemed undramatic. It need not be so. Why cannot the chaplain, provided he is sufficiently trained to know the tremendous potentialities as well as the limitations of his sphere of operation, make more claims for what he can do—in one hundred percent collaboration with physicians and others? We are just beginning to see that he can do this, and that he should do it. It is easier to command attention if one starts his own program, but unco-operative work in this field above all others is self-defeating in the long run.

Just what shall the professional religious worker do about healing? All counseling is closely related to healing, and we have pointed out elsewhere that the minister must be a counselor, whether he wants to or not. Further, every clergyman must minister to the sick. More is said about this elsewhere; but it has already been suggested that he must work co-operatively, yet on the basis of knowing the very great resources which he has at his command. Thirdly, he may make increasing use of prayer and meditation in various ways. Prayer used judiciously with individuals can accomplish something which nothing else can; for it brings the problem into the presence of a God who can give the strength and wisdom to solve it, not automatically in ouija-board fashion, but in the sense in which Christianity has always referred to "mystical experience" in the best sense. Voluntary, and usually small, prayer groups are too little encouraged by ministers. Attempts are now being made to find appropriate methods for family prayer and worship, and these may have sigificance for the ministry of healing.

The pastor may have worship services in which healing and health are central concerns. These should be primarily services of worship. Just as any of the great desires of the Christian heart are held before God in worship, so may the desire for health and healing. If the trend of the services is to request God for "special favors," they are probably not worship. But if they deepen awareness of the availability of spiritual resources for health and healing, and clear away the misunderstanding that disease or illness is punishment, they may be of great value. Such services may be special, held at fixed hours of the week and month and announced as "Services of Healing." It will not make much difference if many of the attendants are "hypochondriacs," provided the services are of the right kind. For the so-called hypochondriac needs above most others to develop the capacity for making genuine affirmations; and this he cannot do unless the level at which he sees his difficulties is both raised and deepened. Such services will not be a substitute for work with individuals. But the widespread notion that they merely reinforce neurotic prejudices is a commentary, not on the potentialities of worship services which have healing at their center, but on the way some healing services are actually conducted.

The minister has many specific resources which he may use in working with the sick. The sacraments are of great importance. Prayer, meditation, the Bible, other literature, listening, quietness, understanding—these are as real as pills and sometimes more helpful.

A good deal of what has been said applies also to the lay religious worker. He possesses some of the "distinctively religious" resources that a minister has, but he lacks certain authorities and certain training. We are not dealing here, however, with the question of whether Christian laymen *should* bring religious resources to bear in relation to health and healing. As with personal counseling, we must accept it as a fact that they *do* bring such influences to bear. The real question is how they can use such resources more effectively.

Greater complexities are involved here than are usually recognized. The human psyche is hardly simpler than the human body. The work of the layman, therefore, cannot be a substitute for the kind of professional religious work that has been discussed. But intelligent work by laymen and laywomen should have a greater place in the future than it has at present. As laymen increasingly gain understanding of the problems involved, they will see the possibilities which have hitherto gone by the board for want of understanding. But they will also be less likely to rush in where professionals fear to tread.

The fact is that most persons who are ill in any way are lonely. They feel stopped, sometimes depressed, anxious, fearful, isolated. The variations are important. But true companionship is always a spiritual therapeutic agent of the highest value. From what has been said before, we recognize that the ability to offer friendship to others depends on one's own state. Therefore the personality of the one who offers and his methods of offering friendship are of great importance. But if this is tendered sincerely, intelligently, and with relatively "pure" motives, it has untold therapeutic influence. Some laymen can do this, usually, of course, with persons they have known before illness came. This is the quality above all others which should be sought in church visitors and developed by further training. Sometimes such people may be very capable, and yet be wholly incapable of understanding how they do it. But for every one of this type, there are a hundred who will profit from further understanding. And no one should be proud of the fact that he does not

understand how he does it. Attributing all power to God is
scarcely a satisfactory excuse for failing to understand His
spiritual laws.

The Church's Faith in Health and Healing. It is an old trick
of the quack to deal with resources accessible to anyone as if it
required a special process to find them.[5] A corollary is to treat
certain results as if they depended solely upon the kind of
experience of which only members of the "in-group" possess.
The scientific forces sometimes unwittingly play into the hands
of such groups by wholesale denunciation of their methods,
which is then interpreted by these groups as an attack upon
their faith. It is in this way that the term "faith-healing" has
come to have an unsavory connotation, as if it were pure magic
to see that attitudes and outlook have something to do with
physical states and processes. Real facts cannot be exploited in
the interests of a special group provided they remain real facts
in the minds of everyone. But if they can be made articles of
faith, a special hold on them is possible. This has happened to
what we may call the "influence of faith upon healing."

Our survey of psychosomatic medicine, inadequate though it
is, has indicated that the reality of psychic influence, not only
upon attitudes but upon somatic processes, is a fact, and that
its presence or absence is merely a matter of degree. Let us not,
therefore, make an article of faith out of this, but rather treat
it as a fact. If we want to "believe" that in a *particular case* the
attitudes (e.g., faith) have had a greater and more significant
influence than the physician or someone else says they have had,
let us be clear that we are talking about the application of a
principle in a specific case and not about the validity of the
general principle. It is misunderstanding on this point which
has put the whole conception of spiritual forces in healing in
such peril today. Because we have not been "person-minded" or

"case-minded," we have put the principle in danger when in reality it is in no danger at all.

If attitudes and outlook can have such a tremendous influence on health and healing, for good or ill, it follows that sound outlook and attitudes have a beneficent influence. Most of the psychosomatic work done thus far has been in the other direction, indicating the influence of unsatisfactory attitudes and outlook upon the production of illnesses. But this indicates the need for more specific work in the other direction as well. Either way the principle is proved, even though at present we can speak more accurately about production of specific illnesses than about production of healing.

These attitudes and outlooks are not to be understood merely as conscious formulations, however much Christian terminology may be used. We say, groping for words, that they must take in the emotional, intellectual and volitional life. What we mean is that the attitude which really represents the person must come from the depths and go to the heights of his experience and must include more than he consciously knows, feels or wills. There is real insight in the cry, "Lord, I believe. Help thou mine unbelief." For only in recognition of the divided interests within the self can one proceed on the path to attitudes of real faith. But if such faith is present, though always in imperfect degree, it may have great therapeutic influence.

Many medical workers are recognizing that attitudes of faith in this sense are therapeutic in their influence .Any surgeon knows that his patient's chances are improved if there is "faith" in the surgeon on the part of the patient. He also recognizes, though we must forgive him for not being an expert on the *psyche,* that the general attitude which he may call "confidence" or "courage" is an asset. Beyond that it may not be necessary for him to go. But we believe, as Christians, that there is a close relationship between the validity of the object of faith, and the operating strength of faith. As a scientist (and the physician is first scientist even though he is also more than that), the physician's concern is with the constructiveness of the outlook present in his patient. If the patient's faith were based on any kind of object, it would make comparatively little difference to the physician, as scientist, as long as it worked. And there are many persons whose level of development in spiritual experience is such that a faith vital to them would mean something considerably less to us, just as there are others who would look on our faith as of a less developed character than theirs. The faith which works will, when analyzed in the light of the best Christian theology, differ a good deal among different people. But it is useless to talk of "rabbits'-foot faith" in this connection; for we do live in a culture which disbelieves in rabbits' feet as objects of faith. Yet we also live in a culture where understanding and appreciation of the nature of God varies more widely than most persons realize. What we are suggesting, in other words, is not complete uniformity in the matter of understanding the object of faith, for that would mean that a person's theology would have to be set completely right—which probably means putting it in accord with our own—before healing forces could go into operation. That is not so, and should not be so, even though we may want and justifiably attempt to improve the level of spiritual capacity.

The degree of "sophistication" is important in reference to the way in which different persons understand their relation to the object of faith. There should be some better phrase to describe this, for "sophistication" has the wrong connotations. Its opposite, "naïveté," is equally unsatisfactory. Perhaps the meaning would be suggested more accurately by referring to those whose thought processes are more abstract and those who always think concretely, or those who tend to deal with symbols "semantically," and those who tend to deal with them literally.

There is a real difference between the meaning which such a phrase as "God's healing force" will have to these two types of person. One type may expand the figure concretely so as to see the image of a line of communication by tubes with heaven, the water of life flowing down by the sheer force of spiritual gravity. This figure may be helpful to both types; but to one it may be more meaningful because it is more concrete. The danger enters if he forgets it is a figure. The other type may perceive the meaning, and also perceiving the danger in turning a line of communication into a private line, he may actually find the figure of negative value for him. To attempt to get this latter group to conceive of the object of faith, or of the processes by which faith is strengthened, in such ways as this, may therefore do more harm than good.

Many have found that meditation on great verses of Scripture, or on other simple phrases of affirmation, brings them great spiritual help. Perhaps a majority of the most sensitive and intelligent Christians have been in this group. But it is not true of all. Where this method is not appropriate, we shall be doing a disservice by recommending or insisting on it. This quality, abstract or concrete-mindedness, or whatever it may be called, must always be taken into account in connection with help toward understanding one's relation to the object of faith. For what we want is to make the Christian object of faith more real and more relevant in people's hearts and minds. A few confirmed intellectuals are still convinced that God does not exist because the picture of the God in whom they believed at the age of six is now known to be immature and inadequate. They, too, may be helped to an object of faith, not necessarily just *our* object, by indicating to them that the lacunae caused by the evacuation of the childish concept needs to be filled with a more mature conception.

No scientific methods can prove the "truth" or "reality" of the object of faith, but they can indicate whether the object of faith works and is tied up with the "whole personality." It is at this point that all our Christian experience becomes concentrated in our conviction that the nature of the object of faith is important. We believe that spiritual experience must be nourished and must grow even as the body grows; that no one has anything but imperfect spiritual perception; that more insight into the nature of what we believe to be spiritual reality is possible at any stage in the process. Let us use the methods of science to prove *how much* certain kinds of religious influences, in certain kinds of people, help to bring therapeutic results. But let us not fall into the error of trying to prove the nature of God because of the use of certain methods which have brought therapeutic results. Science has proved the reality of faith as an agent for therapy or pathology. It is our job to increase faith in the object of faith in which we believe and thus to have it produce more therapeutic results.

CHAPTER VI

MENTAL HEALTH AND RELIGIOUS EDUCATION

There is a wide gap between the teaching of the best Christian religious educators and the actual religious education practices of most churches. For the principles, stated or implied by leading religious educators, generally take full cognizance of the findings in general education, psychology, and related subjects; and some attention has been paid to mental hygiene. Yet even these leaders are distressed that progress has not been more rapid in the application to the educational practices of the churches of what is definitely known. What light can be thrown on this dilemma by our knowledge of mental health?

It is not the purpose of this discussion to present a philosophy of religious education. That has been ably done by the religious educators.[1] It is probably true, as Harrison S. Elliott seems to suggest, that a full and deep understanding of modern mental hygiene will provide some new bases for a philosophy of Christian education.[2] But even apart from any such thorough-going study of the philosophy, our knowledge of mental health throws considerable light upon problems of current Christian education.

To summarize briefly the point of view of leading religious educators, it is emphasized that the child is an autonomous individual who has and must have his own experiences. He is not merely a little adult or candidate for adulthood. In order for him to learn, in the area of religion as elsewhere, he must have authentic experiences of his own. Religious insights will be meaningful to him only as they are experienced firsthand and not merely accepted secondhand from his parents or teachers. While it is the purpose of Christian education to equip him with understanding and appreciation of the Christian tradition and point of view, the methods must be such as enable him to discover and assimilate these for himself. Thus he will come to Christian beliefs of his own, and the tradition itself will inevitably be modified in the process. He will come to have some intellectual understanding of the Christian point of view, but this will occur only as he has authentic feeling for and assimilation of this point of view and only as he attempts to meet situations and make decisions in the light of this point of view. The Bible should mean much to him, as something vitally related to his own life and experience. For the child is growing, and his religious experience will grow in precisely the same ways as do other aspects of his experience. Religious education, therefore, cannot concentrate solely on the "content" which the child is to learn but must pay equal attention to the methods by which he learns.

Not all religious educators would subscribe even to this brief statement of principles. But it seems likely that most of them would do so. It is clear that these educators are far more concerned with the child, as child, than was once true, and that they believe in paying full attention to the emotional aspects of the child's life and growth. This would suggest, for example, that problems relating to the methods of teaching, the personality of the teacher, and the like, would be at least equal in importance to the problems of curriculum.

Yet in spite of the way in which these principles seem to fit in with our knowledge of mental health, in practice this knowledge can rarely be seen at work. Is this merely the inevitable lag between the progressive work of leaders and the practical application by followers? Is it because enough good teachers have not been found? Or might there be other reasons also, granting that these would have some influence? Is it possible that the attention which Christian educators have paid to the philosophy of religious education, necessary though it has been, has itself acted as a stumbling block to practical progress?

One who approaches the thoughtful literature of religious education from the point of view of mental health is struck by a fact which he finds difficult to describe. He finds almost every principle recognized and stated which mental hygiene has led him to believe is significant. But he gets no sense of emphasis. It is easy to recognize and state a principle and then to pigeonhole it. That is what some of the religious education literature seems to have done, excluding thoughtful writing such as Elliott's. One may concede, for example, that teachers should be mentally healthy as well as intelligent in order to do a good job. But if one merely states this, and then proceeds to questions of organization and curriculum alone, only lip service has been paid to the principle.

The quality of religious education is bound to be no higher than the quality of those who teach. There can be no doubt that anything done, and something has been done, to improve the caliber of teachers, and of teaching materials and methods, will improve religious education. But the problem of the teacher is central. And from the mental health point of view, the problem of the teacher's emotional relationship to his pupils is of paramount importance. Is it possible that some light can be thrown on the present situation by looking at the relationship between teachers and pupils in our church schools? To do this is not to examine the entire problem. But it is to take one of the central problems and to throw it into the foreground so that it does not blur into insignificance against the many other problems which are also on the stage.

Teachers and Behavior Problems. Some years ago E. K. Wickman was interested in finding what kinds of emotional or behavior problems school children have and how frequently they occur. In gathering information, he soon discovered that he was studying the teachers' attitudes toward behavior problems rather than the behavior problems themselves. A brief account of his study is necessary in order to understand the conclusions which are significant for our purposes.[3]

From the initial explorations, a list of behavior problems was prepared, and teachers were asked to check how frequently each problem occurred in their experience. The teachers were also asked to rate the behavior adjustment of each child. A different group of teachers was then asked to rate the relative seriousness of different kinds of behavior problems; that is, to indicate which type of problem behavior would be likely to cause most harm for the child. These last ratings were then checked against a list of similar ratings made by mental hygiene clinic workers.

The trend of the results soon became apparent when the teachers tended to stress as serious those disturbances of behavior which attacked their own standards of "morality, obedience, orderliness, application to school work, and agreeable social conduct."[4] At the same time there was a tendency for the teachers to rate as not serious any problems which did not cause them active irritation or annoyance. One might say that the teachers reacted to the children by judging behavior as unsound in the degree to which they themselves were unfavorably affected by it.

The teachers reported that only a few (about seven per cent) of the children had serious behavior problems. Their definition of the "problem child" was one who was antagonistic to authority, did not conform to order and routine, and who did not work hard enough. But few teachers identified children who were shy, oversensitive, fearful, or suspicious as having serious behavior problems.

When the ratings by teachers were set against the ratings by mental hygienists of the relative seriousness of different kinds of behavior difficulties, the contrast was striking. At the top of the teachers' list of the most serious problems (those judged to have the most serious consequences for the child, not necessarily the problems most frequently encountered) were the following: heterosexual activity, stealing, masturbation, obscene notes and talk, untruthfulness, truancy, impertinence and defiance, cruelty and bullying, cheating, destroying school materials, disobedience, unreliableness, temper tantrums, lack of interest in work, profanity, impudence, and rudeness. At the top of the mental hygienists' list of the most serious problems were these: unsocialness, suspiciousness, unhappiness and depression, resentfulness, fearfulness, cruelty and bullying, becoming discouraged easily, being suggestible, being overcritical of others, sensitiveness, being domineering, sullenness, stealing, shyness, being a physical coward, selfishness.

Further analysis of these ratings shows that the teachers regarded sex acts, dishonesties, and transgressions against authority as the most serious kinds of problems; and withdrawing, recessive personality and behavior traits as the least serious. The mental hygienists, on the other hand, considered withdrawing, recessive personality and behavior traits, and the like, to be the most serious types of problems; while transgressions against authority, violations of order, and the like were considered least serious.

The reversal of the two judgments was by no means complete but it was significant enough to challenge our full attention. The teachers tended to believe that what bothered them most was also most serious for the child. The mental hygienists tended to believe that the child who was in some way out of the group had the most serious kind of problem. Perhaps the judgment of the mental hygienists represents something of a reaction. That is, they may have believed that the child whose response is aggressive is bound to get some kind of attention, whereas the child who is merely shy to an excessive degree may not even be considered by the teacher to have a problem.

The Wickman study pointed out that it was the tendency of teachers to greet aggressive behavior on the part of children with aggressiveness in return, which would have the net effect of increasing this type of conduct on the children's part. If the child's problem had been one of learning to accept authority, reaction to him on an aggressive basis would make it increasingly difficult for him to accept authority. Similarly, if the teacher reacted indulgently to the children who had passive or non-irritating traits, then the tendency was to foster habits of dependence in these children. Counter-attacking and indulging were, therefore, unsatisfactory methods.

What the Wickman study suggests is that the teachers *reacted* to the aggressive children, and dealt overindulgently with the withdrawing children. Thus the difficulties of adjustment for both groups were accentuated.

Specific recommendations growing out of the study are worth summarizing. In the training of teachers, more emphasis should be placed on the psychology of child development with special reference to emotional factors. The fact that children are not little adults should be buttressed with evidence and experience. Training courses should give adequate attention to understanding sexual development and behavior in children. Perhaps most important, teachers should be taught to look behind the problems, or symptoms, to an understanding of what causes them in individual cases. The teachers themselves must be taught to believe in, to accept emotionally, the facts about dealing with children's behavior problems.

This study, while penetrating, is not the last word, and at one point it is unclear. Some people, studying it, may say, "But stealing in children is serious in itself; and if mental hygienists do not think so, that is another evidence of their lack of interest in moral questions." There is some justification for this attitude, though it is mistaken as stated. Stealing, for example, is serious so long as we make no effort to understand why the child steals; and as a matter of fact, closer study of the mental hygienists' judgments indicates that they recognize this fact. But they recognize also that there may be many different reasons in the life of the child to make him steal. Stealing therefore is a symptom, a sign that something is wrong; but the essential difficulty will probably be aggravated if attention is concentrated only on the stealing.

There is a realistic social consideration in reference to stealing, as well as a question of mental health. One must consider the child from whom something is stolen as well as the child who steals. But the mental hygienists are right on two counts. First, they imply that we have overdone the attitude of trying to get rid of stealing merely by condemning it; indeed, our overcondemnation of it may be one impetus for the child to steal. Second, they believe it is more important therapeutically to understand what cause is represented by the symptom of stealing than merely to condemn the stealing. Another way to put it is that stealing is morally wrong but that the child who does the stealing is not "bad."

The fact remains that the mental hygienists are mainly interested in the emotional health of the individual; and their assumption is that his health will prove best in the long run for the health and welfare of the whole group. Fortunately this is usually true, especially if methods of understanding the causes rather than merely treating the symptoms are used. But it is not invariably true; and religious workers are more likely than mental hygienists to see the circumstances in which there is real and continuing conflict of interests. Yet the essential point of the mental hygiene group, understanding the causes of behavior difficulties, is something religious workers need.

Church School Teachers and Behavior Problems. Impressed by the findings of the Wickman study with public school teachers, J. J. Van Boskirk and Charles T. Holman recently decided to see how church school teachers compare in their attitudes toward behavior problems in children.[5] They secured the co-operation of church school teachers in five churches in the middle west, most of them having constituencies distinctly above the average in education, intelligence, economic status, and cultural opportunities. To the church school teachers they presented essentially the same questions as the Wickman study had presented to the public school teachers. In the unpublished report of their findings, they point out that the number with which they dealt was considerably less than that which the Wickman survey used and that the results therefore cannot be considered as definitive.

Yet there is no question that the judgments of the church school teachers are almost the same as those of the public school teachers. There seems to be a slight difference, a few of the judgments of the church school teachers approaching more closely to those of the mental hygienists than did those of the public school group. Whether this is due to the years intervening between the time of the Wickman study and the Chicago study, or whether it means that the church school is slightly more responsive to mental health teaching than the public school, is not entirely clear. But for all practical purposes the results are identical. In other words, with only the slightest variations, that which has been said in connection with the Wickman study is entirely true of teachers in church schools.

The Wickman and Van Boskirk-Holman studies are of real significance in helping us to understand one of the most basic mental health problems in connection with religious education. If the findings of these studies are correct, they indicate that most church school teachers have a reactive kind of emotional relationship to their children, that they respond not in terms of the children's needs or possibilities, but in terms of what irritates or does not irritate them or the institution they represent. Church school teachers as a group, therefore, are not able to "forget themselves" sufficiently to help the children face their own problems. If this is so, the essential reason is their lack of understanding of emotional realities, whether in themselves or in the lives of children.

Church school teachers need more knowledge of normal child behavior, especially along emotional lines. The religious educators say that the educational process is not solely intellectual, that it is rather a matter of facing life problems where real issues are at stake and that it is therefore emotional. But what does this mean? The Van Boskirk-Holman study suggested that there were no essential differences in judgment of the seriousness of behavior problems between teachers in liberal or progressive church schools and those in more conservative types of schools, whether considered from the point of view of educational method or kind of religious content involved. This might mean only that the trappings of progressive educational methods were being confused with the more essential characteristics of the church school which the religious educators would desire. Yet this cannot wholly afford the explanation; for at least two of the church schools in question are recognized as being among the best in the middle west.

Perhaps a more adequate explanation may be found in consideration of why this subject has been discussed from the point of view of "problems." Some religious educators may already have said, "These studies are interesting but, after all, they deal only with problem behavior, and religious education deals with development of the normal." No single misunderstanding seems so influential in holding back religious education today as that which is implied in such a statement.

Religious education is concerned with behavior and conduct, and with better conduct—with conduct which brings deeper emotional and religious returns to the individual and the community. But physicians are no longer saying, "You have nothing which I can cut out; therefore there is nothing I can do for you." They are becoming increasingly concerned with preventive medicine, indeed, as has been discussed earlier, in improving and increasing health. But they know they can do this only by diagnosis first of the "problems," and then go on from there.

What, after all, is so unusual about having problems? And why should an approach from the problem point of view be considered abnormal? Why are some kinds of problems considered so much more abnormal than others? Having problems —and problems as we speak of them are always emotional—is a part, though fortunately not the only part, of the whole process of growth, and it is constantly with us. The man who is not facing any problems has already taken the first step toward an unhealthy solution of the problems he has. Indeed, problems should be considered "abnormal" only in so far as they really lead to serious personal and social maladjustments. On the grounds of realistic observation of consequences, therefore, problems involving excessive shyness or cruelty in children are usually more serious than those involving sex behavior or disobedience.

The approach of this discussion, from the point of view of teachers' responses to problems of behavior in children, is not significant, therefore, because problems are abnormal, but rather because they are parts of the normal process of growth and development. It is in crisis situations, furthermore, that more of the child's emotional outlook is developed than at other times. The reaction of the teacher to the child at some point of conduct is bound to produce a crisis in the emotional sense even if one did not exist before. What the teacher does on such problem occasions is, therefore, more important than what he does at other times. Children are exceedingly sensitive to adult criticism. Though a church school teacher may lack some of the disciplinary controls of a public school teacher, he nevertheless possesses a great emotional power over the lives of the children. If the child is more likely to be influenced when he somehow feels an emotional crisis is on, then it is a positive obligation for us to examine the teacher-child relationship from the crisis point of view. To study what teachers consider to be behavior problems is to study the teachers' relationship to children at points of crisis.

If religious education were "normal," in the sense that it did not bother with problems, it would be operating in a vacuum. It would be of no value to use the laws of intellectual habit-formation in teaching a child about religion if the teacher were to neglect the laws of emotional habit-formation to help him actually to experience religion and practice it.

It is not being suggested that a problem approach should be substituted in religious education practice for a "normal" approach, for that is to misunderstand the situation. But this much is urged. The personal problem—whether it be an irritating tendency to steal handkerchiefs or a passive tendency to sit shyly with head down—is not something to be got over as quickly as possible by any means so that the "real work" can go on. It is itself the opportunity for understanding which can lead to real growth. Even if the teacher can understand only enough to avoid counter-attacking or over-indulging the child, much may be accomplished.

It seems a fair hypothesis that the teachers in the progressive church schools which were studied had not much more appreciation of the opportunities afforded by emotional crisis than did those in other schools. This is understandable; for the misunderstanding of problems, crises, and the abnormal has been almost as great among liberal as among conservative groups. Is it not possible that a teacher might accept intellectually the constructive philosophy of the religious educators and yet fail to see such emotional implications as these?

Religion and Emotion in the Life of the Child. In an illuminating article on "The Fundamental Needs of the Child," Lawrence K. Frank makes suggestions which are of far-reaching significance for religious education from the mental health point of view.[6] He begins by pointing out how extraordinarily significant it is that we are now discussing the needs of the child as a basis for his education. Citing the old Chinese practice of foot-binding as an illustration of how this has not been followed heretofore in the physiological field, he says that comparable psychological and social practices have been even more prevalent and important. In reality, he says, we are only on the threshold of knowing the fundamental needs of the child, and much of what we do know is rather negative than positive. "Probably the most general statement that we can make about the child's needs is that he should be protected from distortions, from unnecessary deprivations and exploitations by adults."[7]

He points out the difficulties which standardizations of all kinds have caused in dealing with children. Citing as an instance the very different needs which children have in reference to sleep, he suggests that the standard charts about how long children should sleep have caused wholly unnecessary difficulty. Of great importance is the need for all who deal with children to understand what it means for children to learn to handle emotion. When emotion is roused in the young child, as it often is, the disturbance may be said to "seize control of the child and often impel him to act violently and destructively against things and people and even himself."[8] He must learn how to manage these reactions and free himself from their control. Adults seldom realize the panic the child has, for he finds himself wholly unfree, completely in the grip of something which is not himself. What the child needs at these times is help in learning how to have real control over himself. This particular point has been well illustrated by the Wickman study. "Perhaps the greatest need in these situations is for sympathetic reassurance that will allay the child's panic and so help him to meet the situation more effectively." [9] Often a situation appears terrifying to a child when it does not seem so to adults. Failure to see what the point of view of the child may mean will result in counterattacking or over-indulging types of emotional response which will aggravate the problem. Grief, too, is difficult for a child for, unlike the adult, he cannot have the comforting philosophy which may enable him to do something besides mourn. Though there is no easy answer to this, it is certain that attempts merely to deny the loss to the child are bound to fail.

Frank says it is foolish to think that this means elimination of any repression of the child. Deprivations are necessary, and the child needs "a wisely administered regulation or direction" to relieve him of the burden of learning unaided to manage his

own emotional responses before he is ready. "It is not the order-
ing of life that damages the child, but the distortion, the fears,
anxieties and permanent frustrations and inhibitions that paren-
tal and educational practices unnecessarily inflict upon the child
in the process of establishing these socially and individually necessary repressions." [10]

Traditional teaching, he adds, has paid only lip-service to the
distinction between the child and his conduct. It is the child who
has been called "bad," whereas "it is the behavior that should be
defined as undesirable."[11] This tends to make the child unhappy,
fearful, inadequate and even rejected. Frank suggests that even
delinquent acts may rise out of blind efforts to assuage these
feelings. This does not mean that parents or teachers should be
"impersonal." The child needs "mothering," which means not
pampering, but "giving a feeling of being liked and wanted, of
belonging to some one who cares, and of being guided in the
conduct of life with benevolent interest and confidence." [12]
Though the family is the primary agency where this is supplied,
the school too has to add its contribution.

The child must come at Christianity through the same kind of
learning processes used in connection with anything else. Since
religion goes so deeply into the emotional life, it is even more
important for a teacher in religious education to be familiar
with the kind of thing Frank discusses than it would be for a
teacher of reading or arithmetic. We have some evidence, especially that gained from adults looking back on their childhood
religious experience, that the kind of emotion generated in children by religious teaching is sometimes wholly different from
what was intended by their teachers; and that in many cases
the emotional interpretation by the child is subversive of the real
purposes of Christian education. Theologically we may believe
that God is judge as well as father; but the child whose picture

of God is equated with an all-seeing eye, which is emotionally interpreted as fearsome, has a conception which will grossly impede the kind of understanding of and relationship to God desirable in Christian education.

The church school teacher who confronts this problem is likely to say, "You have outlined a real problem; tell me what I can do to solve it or to avoid it." It seems negative to talk about understanding the child, his fundamental needs, his point of view, his emotional responses, and to place attention on not counter-attacking the child's emotion. It is a little more positive when we say the teacher should help the child to direct and manage his emotion. In the case of the all-seeing eye, the teacher may realize that there is nothing unusual if the child thinks of God with dread; indeed, the teacher's first realization should be that, if she responds to the dread emotion in the child as if it were beyond the pale, that emotion will become more firmly entrenched. She may tell the child, with illustrations familiar to his own experience, something positive about the nature of God; but all this will be of no use if she does not accept the emotional response as a fact.

This does not suggest that the child should come to think of God, for example, in a purely matter-of-fact way, i.e., without emotion. Nor does it suggest that God needs to be only protection and love to children. Just as the child who is genuinely loved by his parents can accept a great deal of discipline without undue difficulty, so a child can appreciate the inexorable aspects of the nature of God if he has had experience of the deeper loving nature. There is also a great difference between matter-of-factness and naturalness. The former suggests an absence of elements of awe and wonder, of the milder types of emotion which scientific workers believe are in themselves of positive value. Naturalness suggests the presence of these "positive" emotions in the same kind of way the child would feel about the love and protective authority of his parents or teachers.

What our knowledge of mental health suggests to religious education is something which seems negative at first glance but which has the most profound positive implications. Our discussion has been devoted largely to problem-behavior, not so much in order to discuss therapeutic methods for solving those particular problems as to see what might be learned about teaching children how to handle and utilize emotion. It is not that religious educators should become guidance clinic personnel in the sense that they should spend their time detecting, diagnosing and helping to solve the personal and emotional problems of children. What is urgently needed is much simpler than that. R. H. Edwards has called it "person-mindedness." If the teacher is genuinely sensitive to individual variations, knows how childhood differs from adulthood, appreciates and truly accepts the facts about the child's struggle to get away from blind control by his emotions, and understands how religion and religious ideas are tied up with emotion—there is a far better chance that the Christian convictions and life-habits with which children emerge into maturity will themselves be mature.

Training of Church School Teachers. If what has been said thus far is accepted, it must be obvious that a main point of attack must be the training of teachers. Matters of organization and procedure in this technical field are obviously beyond our scope. But the groups which are responsible for teacher training work have been, perhaps necessarily, so tied up with problems of organization and procedure, and so limited by lack of personnel, that they have put comparatively little stress, in teacher training work, on the kind of thing which is discussed here. The situation is improving; and whatever can be done along organizational lines—indeed, to have teacher training at all—is very much to the good. But training which failed to include consideration of the emotional psychology of childhood did not help public school teachers much at the crucial points we have discussed, and it is not likely to help church school teachers any more. Training in intellectual matters is necessary but it is no substitute for education in the area of emotion.

Parents are becoming increasingly aware of the emotional needs of the child. This means that they are more interested than ever in what the public school does to their boy as a person and less interested in what skills he acquires for their own sake. Similarly, they are concerned in increasing measure with the whole life-outlook which the child assimilates as a result of church school experience and less concerned with mere skills or knowledge. It is not unlikely that more concern, in teacher training work, with the emotional aspects of teaching children would in itself enlist the interest of a greater number of able teachers.

Why should not a live course on child psychology, including clinical records (life histories of children), be a basic part of the training of teachers and administrators of religious education programs? The kind of discussion involved in this chapter is no substitute for that, though it may point up the importance of the subject. But for real understanding and assimilation the case method is unsurpassed. Some such records are available in print, though to date not many of them have contained significant material on the religious life and outlook of the child. If church school teachers began, however, to study their task from this angle, more case studies containing material on the child's religious outlook and life would be available. No amount of generalization, however good, can be a substitute for this kind of study in connection with teacher training work.

New opportunities and new dangers are involved in the growing amount of week-day religious education work. It is being said, and rightly, that if the church fails to keep its program on a level at least as high as that of the public school, these new efforts will do religion a disservice and tend to drive the child away from the church as he grows older. This is not wholly a matter of securing teachers with intellectual competence, important though that is. Fully as important is the need for securing, and usually training, teachers who are competent in the field of the emotions. However slowly, the public schools are making real advances at this point. Now that the church is in more obvious competition than ever before, methodologically speaking, with the public schools, it cannot afford to neglect the emotional life of the child and of the teacher.

This is no counsel of perfection. This kind of knowledge can in large measure be taught and learned. Such teacher training need not require more expense, equipment, or time than is now used by the best of these courses. And it is possible, though still unproved, that such training might create a wholly new place and status for the volunteer teacher. Professional teaching in the church school is still only a dream in most places and may remain so for a long time, however desirable it may be. Volunteer teachers of children may necessarily continue to be the main resource. A mother who has done fairly well with her own children will not necessarily be an effective church school teacher. But like most mothers, she will be impressed, in dealing with her own children, with the paramount importance of emotional factors. If teacher training work can begin for her at that point, she has an excellent chance of becoming truly competent.

Religious Education for Adults. This discussion has been wholly about the religious education of children rather than about that of adolescents or adults. Our knowledge of mental health has significant suggestions to make in reference to the latter groups, but it is so closely related to the entire practical functioning of the church that it has not been deemed necessary to say much about it in relation to religious education in the narrower sense.

On the formal side, however, there is some evidence at hand to suggest that both adults and young people heartily welcome the type of course which enables them to understand the emotional life, and therefore manage it better. Although frequently the best ways to approach this kind of thing with adults or adolescents are indirect rather than direct, there is no doubt that most people eventually seek some more or less formal help along these lines, even if it be only to read self-help or boot-strap literature. The enormous quantity of such literature now being distributed, quite varied in its degree of helpful or harmful influence, gives evidence of this fact. It calls things by different names and frequently suggests "easy" solutions, but in large measure it deals with the very things on which religious education should be giving help to people. To suggest that the church may enter more directly into this area is not to encourage more introspection. There is introspection enough of the kind which chains people's eyes to a myopic inward-look. But there is too little of the kind of looking inward which is able to focus on the far vision precisely because it has first looked clearly inside.

Mental health and mental hygiene are not the only sources of wisdom from the contemporary world which have significant suggestions to make to Christian religious education. Contemporary sources are themselves small compared to those of the entire Christian tradition and history. But the suggestions implied in the mental health point of view cannot be brushed lightly aside, even if they are only part of the picture.

As Elliott well points out, so long as the educational process confined its attention to intellectual factors, "there was still possible the reservation for religion of the area of the human spirit. But in the developments of mental hygiene, God's relation to that aspect of human personality and destiny was also threatened." [13] Whatever the ultimate theological answer, the practical reply cannot be in terms of denying the truths as made clear by mental hygiene. Yet if the church denies them by paying them no practical heed in its religious education work, it merely abandons the realm of emotional fact to a destiny which does not guarantee to make application on the basis of Christian presuppositions. There are large issues at stake, but none can be larger than the emotional understanding and appreciation of his relation to God which each child may discover and create through the influence of the home and the church school.

CHAPTER VII

THE RELIGIOUS WORKER AND MENTAL ILLNESSES

People may be ill in mind, body or spirit. They are seldom ill in one way without being also ill in another. The practical distinction between "illness," or "physical illness," and "mental illness," has some value so long as we realize that it relates more to the symptoms than to the causes. It is a pragmatic distinction, which arose in a day when people felt that there was no real relationship between "mental" and "physical" disorders.

Fortunately use of the legal term "insanity" to describe severe mental disorders is disappearing. The medical term "psychosis" is being used more frequently; and while it too has defects, it is the best we have. The term "mental illness" is sometimes used as a synonym for psychosis; but the implications of mental illness are really much broader than those of psychosis.

We ought really to talk of "personality illness" or "personality disorder" if we wish to speak from the point of view of causation. For we could make a distinction between those disorders whose causes are such that they can be attacked mainly by the use of psychological or "spiritual" methods, and those whose causes are such that they can be attacked mainly by physical or physiological methods. For our purposes it is sufficient if we have some idea of what the various terms usually mean.

We must assume that there is no rigid or complete distinction between serious mental illness and the kinds of mental illness in the form of anxieties and upsets which all of us encounter daily. Of course there are some differences. There is a great social difference between the person who can get along in society even if he feels upset and the person who must be segregated in a hospital both for his own good and for that of the community. But no evidence has been produced to show that there is a categorical division between the mental processes of all psychotics and those of all "normal" individuals. Some categorical distinctions have been demonstrated about some disorders, as for example with paresis, but this seems to be true only when there are specific organic factors which can definitely be traced.

This means that study of the "pathology" (or gross distortions) of the mind and the personality throws light on the "normal" processes by which the mind and personality operate, just as study of diseased organs of the body throws light on the "normal" functioning of those organs. This is not to suggest that there are no differences between "normal" and "abnormal." But it does mean that the simple distinctions usually made are misleading.

We might say that the efforts made by the religious worker to understand "abnormal" psychology throw light upon his understanding of "normal" psychology—provided the psychology he studies is good. The reverse should also be true. There is no "discontinuity" or definite break between learning about these subjects, although practical distinctions can and should be made.

These assumptions are of particular importance in considering the pastor's relation to mental illnesses in view of the trends within some church circles to disregard them. These are not new trends, but it is high time they were re-examined. One student of this field has well said, "If a person breaks his leg, there are hundreds of church hospitals which stand ready to give him treatment. But if he breaks his heart and has a psychosis, he has to be cared for by the state." [1] The church in days past might have said that it would look after a man with a broken heart so long as he was "rational"; but we now know that the temporary dominance of the "irrational" is precisely what indicates the heart which is most devastatingly broken.

This bogie has appeared in new form in recent years. There has been a good deal of talk and writing about "pastoral psychiatry" and similar topics, which may suggest that the principles involved in handling "serious cases" differ radically from those involved in handling "normal" situations. [2] It is doubtless true that some ministers with special training can deal safely with cases more serious than those with which the average man should attempt to cope. But this area of difference is comparatively small; and in any case it refers only to whether or not the pastor shall try to give help and not to the principles involved in understanding the situation.

Kinds of Mental Illnesses. It is useful to divide mental illnesses into groups in this way: those which have an origin known to be organic, i.e., in which an attack on something organic must be made, if cure is to have a chance of resulting; and those which, thus far at least, have not yielded to cure by the application of treatment to organic factors. It should be noted that this does not divide mental illnesses into organic and functional, as if one were "real" and the other not. This statement is based upon what is thus far known.

It is now generally believed by scientific workers that probably only a few of the disorders falling in the second division will eventually be located in specific organic factors which can be attacked in that way alone. The best known example has been that of paresis, which was classed as a mental disorder because the dominant symptoms related to mentality and general behavior, such as delusions of grandeur, great excitability, loss of competence and the like. The condition was discovered to be due to the syphilitic spirochete operating in the brain years after syphilis had originally been introduced into the body. Pellagra is a more recent example along the same line. But few workers believe that any considerable number of the disorders now classified as "mental" will be found to have equally specific organic points of origin. The more such specific organic causes can be found, however, the happier all workers should be.

It is generally recognized, however, that the best physical treatment, going hand in hand with the best psychological or mental treatment, is of greatest value.

A further distinction about mental illnesses is made between "psychosis," "psychoneurosis" or simply "neurosis" and any other illnesses which do not fit into those categories. The practical distinction is usually that psychosis requires treatment along institutional lines; whereas most neurotics can get along well enough to remain in the open community. This is not a wholly accurate way of examining the matter; but it is a good simple distinction.

Another way of approaching the distinction is in terms of the area of conflict. One psychiatrist has said that the neurotic is in conflict within himself, the criminal is in conflict with society, and the psychotic is in conflict with both.[3] This too is helpful but not definitive.

From the point of view of causes, the psychotic is the person with unhealthy tendencies which have gone relatively deep, while the neurotic's conflicts are somewhat closer to the surface and are therefore more accessible. For example, the person with a deep depression is likely to be psychotic; while the person who is nursing a state of anxiety which is concealed from the casual observer is probably neurotic.

There are some individuals who do not seem to fit into even

these broad groups. There is, for instance, the "neurotic criminal," who steals not so much to use what he steals as he does in order to get caught.[4] There is the "psychopathic personality" (whatever that means), who may not seem to be in conflict with himself or who may not be openly anti-social yet who is basically unstable and unsocialized. Then there are the "occasionally neurotic" normals, in which group most of us fall at least at some times. There are things which most people worry more about than the situation warrants, and the worry usually has no chance of helping to meet the threat. There are some occasions when all of us get angry without apparent cause, or fail to get angry even when the situation calls for it. There is no particular point in pinning a neurotic label on ourselves, but we should recognize the kinship of our everyday problems and responses to those more serious ones of the psychoneurotic and the still more difficult ones of the psychotic.[5]

Complete knowledge of the psychiatric classification of types of mental disorder is a good thing for psychiatrists, but it is not particularly relevant for the minister unless he is chaplain of a mental hospital. It would be well for the minister to know in a general way what differences are connoted by such terms as "schizophrenia," "paranoid condition," "manic-depressive psychosis," and these he can discover in any good textbook on psychiatry.[6] But he will do well to remember that these terms refer in the main to patterns of behavior of patients rather than to fundamental causes or to methods of treatment. This whole matter had best be left to the psychiatrists, though it would be well for the minister to familiarize himself with the terms sufficiently to take the mystery out of them.[7] But it is difficult to imagine a situation, outside the staff meeting of a mental hospital, where he would be justified in talking about "schizophrenia" rather than about the description in commonsense language of the behavior responses of a certain individual. He should particularly avoid that academic trend in some ministers, who have had a closer acquaintance with Greek than with the clinic, which leads them to refer, for example, to "schizophrenia" as "split mind" or "split personality." In any common sense of the word "split," schizophrenia does not indicate "split personality." Understanding of the disorder which is summarized under that term has proceeded some distance since the term itself was introduced. It is probably safest for the pastor to grasp the gist of the technical terms and then let them alone.

The temptation to discuss mental illnesses from the point of view of types is great. From the minister's point of view, however, typologies are of limited value if they do not help him to see the real problems of specific individuals. The function which typologies should perform is important—showing factors or characteristics held in common by more than one person. Some typologies deal with symptoms; that is, they assume that two persons are of a certain type because some signs exist in common. Others deal with causation. Some typologies are created for pedagogical purposes, to help make the meaning of certain characteristics clear. One should know definitely what the basic point of view is in reference to any typology with which he is dealing.

The more or less standard psychiatric typologies are a mixture of various elements, partly causative, partly symptomatic. Those of the psychoanalysts deal with psychological causation. A few workers have attempted to see types in terms of the "life direction."[8] The pastor will probably find that he has his own system of pigeonholes, which may be partly inarticulate. We do not suggest that he have none, but only that he recognize their limitations. Depending on the purpose for which common characteristics or factors are sought, there may be various effective typologies. But all of them become masters rather than servants if they obscure our view of the real persons with whom we deal.

What Lies Behind Mental Illnesses. All of us have a tendency to try to distinguish the mentally healthy from the unhealthy on the basis of certain acts. Thus we may tend to say it is unhealthy to use alcoholic beverages, and healthy to refrain from using them. But in making this type of distinction, we forget a still more important point: what the action means to the person who performs it. We have such words as "obsessive" or "compulsive" to indicate the general difference between healthy and unhealthy acts. One who performs an act under inner compulsions may be "neurotic" or unhealthy even if the act in itself cannot be so classified. Even a potentially healthy action may be made unhealthy if it is undertaken through inner compulsion, i.e., with the "real self" having no control over the act. Thus it is potentially healthy for a mother to show as well as to feel affection toward her children; but if she is driven from within to show affection even on those legitimate occasions when she does not feel it, her reaction is not healthy. Probably the deepest evil in alcoholism is compulsion. For alcoholism is reached, psychologically speaking, when a person must drink whether he wants to or not. Of course there are important objective ethical considerations involved in such a question as this. But there is basic importance in recognizing the difference between relatively compulsive and relatively "free" acts.

Still another distinction has recently been clarified which casts light on the problem of the unhealthy versus the healthy. It is healthy to seek satisfactions in a positive sense, to seek those spiritual and material goods which will tend to produce a state of positive happiness. In contrast, it is a sign of lack of health to have to seek merely for psychological security, to seek to "avoid being hurt." [9] There are probably many more people in the second group than we realize, and all of us are in it to some extent. Yet we know that there can be basic psychological and spiritual security even in the face of external circumstances which are adverse.

A word of psychological explanation may be needed at this point. A child learns to use language not merely through learning to produce certain sounds, but also by selecting out of the early experiments of his "noise-making machine" those particular sounds which have social meaning in his environment.[10] He learns to use and control his emotions by an exactly similar process. He tries out many types of emotional response and eventually learns which ones will possess most meaning in his environment. But just as he learns that producing a certain kind of sound will bring responses of "hush-hush" from people around him, so he learns that expression of certain feelings will produce negative reaction. It is thus that he learns "good and bad" about feelings. A point too little recognized is that he tends categorically to eliminate the recognition of some emotions even more completely than his parents intend. Thus with hostility, for example, the child may have been taught that he should not strike his mother; he may interpret this all unwittingly in such a way that he can never admit having hostile feelings of any kind toward his mother. This then is the process of habit formation, and eventually it becomes systematized into the character pattern.

It is helpful to think of this process in terms of *strategies* which the individual uses in facing new situations. We could understand, for example, the little girl with an alcoholic father and a prostitute mother reacting to life as a whole by a general withdrawal reaction, as if she said to life, "I don't care." She cannot be blamed; in fact, it is doubtful whether any more open and free response would let her pull through at all. A strategy always has some value, therefore, in meeting a situation; that is why we call it a strategy.

But strategies of this sort do not disappear with the disappearance of the situation which they were created or used to meet. They have a kind of momentum, a persistence which runs far beyond this threat or danger which they were designed to meet. In the case of the little girl this was made clear when she was placed at the age of six in the best possible type of foster home. Here she received real affection and attention, and every effort was made to make her feel loved, wanted, and respected as a person. But she would not, indeed could not, respond. For the character pattern which had arisen from her earlier necessary strategy could not be sloughed off at once. It took three years in this ideal environment before there was any marked change in her character and outlook.

This persistent element which disregards external changes is always prominent in mental illnesses. For if one has developed a strategy in a situation where he had no choice but to avoid being hurt or to choose the lesser of two evils, he has saved his life for the moment. But though the situation changes—and it always does—the strategy has tended to fix itself as an integral part of his character pattern. He is then concerned with continuing to avoid being hurt, rather than with the search for positive satisfactions. This attempt to avoid being hurt is therefore compulsive, as we have used the term; and any specific working out in life of this tendency therefore has unhealthy elements in it, even if the action to which it is applied is potentially healthy or good.

An illustration of the degrees of this practical freedom of choice is a man standing in the middle of a mountain road. He may be there because he enjoys walking, or is looking at the scenery, or is searching for wild flowers by the roadside, or for any one of a large number of possible reasons associated with "positive satisfactions." He may choose to walk on one side of the road or the other, or to walk in the middle. But suppose he suddenly becomes aware that a huge motor car is almost upon him. He must jump, to one side or another, probably to the side which is closest to him when he hears the car, even if it is the precipice side of the road. No place on the road seems safe to him. Forgotten are the scenery or the wild flowers; anything offers more safety than the road itself.

This reaction on the part of our hiker is natural and normal. There are many occasions when our sole concern must be a search for safety. But there is a tendency in all of us to jump wildly off the road even at times when no motor car is approaching. This is the element of "momentum," the persistence of a tendency to seek safety even when we are not actually threatened. When we feel this way, we are not making free choices in any practical sense. This is not to say much about freedom and determinism in the philosophical sense, but it does suggest the practical way in which even acts that seem to be free may be determined in part by our reaction to previous similar situations rather than to the real needs which are existent in the present situation.

In summary to this point, we have mentioned the minister's use of types in connection with mental illness and have emphasized the limitations of typological considerations from our point of view. We have examined several kinds of valid distinctions which may be made between healthy and unhealthy types of response and have suggested a few of the basic principles involved in understanding character formation and personality illnesses which would otherwise seem "illogical." Those processes in character development, particularly "sick" character, which are more obviously simple responses to external situations have been assumed to be a part of common knowledge and have therefore been taken for granted.

A further word may be given on the causes of mental illnesses. There are three obvious kinds of causes which have to be considered: physiological, psychological and cultural. Paresis is caused by the spirochete; ill humor may be caused by an upset stomach. A parent who fails to give his child genuine affection helps to create a character pattern in which the child will be predisposed to distrust other people he may meet. We have perhaps said enough about these two kinds of factors to suggest that, as laymen to medicine and psychiatry, we must always recognize the possibility of these two elements being involved in any particular case of illness.

There is time for but a glance at cultural factors.[11] If most or all parents consistently, believing that they are right because they all agree, teach children emotional responses which tend to be unhealthy, then the fault lies in the "culture." Furthermore, if they tend to teach types of emotional response which conflict with each other, the children are bound to be in more serious conflict than the situation "laid down by nature" would warrant. To a considerable extent our own culture may be, and has been called, a wholesale producer of trouble on this score.

There is nothing wrong or unnatural about conflict itself. For this exists wherever a decision has to be made in the face of two or more partly incompatible values. Such choice may involve pain in the loss of one of the values, but this does not produce mental illness. In the deeper or more basic conflicts, however, it may do so. If our culture teaches a child, for example, that it is evil for him to be angry, every time he begins to be angry he is in basic conflict within himself. For the anger, finding not even recognition, continues to have effects which can be measured in the physiological laboratory as well as by the psychiatrist.

Basic conflict may be produced when the culture counsels impossibilities of emotional life or when it teaches acceptance of loyalties or standards of conduct which are contradictory or incompatible.

One of the basic conflicts which all of us are taught, not in words but in feelings, is that of co-operation-competition. We are usually taught from religious sources that we should seek the good of the other fellow rather than our own; the implication is that the other fellow's good will be our undoing. From other sources we are taught that we must try to succeed, and that this will be at the other fellow's expense. Both points of view seem to agree that the welfare of ourselves and that of others are in basic conflict.[12] Christianity, of course, asserts that this is not true, but all too often it is assumed to be true. If the basic notion gets rooted in the character pattern that our own welfare implies the other fellow's misfortune, then a terrific conflict ensues. One does not have to be an instinct psychologist to recognize, once this is understood, that such a conflict threatens the fundamental integrity of the personality. If a person fails to get perspective on the problem, either answer he may give to it will be unsatisfactory. If he decides to "get all he can," he loses his selfhood and personal integrity. If he decides to "give everything to others," he becomes a doormat. The homiletical moral is to help people to understand the difference between "self-love" and "selfishness," to get a new perspective upon the problem as a whole.

The pastor will do well to know something about all three of these possible types of causes which produce mental illnesses. We have implied that his ordinary concern will be more with the psychological or spiritual than with the physiological or the cultural, but he will give too much emphasis to the former only at the peril of failing to understand the basic causes of any particular situation. On the other hand, in his desire to get all the causes in perspective, he will do well to remember that the physiological and organic factors, concerning which he has less training and knowledge, are sometimes considerably more important than he may assume. The moral is constant and complete co-operation with physicians and psychiatrists.

The Community's Treatment of Mental Illnesses. Before considering what the religious worker should do about mental illnesses, we should have some conception of what the community as a whole does about them.[13]

There are more beds available in hospitals for mental patients than for all other kinds of sick people put together. This number in the United States is about half a million. This does not mean that there are more sick people whose symptoms are predominantly mental, and are severe enough to suggest institutional treatment, than there are people whose illness can be treated in general hospitals. For people in the latter class usually remain in hospitals a much shorter period of time than do people in mental hospitals. The fact remains that the problem is enormous. It is estimated that, at the present rate of admissions, one person out of twenty spends some part of his life in a mental hospital. If the present increase in rate of admission to mental hospitals continues, it will soon be true that more people will go through them than through all our colleges and universities.[14]

Care should be taken against assuming that the psychosis rate is increasing simply because admission to mental hospitals is increasing. The rate of admission in some states is two or more times as great as that in other states, which indicates not that people are twice as "crazy" in one state as in another but that the social standards of what constitutes mental health are higher in some states than in others. It is undoubtedly true that if more and better facilities were available for treatment of mental disorder in backward states, or even in the progressive states, there would be a rapid rise in admissions. Progress in treatment accounts for a good deal of the increase, especially as the public begins to realize that mental hospitals are treatment as well as custodial institutions. Although this is admittedly only a guess, it is probable that if ideal facilities were available for the treatment of psychosis the number of persons in our hospitals would be nearly doubled.

These figures do not include that large group of "developmental deficients" who now receive treatment in institutions nor the even larger number who need it but do not now have it. This group is usually but somewhat inaccurately called "feeble-minded." They are persons born with some type of handicap or else have developed quite early in life a deficiency which prohibits their going on to develop full personal independence in our complex culture. Frequently they are able, under appropriate guidance, to become very useful to themselves and to others; but they need an environment with a greater degree of protection than life in the open community makes possible. There are more than a hundred thousand such persons in institutions; and at least five times that many who should be cared for in institutions, temporarily or permanently, if facilities were available.[15]

Apart from psychotics and defectives, there are in every community large numbers of persons who are serious problems either to themselves, to others, or to both. There are delinquents and criminals. These will not be discussed here except to suggest that they are a part of the health problem in the broadest sense. In a more specific sense, they need a greater variety of care and treatment than even the most enlightened community as yet offers. There are the "bums" who do not need institutional care but who do not get along in the community. Most communities do no more than give them workhouse sentences for thirty days or ignore them altogether. Some new type of treatment is needed, perhaps a cross between institutionalization and the open community. There is the great army of alcoholics, about which little as yet is being done, though there are signs that excellent constructive activity is beginning.[16] "Alcoholics Anonymous" has done some excellent work, and is expanding its services.

Of course there are persons who are problems solely because of social conditions, as for instance the unemployed. These are not discussed here because the fault in these cases is naturally with the social order and not with the persons' themselves. But there are serious mental illness problems among such persons, especially because morale tends to disappear as employment disappears. The mental health aspect of the situation may not be so bad when many others are out of work, but it becomes more difficult when others begin to get work and the individual in question does not. It is perhaps true that some persons who have received relief or work relief over considerable periods of time have lost their taste for work; but every objective study of relief shows the other factors to be more influential.

There are still other groups, but this is a discussion of those situations most patently related to mental illnesses. We have not yet touched upon that great body of the neurotics. With them the community as a whole has done very little, in the main because they are more problems to themselves than they are to other people. A study of the history of the community's activity shows that it has been more obviously concerned at each stage with protection of itself than with giving help and treatment to the individual.[17] This is perhaps as it should be; but it has become increasingly clear that the best protection of the community is afforded when the best help and treatment is given to individuals who need it.

The American community began to protect itself by using methods which segregated the undesirables, first by driving them away, then by putting them into institutions. With many kinds of disorders this second development was fortunate, for institutions could be made into efficient places for treatment as well as for segregation. But other methods fortunately have been developed to look after persons who cannot best be helped by institutional treatment. Perhaps most needed at the moment are types of treatment which lie between the institutional field and the open community. Consider a few of the non-institutional methods of treatment which are now available in progressive communities:

1—Social case work.
2—Mental hygiene clinics, or child and adult guidance clinics.
3—Psychiatrists in private practice and on the staff of general hospitals, schools, and other community institutions.
4—Psychologists in hospitals, schools, etc.
5—Visiting teachers (trained as social workers) in schools, even in some rural schools.
6—Increased concern for personality problems on the part of many physicians.
7—Probation and parole services in connection with courts, which give supervision by trained workers.
8—The expansion of group work facilities of all kinds as the necessity for preventing disorders *en masse* has been increasingly recognized.

Others could be mentioned, but these are suggestive. In addition, there are the many types of institutional treatment such as mental hospitals, schools for deficients, etc. There are a few attempts to set up treatment centers which will be different from the institution and yet different as well from the open community, but they have not yet gone far.[18]

In all of these it is fairly obvious that the treatment given is at least as much for the protection of society as it is for cure and rehabilitation of the difficulty in the individual for his own sake. Yet if it is true that difficulty in the individual brings a price for which society pays as well as the individual, then concern should be broadened to include what is done for the person who is a problem to himself but not obviously a problem to the community.

As a whole, most communities have done little at this point. The establishment of guidance clinics has been a great recent achievement; but four-fifths of the expenditures for clinic care are in sixty-six of the largest cities which constitute only a fourth of the national population.[19] And even in the most progressive cities the resources are insufficient. The number of psychiatrists, trained social case workers, visiting teachers, and other mental hygiene workers is exceedingly inadequate. Of course it is true that the public would demand and get more such services if it was educated enough in these directions to want them. No one has a more effective opportunity to carry out such education than the religious leader.

The public schools are at least beginning to do a better job with the neurotic. As this discussion evidences, the churches are becoming concerned about him. But in all too few sources is there evidence of a real understanding of what is necessary to try to help people with such illnesses. No short answer to this question can be given; but at least a first step is a radical change of the public mind to the point where it believes that it is normal for people to have personality problems and to seek the best help in trying to solve them. Meanwhile, the religious worker need not wait with hands folded until the community gets the point sufficiently to reach into its pocketbook. There is much he can do now.

The above was written prior to the entrance of the United States into the war. Two things have become obvious since then. The first is that many of the mental hygiene services of the community have been curtailed for the duration, in some cases to an alarming extent. The second is that the new sense of community co-operation arising all over America should find one of its continued expressions after the war in the field of community services in mental hygiene. At least we may help bring this about.

The Minister As "Detector." The religious worker has three kinds of function in relation to mental illnesses: as a "detector," as a counselor or therapist, and as a preventive mental hygienist. We shall consider here his function as a "detector." It is hardly necessary to point out the opportunities for seeing people which he enjoys. He comes into contact with his parishioners not only in his office and on many occasions within the church but in their homes and places of business. The school teacher has a real opportunity with children but with no one else. But not even the family physician has as much opportunity with adults as the minister.

It has been suggested repeatedly that the pastor's first obligation is to understand something of how difficulties arise. If he has such understanding then he will have a good chance of spotting them before they become too serious. This is what we mean by his "detector" function. It must be re-emphasized that the minister should have no ulterior motives in keeping his eye open for signs of potential disorder. He should not do it to make himself feel clever, nor to gain power over others, nor to convince people that he "knows all about psychology." His sole aim must be to want to help people by getting to them before a crisis makes it difficult to give any kind of help. Of course he is not interested merely in "alarm signals." He keeps his eye open

equally for unrealized potentialities. But the fact remains that
if he looks only for the good features he will fail to save many
persons from spiritual agony and even catastrophe.

The next most important consideration is for the minister to
understand why certain kinds of symptoms are likely to be
followed by certain other symptoms, and something of the causes
of illnesses. Phases of that subject are discussed throughout this
volume. But it is relevant to help him to have some idea of the
relative seriousness of certain symptoms and to let him know the
kinds with which he should be most concerned.

Perhaps the best single idea to guide him is "excessive." If he
sees any response which is excessive in the apparent presence
or absence of emotion, it is at least worth taking another look.
He will find dangerous symptoms not so much in peculiar acts
as in peculiar attitudes toward acts which, when he can analyze
them, will usually be found to be the result of deep-rooted patterns of anxiety, search for safety alone, and the like.

The first kind of "excessive," and one of the most dangerous,
is excessive withdrawal. The child who throws things always
gets attention, and something will be recognized as wrong. But
the child who retreats quietly into himself is too often considered
all right. We are not suggesting that a child is unhealthy if he
is something less than a hundred percent extrovert. But there
are certain symptoms of exaggerated withdrawal which ought
to be in the mind of the pastor. Continued day dreaming, often
present in persons who become abstracted, is such a sign. Failure
to mix at all with other people in church groups, no apparent
interest of any kind in the opposite sex, a phlegmatic attitude
combined with the facial lines to be expected in a chronic wor-
rier, are other signs. A person who turns out to be unduly sensitive on many subjects is probably of this type. Some of the signs
will be action symptoms, i.e., things which show up only in

particular types of activity. Others will be character symptoms, showing themselves not so much by particular actions as by particular attitudes toward all actions.

The second type of danger signal is excessive mood swings. The person who becomes quite elated at the church party should require a second look, especially if he is in low spirits the following Sunday. The pastor is likely to see a good many who suffer from self-recriminations, for people are likely to think he will approve attitudes which involve saying nasty things about oneself. A young man who was planning to enter the ministry, for example, was talking with a wise old clergyman. "I am entering the ministry," he said, "because the Lord has called me and not because I have any ability." "Young man," said his friend, "if you have no ability the Lord hasn't called you." This was bad therapy perhaps, but it certainly illustrates the fact that most people believe the clergyman will approve their "playing themselves down."

A single woman of forty came to see her minister every two or three weeks for some months, each time recounting her difficulties in getting along with people in the face of the new resolve she said she got after each visit. It must be, she hinted, that she was incapable of getting along with people. After reassuring her for a few visits, the clergyman sent her to a psychiatric friend, who discovered that the woman was unwittingly resorting to the device of blaming herself every time she got near the "real problem" in her talks with the pastor. Self-blame can itself be a screen. Sometimes it may be a bid for sympathy; but when there are real self-recriminations, with considerable depression of mood, the pastor should take the situation with the utmost seriousness. It is not true that everyone who threatens suicide is merely bluffing. Most suicides do not have consultations first; and there is usually hope for those who do. But horrible though suicide may be, it is only a more extreme form of self-recrimination or self-punishment, psychologically speaking. Since all responses of this type indicate an excessive preoccupation with blame, apparently directed to the self, it is necessary to change the perspective in which the problem is seen. If the minister can keep his eyes open for excessive self-recrimination in its earlier stages, there will not be so much occasion for him to catch suicides on the brink.

Excessive outbursts indicate danger. The pastor should bear in mind, of course, that not every outburst is of this type. A child who is being kept quiet more or less forcibly during the minister's visit may quite naturally become tired of it and burst forth in yells or wails. But outbursts without much apparent cause, whether they be anger against someone, or weeping, or self-condemnation, indicate that something is wrong, though probably not what the person thinks is wrong. Undue sensitivity on one or two subjects, combined with outbursts, is another sign, even if the person forcibly keeps the outbursts under control.

The most common signs the minister will see are evidences of fear, anxiety, insecurity, undue submissiveness or dominance. These things can hardly be detected merely by noticing externals; things that are noticed must be put together to form a pattern. But let it be noted that excessive attitudes of submissiveness are as dangerous as those of dominance.

There are many types of "excessives" which have not specifically been mentioned. The person who continually apologizes for himself or his tardiness, or who says repeatedly that he is taking too much of the minister's time, is showing a danger signal as much as the person who makes obvious efforts to impose on him. The person who expects the minister to be perfect is sick; basically, he expects the minister to be good *for* him. The person who tries to get the pastor's help on the ground that pastors are supposed to love people and therefore should do anything to help them does need help, but not the kind he thinks.

Anti-social behavior is always a danger signal, but not always in the way it seems. The boy who steals gloves from the cloakroom may do it not because he wants the gloves but for some other reason. The minister should have his eyes open to see that there is no jumping at conclusions about such incidents, that they get proper care and attention, beginning with efforts to understand why.

When the minister sees something which he feels indicates at least potential danger, this does not necessarily mean that he will act upon it then, or even later. This is perhaps the greatest corrective which most religious workers need in order to help them do effective work with individuals. If a situation is seen, and its probable causes recognized, how can one restrain himself from action when he is not clear that the particular action is indicated? Actually, that is the wrong question. Of course one is never absolutely certain that the course he follows is right, but there are few occasions when one should barge into a difficult personal problem without previously having made careful assessment of it and drawn the rational conclusion that some help could be mediated. Religious workers need "tension capacity" in their work of helping others. The ability to see more problems than one can possibly solve, even if he had time, is a prerequisite to good pastoral work. The minister does not create the problems; life does that. Even if he fails to see them, they are still there. But in that case he gradually builds the habit of seeing only those problems which he himself can help. The image in which man was created is not so compartmentalized.

The minister should not concentrate on looking for danger signals to the exclusion of looking for unrecognized potentialities; he should do both. He should, when he notes a probable danger signal, ordinarily keep this to himself, at least until he has seen more and gone over the whole matter carefully in his own mind. And he should not be too sure about it, even to himself. Harm can be done by the clever pastor—the one who is really clever—if he notes symptoms of anxiety in Mrs. Muggins and breaks in the next moment with the direct question, "Now just what are you afraid of, Mrs. Muggins?" If the contact has been built up over a period of time, if the minister has looked at the situation carefully, and if he finally decides that Mrs. Muggins is longing to have a chance to discuss it, that is fine. But that is very different from suggesting, "I know more about you than you do about yourself." That is never really true, even though we may have more perspective than the other person has, and therefore more helpful knowledge.

In short, the pastor may be a "detector" or a "detective," but he is a "plainclothes" man. The fact that he is a pastor makes people realize that he has a badge; he does not need to flaunt it. This is in no sense deception on his part. To try to tell someone else everything we think or suspect about him without regard for other considerations is to display not absolute honesty but fairly serious neurosis in ourselves.

The Minister As Therapist. The principles of counseling are examined in the chapter of that title. Here it is proposed to examine what the minister does with people whose disorders or danger signals are quite serious.

The pastor is not the therapist for psychosis or serious neurosis of any variety. The reasons are so obvious that they need but be mentioned. He is not trained to do this; especially because the more serious the disorder, the more important that medical knowledge be applied along with psychological knowledge. Further, the processes of getting to a problem which lies deeply buried in the unconscious are more difficult than of getting to problems which are less deep. Sometimes it is easier to understand the root of the psychotic's problem than it is that of the "normal" person; but to make the contact which may help to remove it is quite another thing. Secondly, the minister has not the time to deal with serious disorders, even if he should have had medical training as well as a theological education. If he takes the time, he will have no church. Thirdly, his rôle prevents him from being an active therapist in serious personality disorders. Persons who have had both medical and theological training find that the values of the dual training emerge much more significantly in their understanding of the situation than in what they can do to help it. Therapeutically, they must be either clergymen or psychiatrists to the person; they cannot be both. This is largely a practical matter. Apart from the personality of a particular minister or psychiatrist, people think of their position in terms of different rôles. In general the person who is seriously ill mentally should have major help from the person in the rôle of the physician.

But this does not say that the minister should wash his hands of the whole matter which, by and large, is what the church has done with psychosis. It has been entirely content to leave psychotics completely in the hands of the physician. There are not half a dozen mental hospitals in the country which have trained and able full-time chaplains on their staffs to co-operate with physicians in ministry to the patients, and not half of those receive any support from the churches. Yet the significance of the pastor's working side by side with the physician, even in cases of serious mental disorder, is very great. Experience has shown that patients, even in the deepest psychosis, may derive much value from a service of worship or from a call by the minister.[20] And a minister trained to work with psychiatrists in such a situation can be of great therapeutic value.[21] Sometimes the parish

minister should stay away from a psychotic patient, especially
when the pastor—or any pastor—represents something to the
patient which is negative—and this is sometimes true. But generally speaking, a pastor who knows something about mental
disorder, and who will consult carefully with the psychiatrist in
charge, can be of real help to his psychotic parishioner. This may
be especially worth the effort in those cases where the psychiatrist
believes that the outcome is still to be determined, usually when
the patient is confused, excitable, and partially disoriented—that
is, when a clear psychotic character trend has not definitely
emerged and taken control.[22]

With psychotics or others who are seriously ill mentally, what
may the pastor do when there is no therapist in sight? This is
especially likely to be true in small towns and rural areas. This
fact is sometimes cited as warrant for the pastor to "try anything" since no one else is available to help. This is a dangerous
philosophy, dangerous not only to the patient but to the pastor
as minister of the church. There are always constructive things
to be done; but sometimes it is better to do nothing directly
than to do anything short of the most expert.

In such a case, the minister can almost always carry on constructive work with the relatives. People so frequently think of a
mental illness as family disgrace; and if the minister does no
more than change that attitude, he has accomplished much. He
may remember that there have been factors of interpersonal relationships involved in the causation of the difficulty; and he may
use the crisis constructively to help change the human environment in which the trouble has developed. Sometimes the relatives may be helped to change their attitude toward the patient,
to understand him better. To know that there is logic—even if it
is not their logic—in his actions may be valuable in itself.

The pastor can sometimes help the local physician, who may

have had his medical education in the period when mental ills were considered "imaginary," to get a better understanding of the situation. He may be able to manipulate small things in the patient's environment to improve conditions in some respects.

If the condition is serious, he should of course try to get the person to a place where he can have at least a psychiatric diagnosis, even if this involves a considerable trip. There are few points in the United States where an adequate, though not necessarily the best, diagnosis cannot be had within a distance of two or three hundred miles. When this is not possible, the pastor and the family physician will have to use their heads about the relevance of institutional care. Generally speaking, institutional treatment should be one of the first recourses and not one of the last if the disorder is serious. When there is any real doubt, it is a good rule to recommend institutional care. There are excellent private mental hospitals, but these are usually prohibitively expensive to the person of average income or below. State hospitals have been improving; and while those in a few states are inadequate, those in most are fairly good—at least they are so much better than any other kind of care which can be afforded that there should be no hesitation in sending the person there. The pastor, along with the physician, has a great responsibility for educating the community at this point.

Fortunately a remarkable book to aid both the pastor and the family has just been published. It is entitled *Mental Illness: A Guide for the Family*. With complete accuracy, it deals in simple terms with such matters as getting the patient admitted to a hospital, taking the patient to a hospital, the patient's first month in the hospital, life in the hospital from the patient's point of view, when the patient comes home, and similar matters. It is strongly recommended not only for the minister's library but to be recommended to one's parishioners.[22a]

The pastor may ordinarily continue to have pastoral relationships with the patient. If the person is not institutionalized, the minister should of course be guided by all the principles he knows. If the patient has delusions and believes the pastor is tuning in on him with a secret radio, the minister had better stay away. But a quiet attempt to show interest, especially if he has shown it in the same way for some time previously, usually is valuable. The pastor may listen to the person and follow roughly the same principles that he would in any counseling. But he should not give any interpretation of any kind; and he should not listen too frequently. In incipient stages he may use counseling principles to help toward a saving insight; that is of course what most counseling does. When psychosis or serious neurosis is in evidence, he had best apply only the most conservative of his principles on the patient himself, and expend his energy on the patient's environment.

To turn to neurosis, some psychiatrists say that a pastor should never attempt to counsel with a neurotic. This would seem to be going too far; and there seem to be no reasons why the minister may not give significant help to many neurotic people. But the principles of counseling should be applied, and he should not allow his contact to become any deeper than his time or training will permit him to follow through. As a matter of fact, we have hardly begun to explore the indirect ways in which the minister's understanding may be put to use apart from the possibility of his doing direct psychotherapy.

The Minister As Preventive Mental Hygienist. The task of preventing mental illnesses is the most important which the pastor may have in connection with them. Various phases of this subject are discussed elsewhere in this volume and are mentioned here only to emphasize the fact that they are an integral part of the pastor's function as preventive mental hygienist. Group counseling and group work generally, religious education, work with the "physically" ill, pastoral calling, pastoral work in crisis situations—all these have health implications for the prevention of mental difficulties and illnesses. The minister has no choice about whether they will have health implications. His only choice is whether he will become aware of those implications so that they may be better guided.

Three main facets of his ministry deserve additional words of discussion: worship, preaching and parish administration. It should be plain that we have nowhere stated that health—even personality health of body, mind and spirit—is the *only* aim of the religious worker, or that health is the only point of view from which the minister surveys his task. In referring, therefore, to health implications of worship, we are not suggesting that this is the only valid way, nor even the most important way, to look at the subject.

Whatever the theological meanings believed to inhere in worship—and there is more agreement about these across Christendom than is commonly believed—there are certain practical suggestions which follow from our knowledge of health. The service of worship, to be effective, must make contact with the emotional life of the worshiper. Something must be done after contact is made, but little can be accomplished unless such contact is made. People differ in that to which they will respond. A person who has had such contact made only in a formal type of service will probably be repelled by a more free and easy type of service; and the reverse is also true. Probably the index of denominational membership gives a fairly good indication statistically of the capacities of people for being reached by services of greater or lesser degrees of formality when this is compared with the degree of formality to be found in each communion. Some say with justice, however, that this is only a difference in training, that all worshipers could be taught to appreciate types of formality or informality in worship which now repel them. In either case, we now have habit patterns of worship which indicate what people believe they like.

There is one danger in the growing formalism of worship which should be carefully watched. Formalism is, after all, only the habit process in action, learning to reverence quietly not only because of the emotions spontaneously generated at the present service but carrying the background of previous experiences to enhance the total meaning. But as we have seen elsewhere, the more firmly habit becomes fixed in the personality, the more tendency there is for it to work automatically, i.e., without consciousness of meaning. This would not be so bad were it not for the compulsive element which sometimes is present. If one worships only according to certain forms, he may come to feel, even if he does not believe, that worship with any other than those forms is not worship; and he is also likely to feel uncomfortable if he does not worship by use of those forms. This is merely one specific instance of the question of how to produce meaning through formation of habit into character pattern without letting it become purely automatic or compulsive. The worshiper who is less concerned with form may be compulsive in that he feels no positive satisfaction in worshiping, but merely feels uncomfortable if he does not. This is a neurotic state, whether it be centered around worship or something else.

The leader of worship, whatever his communion or his personal convictions, must find some happy dividing line between attempting to make the current experience in itself as meaningful as possible, and trying to make the association with other worship experiences enhance the current experience. This of course is the old problem of tradition versus experience in a psychological setting.

It is sometimes stated that the worshiper should leave a service with something positive to help him during the ensuing days. It is also stated that his heart should be touched by the evil realities of the world in which he lives. Both of these statements are true. Psychologically he must be touched; but if the service has given him no sense of the resources available in Christianity both to solve difficulty and to meet it when it cannot be solved, it has done little good merely to reach him. The center of meaning is feeling; but the depth of feeling has little or nothing to do with the "expression of emotion" in the ordinary connotation of that phrase.

The pastor has also a great opportunity in connection with private worship, prayer and meditation. Rightly carried out, the results of these practices for health are of tremendous importance. What has been said about the compulsive elements in public worship applies even more forcibly here. There is a vast difference between the person who, prevented from his period, let us say, of morning prayer, looks forward to having it the next day, and the person who feels that his whole day has been thrown out of kilter by missing it. The first comes to prayer with a sense of need which will result in new strength; the second has attached neurotic meanings to his prayer life. He merely feels bad if he does not pray. He gets little positive strength from praying.

Some say that private prayer should be carried out for a stated period each day; others emphasize prayer on many occasions. Some, of course, recommend both. There is no doubt that the most meaningful life of prayer will gradually tend to have some habits built up in connection with it, making a practice of using a certain period or periods of the day most desirable. But people differ greatly in the way meaning comes to them through relative systematization or lack of systematization. Pastors have scarcely made a beginning towards learning "spiritual direction." When they do, it will make for health as well as other positive values.

Family worship, worship in small informal groups, and worship in other ways than through the main public services of the church are full of potentiality for health. Services of worship for children and young people's groups which contain real meaning in themselves and which tend to build habits of recognizing meaning in experience are being improved every day. Exploration is being made into family worship, trying to find ways in which worship can be meaningful and practicable in view of the changed sociological circumstances of the modern family. Worship in small groups, where more intimate inter-personal relationships are possible than in large groups, is of especial value for some types of people. Wisely conducted services of worship for "health and healing," as has been suggested previously, may be of value even when they tend to attract only relatively unhealthy people, and this circumstance is not always true. Some of those now being conducted are not wise in that they stress only "good" or "happy" things, and therefore act more as an escape than as a means of making contact and then applying the resources of Christianity to that contact, once made. There is a significant psychological reason for having the phrase, "He descended into hell," in the Apostles' Creed.[23]

Comparatively little has been written about the relation of mental health to preaching.[24] Psychological understanding, it has been well said, does not suggest so much what to preach as what not to preach. Another way of saying nearly the same thing is that preaching begins with the preacher. One minister who had had supervised clinical training reported that he realized afterwards that he had been very bombastic in his preaching, had been taking out some of his own hostilities on the congregation with no awareness of the fact that he was doing it. It was not, he said, the ideas themselves that were wrong; it was his outlook toward them, which had an emotional tinge that had to be transformed. This is the first and probably the most important contribution of mental health knowledge to preaching.

The second way in which mental health and preaching should be related is in using real psychological facts to help demonstrate Christian truth. Psychology does not prove or disprove the existence of God and it is not this kind of fact which is intended.[25] But it does give insight into such things as the nature of love and of hostility. There are endless messages, integral parts of the Christian gospel, and abundantly documented in the Bible, upon which psychological and health knowledge casts illumination. More has been said along this line in an earlier chapter.

The minister may occasionally preach "mental health" sermons; but ordinarily he is wiser, as he is in dealing with social issues, to include a mental health paragraph in a sermon directed at the great driving centers of the Christian gospel. If he feels that he has to "insert" such a paragraph or section out of the context, he has not well understood either the health implications of the gospel or modern knowledge of health and personality.

The kind of knowledge we have been discussing should teach the preacher something more about when he is and is not making contact with his congregation in a vital way. No man can make a touchdown every time he carries the ball; but it is valuable to know how many yards have been made or lost.

The layman's knowledge of mental health should be of significance in his interpretation of sermons. Of course this is tied up with the whole question of the critical function of the layman in the church. But the layman who finds his preacher's sermons never touching the life problems which he and others are facing is justified in wondering whether something should not be done to make the preacher aware of the problems. The whole subject of preaching, even in its relationships to health, is so vast that only these basic aspects can be touched on here. But it should be noted especially that it is a concern of the layman as well as of the preacher.

Finally, there can be real mental hygiene in church administration. Ministers sometimes waste hours trying to convince a stubborn deacon about something; whereas if they had recognized that such persons can never be convinced by rational argument of any kind, they might have saved time and energy. Other ministers try to dominate their official boards not because they like to dominate but because they are unaware of their own basic distrust of opinions which disagree with theirs, and therefore of their distrust also of their own. Still others acquiesce in anything suggested by the official board, and become administrative chameleons. Self-knowledge is certainly the first thing, but it is by no means all. A minister who continues to allow a crotchety and ill-natured secretary, or a gossipy or unsympathetic one, to remain in her key position in the church, at least without some attempt to change her outlook, is doing a tremendous disservice to the whole life of the parish. Exaggerated kind-heartedness of this type indicates, not Christian love, but administrative incompetence.

Enough has been said to suggest that the health function of the minister goes far beyond interviewing individuals, important though that is. Not all, nor necessarily the most important, suggestions about religious education, preaching, administration and the like come from the kind of knowledge we are considering. But more of them do than is commonly realized. Whether the pastor realizes it or not, these things are potential agents of preventive mental hygiene. No Christian minister is content to stop with "prevention" of mental illness or other evil; he wants to go on to the positive resources of living the Christian faith. But unless his eye is on prevention and cure of ills as well as on positive Christian living, he is something less than a shepherd of the sheep.

CHAPTER VIII

PASTORAL COUNSELING

What It Is. Pastoral counseling is the endeavor by the minister to help people through mutual discussion of the issues involved in a difficult life situation, leading toward a better understanding of the choices involved, and toward the power of making a self-chosen decision which will be as closely bound up to religious reality as the people are capable of under the circumstances.

It may mean giving comfort to a mother whose son is somewhere "west of San Francisco." It may involve a man whose business has just gone to pieces, or a child whose parents have mistreated her. It may involve dealing with the sick in body, mind or spirit—or with those going through the difficult crises of normal growth. In short, it is the eternal wisdom of the Christian church going into action in the face of specific human need.

Pastoral counseling is in some ways a misleading term. Many think of it as implying things like this: giving advice, helping only a single individual, carrying out a formal office interview. They think it is no one's business but the minister's or that, because it is religious, it can be carried out only through the use of language which is traditionally religious.

We should rid our minds of these misconceptions if we are to retain the term, and it is worth retaining. Pastoral counseling does not mean giving advice, that is, "telling" people either what to do or why they have not already done it. It frequently happens to most of us, ministers and laymen alike, when we see some one wrestling with a difficult problem, that we see clearly the course of action he should take in order to find a solution. We have the advantage of perspective, of seeing the problem from the outside. When we think we see the solution, we may be right or we may be wrong. We may be right because we do have the advantage of perspective. But we may be wrong because we do not have all the "emotional" facts which the person has who is actually facing the problem.

What happens if we give advice? It is obvious that nothing constructive will be accomplished if our advice is not wanted. But what will happen if it is wanted and requested? If it is accepted and it turns out to be wrong, we shall probably have lost a friend, and certainly have lost our chance of helping the person on another occasion. If it is accepted and we are right, the person may become dependent on us the next time he is confronted with a problem which needs a solution. If the advice is rejected, we have lost our chance for usefulness in the situation.

When we say then that pastoral counseling should not mean giving advice, we mean it. For we believe that the decisions which people make must be autonomous decisions, that is, that they must be made without coercion of any kind if they are to be a real part of the person who makes them. But counseling comes in because it helps to talk things over with a wise listener. To make any decision implies not only that we gain something, but also that we lose something else; for there can be no conflict without two or more values being involved. If a person accepts a solution to a conflict (accepting one value and leaving another behind) without the free concurrence of his "whole personality," he becomes something less as a person than he was before. Pastoral counseling is not giving advice.

Neither is pastoral counseling helping only a single individual. Ordinarily it involves a method of working with or through an individual; but some of the best counseling is done with families or with other groups. The minister who discusses marriage with an engaged couple, for example, is counseling fully as significantly as if he had each member of the couple alone with him. We shall have a word to say later about counseling with larger groups; but if the minister by dealing, for example, with a group of engaged couples in a free and mutual discussion of marriage, accomplishes part of what he could accomplish with each individually, a counseling process is going on. He will certainly want to supplement this with individual counseling, but the fact remains that such work with the group is a part of pastoral counseling.

Counseling is not confined to office interviews. Because the process of helping people needs to be done with a minimum of interruption and of disturbing factors of any kind, it can ordinarily be carried out better under conditions which the counselor can control. If, therefore, there is a completely free choice of where the problem is to be discussed, the office or "counseling room" of the minister is ordinarily the best place. But there is seldom such a free choice. There are literally thousands of people every day in our country who have reached a point with some problem where they would be perfectly willing to discuss it with a minister if he came to them, but who would not think of going to him.

Pastoral calling is, or should be, one of the great opportunities of the Protestant ministry. For here the minister has a chance to meet people who would not come to him, but who want his help. The size of this group can scarcely be overemphasized. We shall have more to say about pastoral calling. But it should be evident that where the process of helping another is going on it is definitely pastoral counseling whether it is in the pastor's office, the parishioner's home or office, or over the luncheon table.

Pastoral counseling is commonly thought of as the concern only of the minister. It is true that pastoral counseling can be carried out only by pastors. But this should not make it of less concern to the layman. The layman may not be an expert on preaching; but from the receiving end he has some ideas, and frequently good ideas, about a few minimum standards which his preacher should live up to. It should be so with pastoral counseling. This service by ministers will reach its level of potential usefulness only as laymen understand a few of its basic principles and urge their ministers to practice them.

Few of the principles of pastoral counseling are "secret"; and it is perfectly possible for some types of counseling to be done by responsible church workers who are not ordained. But the "rôle" of the minister is important in distinguishing pastoral counseling from other types of personal counseling. If the non-ordained church workers keep this in kind and take into consideration their comparative lack of professional training, there are few of the principles, discussed here, which are not also relevant to any help which they may give.

Pastoral counseling is not distinguished by reason of its use of traditionally religious terminology. Whether the term "God" appears in the counseling situation, for example, depends upon the spiritual maturity of the counselee and upon his degree of psychological understanding. A young man who has always associated God with a tyrannical father is not likely to be helped to understand God until he has come to terms in his relationship to his father. Certainly pastoral counseling is not a process of dealing out sermonettes which are supposed to be acceptable because they use hallowed words. Counseling seeks to get at emotional realities, and pastoral counseling seeks to get at them especially with resources which the pastor and counselee find in religion.

Is Pastoral Counseling New? From the point of view of some of the principles which will be discussed, pastoral counseling is rather new. But in some form it has been a real concern of the church from the days of the New Testament. Jesus was so plainly interested in helping people—in body, mind and spirit— that even in its periods of greatest doubt the church has never ceased to make an effort.

Modern pastoral counseling flows from three streams within the history of the church and from a large number of modern scientific trends or studies. So far as the church is concerned, the first stream is that of penance or confession. In the early church there was need for discipline over the ethical conduct of members, which usually seems to have been public. But before long the practice of hearing confession by priests, and then of forgiving offenses in the name of God, often came to be done in private. Certain duties in token of recognizing forgiveness usually had to be carried out by the penitent.

Since guidance was needed on the part of those who did the guiding, the sixth century saw the beginning of books to guide priests. These came to be known as "penitentials" because they dealt with handling penitents.[1] In the thirteenth century confession at least once a year was made obligatory for all church members. Confession, in practically the same form, continues to this day in the Roman Catholic Church.

The Protestant Reformation did not get rid of the confessional, though it seemed to do so. It did remove from the priest or minister any automatic power to forgive sins on behalf of God, but it permitted the minister to assure the parishioner that God had already forgiven him. It must be admitted that this function of the ministry, in spite of the warrant which the

Reformers gave it in this form, was generally allowed to lag, although there was a great deal more of it in the centuries following the Reformation than is generally supposed.

But the confessional rests on at least one assumption which makes it of less value today. This assumption is that the thing about which the person feels guilty has a close relationship to the thing about which he *should* feel guilty and, therefore, for which he should seek forgiveness. Although this is true in some cases, we have been learning that the transformation needed to cleanse the personality often has little relation in the conscious mind of the person to what he thinks is troubling him. An illustration is the man who wanted to be assured of God's forgiveness for having uttered an oath against God; what he needed first was a conviction of sin about the way he was exploiting his children. After that might come forgiveness of his real offense, and the restoration of right relationship both to his children and to God. The traditional confessional has dealt, and to some extent must deal, with what the individual feels is wrong rather than with what actually is wrong. Pastoral counseling is not guilt-centered in the same sense as the confessional.

The second source of pastoral counseling in the church has been the ministry of crisis and of consolation. Work with the sick, the dying, the bereaved, and those afflicted with other critical difficulties has always been a function of the clergyman. Reading the history of this ministry brings the conviction that the church has always used the best resources available to bring consolation, relief and new courage in the face of crisis and suffering. The modern age accepts the legacy of this ministry and contributes new understandings of how to accomplish it.

The third source of pastoral counseling within the church was informal practical counseling. Like the old country doctor, the old country minister, who had been in the community for many years, was looked to for help and guidance on all kinds of problems, not so much perhaps because he was the minister as because he was known personally to be able to help. The history of this source lies in the experience of individual priests and ministers. Though a less formal aspect, it is as important as the others.

From modern science have come many resources for use in pastoral counseling. We usually sum these up in the term "mental hygiene." But the essential thing which modern science teaches the pastoral counselor is how to understand the parishioner's real problems. It has emphasized the need for getting personally in "rapport" with him, of being able to help only where help is wanted, of various dangers which may be avoided and resources which may be used; but basically its contribution has been in the direction of understanding the "how."

The Requisites of the Counselor. Counseling depends first upon the counselor.[2] It is therefore pertinent to suggest at least a few of the qualities needed by the pastor who is to do the counseling; and there is no minister who can avoid doing counseling unless he locks himself in his study. These suggestions are rather counsels of perfectibility than of perfection.

The counselor should first understand himself. This is so often stated that it seems a Polonian cliché. But when we use it in connection with the counselor, we have some specific things in mind. Here is a minister, for example, who is very shy. He never makes a positive statement about himself without the use of some phrase suggesting his own modesty in saying it, or without ascribing all power to God. In his contacts with individuals he is restrained. "We never feel really close to him," the people say, except the shy ones. The latter receive great help from their minister, who is, after all, a pretty good fellow if one can break through his shell. But he shuts up like a clam if an enthusiastic deacon or matron suggests a possible new way to arrange the flowers in the chancel. This man's failure to understand his own bias has cut him off from the power to help large sections of his congregation. If he understood that excessively shy reactions are based upon a fear that others will take advantage of him if he opens up, and that this fear is based on a feeling of insecurity about life, and that the feeling of insecurity probably stems from childhood experience in which more was expected of him than he could reasonably have been expected to fulfill—he would probably not be so shy. Learning this, and much more, about himself would be a painful experience at the start; but it would be worth it in the long run. This is what we mean by the counselor's understanding of himself and his own biases.

Another minister had gone a long way toward being a good counselor. But he could not forgive his father for having been excessively cruel to him, and could not assimilate that experience. His counseling went well until he met people who did not resent their imperfect treatment by their parents as much as he did his. He would then launch into a sermonette on how nasty nineteenth century parents were. Of course it was much to his credit for having discovered in his own childhood some of the sources of his feelings of resentment, and of realizing that they should not merely be repressed. But, more important, they should have been assimilated and certainly not foisted on unsuspecting parishioners. There are few unpleasant experiences of life which, if they remain unassimilated, cannot become the counselor's Achilles' heel. It is plain that self-understanding has a meaning.

The pastor must learn, too, what a variety of responses people can and do make to similar situations and not assume that they feel as he does. The minister in the illustration above assumed that other people would feel as resentful of the way their parents had treated them as he did of his own parents. Another minister, finding a woman frankly relieved at the death of her crotchety and domineering husband, missed a wonderful opportunity to give help where it was needed by being utterly unable to understand "how she could feel that way." More than one minister has wasted precious hours in attempts to convince alcoholic addicts that they should not drink, without any attempt to discover the emotional reasons for drinking in the life of the particular alcoholics. The minister does not need to agree with the parishioner or with his point of view. But he does need to understand that it may be different from his own and that it may at times be just as understandable provided its causes are known.

Another variety of this error is to "type" people, put them in little pigeon-holes. Pigeon-holes are a good thing as long as they remain merely pigeon-holes. To have in mind a few types has some real value. But there are always individual factors in every person, and too much thinking in "types" is to miss the personality itself.

In the third place, the pastor must be more interested in seeing that people get help than in helping them. A psychiatrist recently told an instructive story in this connection. Two ministers had telephoned him some weeks previously. One said, "There's a woman here in my office who has a mental problem— something about sex, and of course I couldn't help her on that. Will you see her?" The other said, "I've just had a talk with a woman who needs some help. I was careful not to give her false reassurance or to excite her, but I'm afraid I have neither time nor training to get into it in the way it should be done. Can you talk with her?"

In the first case the minister did not care, because his province was "religion" and this was not a "religious" problem. He was even a bit incensed that he should be consulted about a sex problem. The other minister wanted to help; he did care. But he recognized that the roots of his parishioner's problem went deep, that it would require both more time and more skill to deal with them than he had, and that the most important thing was having the woman helped rather than in helping her. In both cases the problems were referred, but with what a difference.

Even today we sometimes find ministers (and parishioners) who believe that it is a confession of the weakness of religion to seek help elsewhere than in the church or through prayer. This is equivalent to saying that God works through prayer but not for example through the surgeon's knife. We should use every legitimate resource available and teach our people to do the same. Further, ministers should not think that a referral is any confession of incapacity on their part. The minister who always wades into every situation where he is asked to help is indicating that he is more concerned with his own place in the situation than with that of the parishioner who needs aid.

The counselor cannot succeed if he has a personal or theological ax to grind in his counseling. We have spoken enough of the personal ax to indicate why the statement is true in that case. But the situation is no better if a minister cannot counsel without dragging theology in by the scruff of the neck— even good theology. Here was a layman of middle age, deeply troubled, confessing to a minister for the first time certain acts of his adolescence in an attempt to get at the heart of his present problem. Suddenly the minister stopped him and launched into a discussion of human imperfection in the face of God's perfection, of the place of freedom and determinism in all human acts, and of the meaning of sin. The confession stopped, and general discussion about theology ensued, but no further progress was made toward solution of the man's problem. There is a place for theological discussion and a place for it in counseling;

but it is never in the midst of an emotional revelation and never until the parishioner is ready for it.

It is entirely possible that this man, having assimilated his earlier experience, would then have been drawn to think of other "imperfections" in his life. He might eventually have seen a pattern of them; and at this point a discussion which aided him to see that this was exactly the kind of human dilemma which theologians have called "sin," might have been greatly helpful.

In the fifth place, the counselor must be reasonably objective toward success and failure in his counseling. There has been much discussion of this point. Some have said that being objective means that we do not care and therefore out with it. Others have said that we cannot help a person if we have any "feeling with" him. Both of these extremes are incorrect, especially the first. By objectivity of a reasonable variety is meant something of the attitude a surgeon must have. He may be tremendously concerned with saving an individual's life but, unless he is calm and free from anxiety during the operation, he decreases the patient's chances. The best way to help an individual is to keep from being so tied up with him emotionally that we fail to have any perspective on his problems. Someone has well said that the counselor shares the counselee's emotion but not his logic. There must be a basic feeling of wanting to help, of the same sort the surgeon possesses, and even more of a basic "feeling for" *this* person who is to be helped. But this is not to be confused with "feeling with" the person in the sense of accepting his feelings as the only possible ones under the circumstances.

There are counselors, but not good counselors, who cannot bear to tell of their failures or even to recognize them. Such workers are either very insecure within themselves or they have unconsciously dealt with but a single type of person whom they are able to help, such as the type which believes it needs a dominating parent person to make decisions on its behalf. There are a few ministers at the other extreme, who have seen so much failure in their own counseling efforts that they have decided it is all a waste of time. Probably these latter are good men who, with a little more understanding of the principles of counseling, could achieve good results. But sometimes they are men who will undertake nothing at which they cannot be very successful. Certainly a real though not a perfect objectivity is needed in counseling—a willingness to accept both success and failure without being inflated by the one or deflated by the other but with sufficient desire for success to work to improve their capacities.

The counselor must also be relatively "unshockable" and able to "take hostility." Being shocked in this sense used to refer chiefly to the counselor's attitude when hearing of sexual irregularities when he had not suspected them. But it means vastly more. It means that the counselor is seriously and earnestly so much *with* the person as a whole that he cannot be emotionally deflected by a part of the person in the form of some act or attitude. The psychiatrist speaks of this as "keeping on the side of the ego." It means more than that a counselor would not express surprise upon learning something unexpected or morally shocking, though it does mean that too. It means also that his knowledge of the "so much bad in the best of us" prevents him from ever withdrawing his sympathetic interest from the person as a whole on moral or any other grounds.

Being able to "take" hostility is closely related to unshockability. Many psychiatrists point out that basic anxiety is the root of neurosis, and that its cause lies frequently in the realm of hostility which has failed to have not only expression but even recognition. It is certainly true that any human relation which goes very deep encounters currents of hostility as well as of love; and this is particularly true in counseling, where an attempt is being made to get at problems in which hostility has often been a bottled-up factor for years. This hostility in the counseling situation may show itself fairly directly, as in the form of an outburst, or of quiet irony, or of overt irritation; or it may come out only through forgotten appointments, distractability, or in other ways. But when the counselor is aware of its presence, he must be able to "take it." If he understands that it is not really directed at him personally, this may help. But it often seems to be directed personally. By "taking it" we mean refusing to deal with it on its own emotional terms, to fight back, or too pointedly to ignore it entirely.

The counselor finally must know when counseling is called for and when it is not, in view of the practical exigencies of the situation, and what kind of counseling it should be. Reference has already been made to persons whom the minister is not equipped to help single-handedly, and his referring of them to other specialists in human problems. But there are different ways in which he deals with people whom he can help. With some, one or two chats will suffice; with others, a more extended series of consultations is needed; with still others, individual interviews and then a family discussion should be held. Many ministers counsel beyond casual meetings only by importunity; that is, the person who demands most gets most. This is an unsafe criterion. Granted that the minister cannot help when help is not wanted, he can say to someone who has asked for help that they should meet once a week for six weeks as easily as he can suggest that it is all over. There must be judicious handling of time in view of the small amount which the minister has available.

In summary, the minister should be the kind of person who will give people confidence that he wants them to be helped and can do at least something about it himself. Without some measure of this, which comes from training as well as innate ability, he will be of little value as a counselor. It is hardly necessary to suggest the obvious fact that his own spiritual experience must be genuine, but he will certainly not try to have all his parishioners duplicate in details his own particular brand of experience.

Principles of Interview-Counseling.[3] There are relatively few principles of counseling which can be communicated through the mere medium of words on paper, and no formulas at all. The fact is that every individual does differ sufficiently from every other to make all universal categories somewhat misleading. Furthermore, the principles must be applied not only *to* an individual but *by* an individual; and the counselor cannot do something which is beyond or beneath the range of his own personality. The counselor's principles must be conditioned by his personality. Even though he attempts to work around his own biases and handicaps, he does not disregard them or believe that he can "think" them out of existence.

In this discussion of principles, it will be assumed that the minister is alone with the counselee in a place where they will not be interrupted. Most of the principles applicable here are also relevant to counseling in other types of situations.

The Contact. The first step is making the contact. Most ministers will already know the person from other kinds of contacts within the parish. If the person is a stranger, one starts from the beginning. There will usually be little difficulty if the minister evidences liking and respect for the person. But contact must be established before anything further can be done. The problem of the average pastor is not in making a new contact but in utilizing or changing a contact which has already been made in other ways. The difficulty at this point has probably been exaggerated; but it will be a real difficulty unless it is faced by the minister at the outset. If the person has known the minister as a preacher, or as an administrator, or as a teacher, and now comes to him as a counselor, there must be an immediate awareness on the pastor's part that the relationship has undergone a subtle change. This is not to make a chameleon of the minister but only to suggest that inevitable change must be recognized. The minister may have been hearty and cordial in greeting the parishioner after the previous Sunday's worship service. Now he may be cordial but not hearty. He is not a prophet now but a priest. We emphasize that this is not a change in the minister's personality but the recognition that he has been sought out for reasons which are somewhat different from those which brought the parishioner to worship the previous Sunday. His "rôle" has changed whether he likes it or not. If he recognizes the change, there should be no difficulty in establishing contact.

In a short while the pastor should make some decision about the "level of rapport" which should be sought. This level may be changed later, but it should be considered from the start. If not, the relationship's depth will be guided entirely by the parishioner; in some cases it will become too "sticky," and in others it will scarcely get under way at all. Merely to aim at the deepest level possible is of little use unless the minister wishes to become emotionally involved with the few parishioners who covet that kind of relationship. A good rough list of categories might be stated as follows: [4]

1. The level of conversation, where problems are discussed mutually by two people who are looking at a problem more or less objectively;
2. The level of occasional deeper contact, in which a few elements that are below the surface will be brought up with the counselor's aid for examination;

3. The level of occasional interpretation, where the counselor will offer suggestions as to the deeper problem areas toward which the parishioner might profitably direct his thinking;
4. The level of frank re-examination of character as a whole, together with reasons for its nature;
5. And the level of deep psychological therapy.

The minister with some training is safe in the first three levels, provided they are adaptable to the needs of the parishioner, but he must be cautious about the third and even the second. The fourth level is usually a job for the professional psychotherapist. Even here the trained minister may deal profitably with an occasional person, though this is not generally recommended. The fifth level is for the professional therapist only. The untrained minister will do well to confine himself to the first level, with occasional use of the second.

Getting At the Problem. By the time some contact has been established, the counselor will probably have learned something about what the parishioner feels the problem to be. This is especially true when the minister has been sought out. It may not be so true when the counseling situation occurs during the course of a pastoral call. When some statement of the problem has been made, it is obvious that the pastor should refrain from concluding finally that this is the "real problem." But to assume the opposite, that the problem the person feels has no relation to the real problem, is equally fallacious in most cases.

Through the next pages of this discussion on principles of pastoral counseling we shall be considering a single "case." A parenthetical word is needed in explanation of this method. The more usual method is to use brief "cases" to illustrate various points, making sure that the "cases" cover a wide range of problem areas. This approach is easier to use (as is done elsewhere in this volume), and is grasped more readily by the reader who wants "to hit the high spots." But in one important respect it tends to give a fallacious impression, for it suggests that the principles of counseling are "applied" in specific cases, rather than that they are "induced out of" specific cases. The use of a single extended "case" helps to suggest that the principles emerge from specific situations. In fairness it must be agreed that no one "case" contains material for inducing all the important principles of counseling. But a case which is *representative* may show more of the basic principles than a series of "illustrations."

The "case" chosen for this treatment is believed to be fairly representative. It does not involve illness in the physical sense, nor illness in any of the usual senses. It deals with a rather "normal" crisis in a family's growth, with some complications ensuing from underlying patterns of character. It deals, therefore, with "illness" in the sense of mal-functioning of the whole personality, and with "health" in the sense of attempts to restore and enhance that whole personality. Whether we call the situation of difficulty "illness" or not makes little difference. The fact is that the health, security, and happiness of the total person (and family) are involved.

The fact that the problems and symptoms involved in this "case" are not extreme is not what makes this situation "representative." For we are convinced that sometimes extreme "cases" represent the basic problems more accurately than more "normal" ones.

Here is Mrs. John Huggins, who made it clear to the minister in the first few minutes that the problem was with her fourteen-year-old daughter, who had been stealing small sums of money around the house but denied that she had done it.[5] Having this statement of the problem, the minister was not justified either in concluding that the fault was wholly with Mary, the daughter, or that it lay within Mrs. Huggins herself. But he had Mrs. Huggins there, and his opportunity was with her. He did not share her logic but he did share her feeling that the situation was important and should be considered seriously.

He felt that more facts were needed, not so much about the stealing as about the personal relationships of the Huggins family. He knew that father, mother, and daughter were regular weekly attendants at worship but had never participated in any other activities of the parish. In his pastoral calling he had sensed that the Huggins parents had feelings of being "cheated" in life, and that all was not happy between them. But he had never had an opportunity to talk intimately with either of them before. He knew Mary from the church school and knew that she was a bright and popular youngster. Her teacher had indicated that Mary did not seem to get much help from home in thinking out religion. The opportunity had arrived to find out more about the family.

Mrs. H. said she could not imagine why Mary would steal, especially in such trifling amounts, for she had an allowance as adequate as her parents could afford, and the total of the amounts stolen had been less than the allowance even for a single week. The pastor indicated that, whatever it might be, Mary must have had some reason for taking the money, even if she herself did not know what it was and that, to get at this reason, more should be known about Mary's family as well as about Mary. Seriously desiring to cure her daughter's stealing, Mrs. H. came to talk more intimately about the family situation.

It was eventually disclosed that Mrs. H. had been the youngest child in a family of five, having been born when her parents were about fifty years of age. She had been told she was a delicate child from the time she could remember anything, and she had participated little in sports or outdoor activities, but in her childhood had spent much of her time reading and playing by herself. She went out with boys only a little until she was twenty. Though her casual contacts with them in adolescence through parties and dances seemed normal, she had never become at all intimate with anyone. She had had a number of girl friends, but none who were close friends.

When she was twenty, she met her husband. He had been reared in a small town in the same state, had managed by diligent work to go through a small college, and had a minor job in the local bank. He too had not had many close friends, though he had had a few. He was prevented from having more by the way he had to work to get through college.

When these two met, their romance was slow. They had never really discussed their deepest thoughts and fears; but gradually Mr. H. concluded that he wanted to marry this girl. She was dissatisfied, thinking that his economic prospects were not very good; but after they had known each other for four years they became engaged, and a few months later were married.

Mrs. H. made a few efforts to get into community life in her new status but slipped into spending most of her time in housework, listening to the radio, and in occasional parties. Both she and her husband considered themselves religious and attended worship services at least once a week. They occasionally entertained friends at home for dinner or went to the homes of friends, but not often. Mrs. H. found sexual relationships to be less interesting than she had thought they would be, and since the first few months of her marriage these had been engaged in only infrequently.

Mary was born about a year and a half after the marriage. Mrs. H. had felt nervous during pregnancy and was sure the child would be nervous too. The child's birth was not so difficult as her mother had expected; and as Mrs. H. mentioned this, she seemed to be a bit disappointed that it had not.

Mary had been a lively child. Her mother felt that like herself Mary had always been nervous. When asked whether the child was more nervous at home than when with other children, Mrs. H. confessed that this seemed to be true. The mother described the way in which she looked after her daughter's welfare, how much care she took of her health, how she wanted Mary to bring her little friends home, and in other ways how generally solicitous she was on Mary's behalf.

Mrs. H. confessed that her husband had not been advanced at the bank as they had hoped, and that they both had been disappointed when a younger man was recently advanced to a responsible post over her husband. He was spending an increasing amount of his spare time on the golf links, she said, and when he was at home he seldom did anything but read or otherwise keep to himself.

Mary had done rather well in school. But she had made friends with two girls, reported her mother, who were not quite the right type; and although she had not forbidden Mary to bring them home, she had tried to suggest to her why they were not the kind with whom her daughter should associate intimately. Mary seldom brought any friends home, she admitted. Instead she had recently taken to spending considerable time in one of the local drug stores with young people of both sexes from the school. She liked pretty clothes, and dissatisfaction with her own clothes was the one thing about which Mary frequently complained openly at home. Mrs. H. could not understand this because she made the child's clothes herself and was known to be an excellent seamstress. Upon questioning, the pastor was not surprised to find that Mrs. H. used her own "designs and patterns."

The story might be extended, but enough has been given to suggest the relevant facts which the pastor needed and which he could get by judicious discussion with Mrs. H. The way the story is written, and a few of the matters accepted as "fact," are obviously inferences on the part of the pastor; but the limited space available does not permit a more strictly accurate separation of fact and inference.

It is to be noted that the minister did not isolate his getting of information from the process of cementing his contact with Mrs. H. In the actual situation he did not secure all this information in one interview, but in three; and the process of doing something about it was well under way before all the information was available. But the general outlines were reasonably clear after the first interview.

Since the story must be told in shorthand style, it may not be evident that the pastor's approach was more indirect than direct. He did not ask, "Now, Mrs. Huggins, are you really happy with your husband?" He made the inference that neither Mr. or Mrs. H. were very happy with each other, after having asked questions about how Mr. H. spent his time. The entire procedure at first was of this type. If he had been too direct at any point early in the relationship, Mrs. H. would have felt that he was attacking her instead of trying to find out about her daughter. After all, it was the latter problem, as she saw it, which had brought her for guidance to a minister for the first time in her life.

At the end of the first interview, the minister felt that he was getting somewhere about the real problem involved. Tentatively he concluded that while the problem lay with the family as a whole it could be solved only by working through Mrs. H. herself. Accordingly he left the matter in such a way that Mrs. H. would come to see him a second time. He decided that the

level of "occasional deeper contact" was what he would aim
for, that if this were not sufficient to solve the problem it would
have to be referred. Meanwhile, he asked Mrs. H. if he might
consult with the teacher at Mary's school, and thus made the way
clear to secure further information about Mary, and at the same
time reassured Mrs. H. that he was concerned with the possibility of the problem's being in her daughter.

He had applied the principle of listening in this interview.
As has rightly been pointed out, this is an active rather than a
passive principle. It does not mean sitting with clenched teeth
refusing to say anything while trying to drag the inmost life
out of the other person. It means rather that he put himself
wholly at Mrs. H's service, continually making it clear by his
attitude that he needed to know more that only Mrs. H. could
tell him, and then considering the information given sympathet-
ically but objectively. He did not tell Mrs. H. that he had dealt
with another case of stealing in another parish, that he had been
able to fix that up, and that therefore this would be easy. That
would be violating the listening principle to the nth degree. He
did not talk about his own daughter, or his own married life,
in an effort to give premature reassurance. He asked questions,
but not before it had become reasonably clear to Mrs. H. that
the answer to any particular question might have some bearing
on the situation. Some of the questions embarrassed Mrs. H. a
bit; but it was the logic of the questions, and not the pastor
himself, which did the embarrassing.

Even after the first interview, the pastor realized that Mrs. H.
had told him certain things which she had never voiced to anyone before. He knew there was a danger of her reacting against
him at their next meeting on this account. He did not attempt
to give her false reassurance; but was quite prepared when there
was a little burst of resentment soon after their second confer-

ence began. He "took" the hostility and was soon in fact able to use it to help Mrs. H. to see the emotional factors in the personal and family situation which her hostility showed she was beginning to recognize in spite of herself.

Of course he assured her from the first that their conversations would be confidential. He did not reassure her several times on this point; for that would have been to make her wonder whether they really would be. Later he was able to help her see that the family problem was not so unusual and extraordinary as she had always imagined, and that discussing this *type* of problem was by no means to "give her away."

It is to be noted that the pastor refused to "assign" guilt about the situation even in his own mind. Mrs. H's emotional impulse had been to get reinforcement in her conviction that it was her daughter who was in the wrong; the emotional impulse of the pastor was to believe, and tell Mrs. H., that it was she who should be blamed. But Mrs. H. would not have come to her minister if there had not been a suspicion, however unwitting, that there might be something in the situation beyond the faults in her daughter. Of course the pastor would have broken the contact if he had attempted to tell Mrs. H. that the fault was hers. What he had to do was to get beyond the question of guilt or blame, to the point where he could think of "understanding" the situation. Finding causes is not the same as assigning blame. He became reasonably convinced that the ills which could most profitably be attacked lay in Mrs. H., but this was very different even from thinking in his own mind that Mrs. H. was the guilty party.

Doing Something about the Problem. Considered superficially, the things the pastor did about the situation were as follows. He talked with Mary's teacher at school; he talked twice more with Mrs. H.; he talked once with Mr. and Mrs. H. together;

and he had a final conference with Mr. H. It turned out to be unnecessary to have a talk with Mary.

As he delved more into the situation, it shaped up in his own mind somewhat like this. Mrs. H. had been brought up by parents who were so old compared to her that they were unable to comprehend her interests as a child. Their attitude made her think of herself as delicate, and she did not enter fully into the emotional experiences of childhood and adolescence because she had doubted whether she was a worthy kind of person. She fell into a kind of character pattern of lethargy, not extreme but nonetheless unsatisfactory. Church for example was a passive thing to her. She married her husband believing that she had better get him if she could get no one better, and she had taken few steps to deepen the emotional relationship with him.

In his turn, Mr. H. had had to struggle so hard in his early life that he desperately wanted, as so many "self-made" men do, the symbols of "success" in advancement and promotion. But this single-mindedness, while it made him a valuable bank clerk, made his judgment on important matters so poor that he could not be trusted with a responsible position involving policy. Not having found his marriage as fine an experience as he had wished, he came gradually to draw further within himself and away from his family. He assumed that it was his wife's job to rear their daughter; and he scarcely took it amiss when his wife announced that they were to have no more children.

Mary probably had no good idea in her own mind as to why she stole trifling sums from her mother's purse. But the theft in her case was a symbol of resentment at the way her parents, and especially her mother, treated her. The ordinary meaning of money had little or nothing to do with her stealing. Her parents professed to give her affection but their emotional contact with her was so lacking in depth that she unconsciously wanted to reject affection if this was it. When she was at home or when she thought of her mother, she thought of herself as "nervous," as she had been taught to think. But when with other young people she forgot about this nervousness and enjoyed herself. Her mother's partial repudiation of her best girl friends seemed to be (and in a sense was) justified, but this only made her more resentful in having a lingering suspicion that her mother was right.

Her father's love was too casual; she really scarcely knew him. That of her mother professed to be solicitous but was actually in part exploitative in nature. Part of Mrs. H., to put it crudely, was trying to prevent her daughter from being happier or more spontaneous in her attitude to life than she herself had been.

If this were all the story, the end might have been sad. Fortunately both Mr. and Mrs. H. possessed a genuine love for Mary which had become obscured by the other motives. They had developed, too, almost in spite of themselves, a real yearning for each other's affection which was capable of being transformed into genuine love. What they needed was to get together, to discuss their resentments heatedly but affectionately, to explore the possibilities in each other. They needed, too, to understand that Mary was a person in her own right, that they could not express real affection for her without first recognizing that fact. They needed some information about adolescent reactions and some interpretation of adolescent tendencies. Mrs. H. needed to learn that she could be the best seamstress in the world, yet if she made Mary's clothes with home-made designs, she would be putting new wine into old bottles so far as her daughter was concerned.

The pastor "explained" almost none of this to the Huggins's. After discussing, in the second interview, some aspects of the

relationship with her daughter, Mrs. H. found some light break-
ing for herself and asked, "Do you think I have loved my
daughter too much?" This was a golden opportunity for the
counselor, who was able to suggest aspects of "loving too much"
for Mrs. H's thought in such a way that she soon was able to
say, "It isn't that I loved Mary too much or too little, but I have
had other motives than love which prevented me from loving
her in the right way." It might have taken a long time for Mrs.
H. without help to find out for herself—and she really did find
out for herself—this important truth. It would have been useless to her if the pastor had "given" it to her. Insight cannot be
given; what the counselor does is to set up the conditions so
that there is a chance that it may come. Insight means the
recognition of connections between elements that have been
present but whose relationship has not been understood; and
it may often involve recognition of the presence of elements not
previously accepted as being there.

The minister attempted to encourage as much insight as he
felt Mrs. H. could stand at the moment. He did not believe an
extended character analysis was called for in this situation either
by the problem or by his own capacity to help carry it out. When
he finished his consultations, he felt that he knew a good deal
more about some of the basic problems of the H. family than
the family itself knew. But he was not concerned to get these
ideas over to the couple except in so far as a few basic insights,
achieved by the H's themselves, would set their path in a new
direction.

The counselor suggested a good many things for Mrs. H.,
and later Mr. H. also, to think about, but he used no "suggestion" in the ordinary sense of the term. The influence of
suggestion is ordinarily to minimize forthright consideration of
the problem itself or to urge a solution before sufficient under-

standing is available to make the solution an autonomous decision of the person or persons involved.

Religious Elements in the Situation. Where does religion come into this picture? Might not this family have been aided by a psychiatrist or by some other type of counselor than a clergyman? Of course they might have been; but in very many cases, the pastor is either the only counselor available or is the preferred counselor by reason of what he represents personally or as a minister of the church. Further, even if the pastor had not said a single word which the H's might have interpreted as religious, their relationship to the well-springs of Christian experience through the church would have deepened.

Besides, the whole problem of the family was basically religious. Much more striking cases could have been chosen to illustrate this point, but it is perhaps better to take a situation which is more general and usual. The H's were "good people" and "good church members" in the eyes of the community, by which is meant that they did not get into trouble, paid their bills and went to church. But real Christianity had touched them only superficially. Deep in their beings they wanted to belong, to themselves, to each other, and to God. But they had allowed themselves to drift into attitudes and patterns of life which affirmed only the shadow but not the substance.

It was a life situation which awakened them. Sometimes the minister can be more active in awakening people; he has an opportunity especially through his sermons. But frequently it takes come kind of crisis, not designed by anyone but by life itself, to rouse these unawakened people into seeing that something is wrong which ought to be made right. It is the counselor's privilege and obligation to be at hand when this occurs so that it may be guided into constructive channels. This is as true of suffering as of shock or guilt. Attempts should rightly be made to relieve pain and suffering; but it is also necessary, and sometimes only this is possible, to help turn the newly roused emotion into constructive channels.

Then, too, the counselor did eventually discuss religion itself with the H's. By the time of the third interview with Mrs. H., she was at the point where she recognized certain ways in which she had simply evaded many problems through her apparent passivity. Through a process too long to describe here, it was possible for her to see that she had been applying this same technique to her religious thinking and activity. For the first time in her life she began to experience religious growth. At the conclusion of the interview the pastor suggested a prayer, which was very brief. The same thing was done in the later interview with Mr. and Mrs. H., although the pastor avoided having the prayer interpreted as a symbol indicating that what he had said was true.

The use of a single illustration is almost bound to emphasize certain points at the expense of others which are equally important. Yet several of the basic principles are illustrated and have been described in the case of the H's. We may review them briefly: listening is sometimes valuable in itself; sometimes information is needed, but usually the problem cannot be solved by information alone; the counselor helps to lead to insight, but not to give it; emergent insight is encouraged but not pushed too far; helping one person in a situation often helps others who are close to him; the counselor may suggest hypotheses, or help to define alternative courses of action, but not advise or suggest which should be followed; the use of prayer should be consistent with the entire counseling situation; and the counselor should know more than he tells or interprets.

This particular situation worked out fortunately and at a rate which was much faster than usual. Had Mrs. H. not had the constructive resources which were quickly revealed in her, the whole situation might have been beyond the scope of the minister because of lack of time and training. Had he found himself against a stone wall after the third interview, he would have had to consider referral, which would have been delicate in this case. In all probability he could have done it only if he had been able to say, "I should like you to see *my friend,* Dr. Smith." The referral would have had to be on a personal basis, or Mrs. H. would have balked. This suggests the importance to the minister not only of knowing what resources are available but of knowing personally the persons in charge of the resources. If there were more of this kind of personal friendship among ministers, physicians, and psychiatrists, mental hygiene clinic workers, social workers, and others, there would be less talk about the too easy solution of having "church clinics."

Concluding the Counseling Situation. Especially if the pastor has given some real help, those who have been aided will find themselves with a tendency to avoid closing the consultations. The minister must close them actively at the point at which he feels the person is able to move on his own. He should make it clear that his services are available at any time in the future that they are felt to be needed; but he should not permit parishioners to become dependent upon him, for their own good as well as his. When the Gadarene had been healed through Jesus' ministry, he begged to go with Jesus, but Jesus sent him away and said, "Go back to your home." [6] He was healed sufficiently to move under his own steam. Once he had found a source of help, the easy way would have been to stay with it. But the proper way was to move once again under his own power.

The minister will probably meet his parishioner in other kinds of situations after his consultations. It is wise never to refer, in casual contacts with the individual, to the material that was disclosed only in the counseling room. It is certainly wise to give no sign in any way to others that one has given special time and attention to a particular person. As with the start of the consultation, this change is not difficult if one recognizes its inevitability. The relationship with the person who has been helped cannot be exactly as it was before. But no advantage should be taken of the deepened relationship.

The situation must in any case be concluded. The psychiatrist indicates his conclusion by ceasing to render bills. The Roman priest indicates conclusion by giving absolution. We must have the equivalent of such conclusions, not merely (and not always) prayer, but also a formal kind of indication that the present relationship is being changed. In most cases the suggestion that the pastor will be glad to see the parishioner at a future date will be sufficient. But sometimes a more direct statement is necessary. Sometimes gratitude for help received will make the person want to make a contribution to something. The wise minister will have in his mind a few special causes to which such contribution can best be made. It is sometimes wiser not to allow them to be made to a cause of the parish but to something having wider church significance, as one of the mission stations of the church or an interchurch agency.

Concluding the situation where the counselor has not been successful but has gone as far as he can go is no less important. To have a special counseling situation drag on without much practical hope of success is a waste of the minister's time and of the parishioner's patience. The pastor should in most cases either refer the person to someone who may be able to help or tell him frankly that he cannot be of much practical value at the present time.

Setting Up a Counseling Program. Strictly speaking, the problem is one not of setting up a counseling program, for every pastor does some kind of counseling whether he realizes it or not, but of extending and improving the program he has. For many ministers "setting up a program" may mean chiefly becoming more conscious of the significance of activities in which they have long been engaged. Increased awareness of the implications of counseling is, of course, a prerequisite to improving the program.

The first step on the part of the minister who wishes to improve his counseling program, or who becomes aware of it as counseling for the first time, is to examine himself. Enough has been said previously about self-understanding to suggest why this must be done. It should also involve some sincere evaluation of the limitations which his training, as well as his personality, may impose upon his counseling activities. And it should involve serious efforts to improve his knowledge and understanding before launching any "new program."

Reading is the easiest, and in some respects the most unsatisfactory, way in which to improve his knowledge. If he reads not much but carefully, however, he will be able greatly to increase his wisdom. Some of the best literature now available contains little direct mention of religion, and the connections will have to be drawn by the reader. But if he is unable to make these connections in his reading, it is even less likely that he will be able to make them in his counseling; and most problems about which he will be consulted will not seem superficially to be religious. Bibliographies are available which indicate the best literature for the pastor in this field.[7]

The great difficulty about getting knowledge in this field by reading is that the knowledge one gets is general, while the people one meets are always particular. The pastor who has the opportunity to take a course of supervised clinical training should seize it.[8] Conferences and short courses are being offered in various quarters which are excellent supplements to books though they are not in the same class with clinical experience under supervision.[9]

One means of improving one's wisdom in the field, which is more effective than it seems because it is so simple, lies in recording a few of the counseling situations with which the pastor is now dealing. This should be advised in any case before any new kind of program is launched. An amazing amount of new insight comes from the careful recording of everything the minister knows about the person with whom he is counseling and a detailed accounting of the relationship. In many communities the value of this process may be enhanced by discussion of the notes with a brother minister or with a psychiatrist. Even consulting someone by mail, who has had special experience in the field, is valuable in checking one's own insights.

If there is a chance to have a few consultations with a professional psychotherapist in order to secure increased insight into one's self, that is to be highly recommended. But it is not often possible. Where it is, the minister should welcome the opportunity.[10]

Once he has taken certain steps to improve his own ability, the pastor faces the question of publicity. He has numerous avenues through which he can make it known publicly that he wishes people to feel free to ask for help on personal problems. He can speak from the pulpit, put notices in the church calendar or paper, speak to people personally or in small groups. But the fact is that unless he is very careful such publicity will scare his parishioners away. Any means of publicity which are too obvious may keep away those who most need help.

The "new" program should at first, therefore, be "new" mainly in the mind of the pastor. The general principle is for him to let it be known quietly and casually that he has a renewed interest in helping individuals. The experience of many ministers shows that this not only works but works better than any other means they might choose for getting the people to come who need help. There is certainly no harm in putting a modest note in the calendar to the effect that the pastor is available for consultation with individuals at certain hours and by appointment; it is often a good thing to have certain hours free when people may come without appointment. Even if they do not come at first, continuation of the hours will eventually be found productive. Occasional modest announcements from the pulpit, similarly, that the pastor is available for personal conference may do good. But to announce from pulpit, calendar or bulletin board that the minister "has now opened a clinic in pastoral counseling to help individuals solve their personal problems" is exceedingly unwise.

Giving courses on "personality development" or on some related theme is a legitimate means of making the congregation aware indirectly of the pastor's interest in personal problems. These may be Sunday or week-day evening meetings, may be led by the minister if he feels competent, or by guest "experts." [11] But the course or series of lectures should be relevant, and should not merely be in ordinary sermonic vein appropriate rather to a service of worship. Sermons may indeed be preached, in services of worship, which have mental health implications, and these should be an indirect stimulus to the use of the minister as a counselor. But care should be taken not to use illustrations involving any counseling experience in this parish.

But most of the change will be within the attitude of the minister himself. He should keep his eye open in his pastoral calling. Of course he is not a mere "detector," looking for the signs of crisis and maladjustment, but to some extent he must be just that. This does not mean that he goes around "psyching" his parishioners, for that implies an attitude of exploitation on his part. It is a very different thing for him to have his eye open in a new way for unhealthy situations which, if checked soon, will probably not have the disastrous consequences they might otherwise have had.

An understanding psychiatrist recently described the story of a patient now in his mental hospital. A woman in her fifties, she had been chained to her mother for fifty years on the mother's plea that if the daughter loved her she would stay with her and care for her. The daughter developed no personal life of her own. When the mother died, the daughter became seriously ill and had to be committed to a mental hospital. The prevention of this condition would not necessarily have involved getting the daughter to leave home, certainly would not have meant getting her to "dislike" her mother. But it would have meant having her achieve some insight into the fact that she was not developing as an autonomous person but was being swallowed by her mother. What makes the story more tragic is that the pastor of these women praised this as "one of the most beautiful relationships I have ever seen." Had he had his eyes open, he might have been able to prevent a tragedy.

The pastor, too, will make new use of the crisis situations with which he is constantly confronted. He will have a new conception of the significance of pre-marital counseling, not merely as the giving or checking of information, but as helping the couple toward an emotional and spiritual comprehension of what marriage means. Do they understand that considerable hostility in the relationship is normal and should have expression? Do they recognize *emotionally,* deep in their being, that the nature of the relationship will change, and that with understanding they can guide the change toward deeper levels of love but only through a process of give and take which involves some pain? The pastor can help to give them some perspective on their marriage, not so much by talking to them as by listening and mutual consideration of their attitudes.

In the other general crisis situations of birth, death, bereavement, going away to school or work or war, and the like, he may make great use of his insights. The same is true of the specific crisis situations which may occur at any time: illness, crime, loss of money or prestige, unemployment, and the like.[12]

In short, the minister may develop new elements in his program but his most effective means of expanding his counseling program are quiet and judicious.

A final word needs to be said about the amount of time he should spend in counseling and about different kinds of counseling. Most ministers who work successfully in this field say that they cannot deal with more than a dozen or twenty persons or situations a year which go beyond level number one of rapport as outlined above. That is, their time does not permit them to counsel for more than one or two interviews with more than a dozen to twenty people a year. Of course they are able to see a good many other people for one or two interviews in their office. But all indicate that office interviewing is no substitute for pastoral calling at the parishioner's home, or office, or luncheon table. If the minister remains in his office, he may do useful counseling; but he will fail to see many problems, and be asked for help about them, which most need and deserve his attention.

Certainly some of his counseling time should be set aside for work in connection with teachers of the church school, young people's groups, and the like. Whether this is group or individual, its importance is equal to the more dramatic counseling when problems have "broken out."

Group Counseling. Almost any small group which meets on

the basis of some natural interest may be used at times as a group counseling situation.[13] Groups of older young people who are thinking of marriage, adolescents who are confused about jobs and marriage, parents with young children, church school teachers, older single women—these are but a few of the groups with which the minister may carry on a group counseling process.

The process should be one of mutual discussion of the real problems, starting with the group itself. Such devices as getting each member of the group to write out what he feels is the major problem of such people as those who make up the group may afford a good beginning. These methods must, however, be used with care, and it is dangerous to have people write autobiographical material unless sufficient time is allowed for discussion of it with the person individually.

Care must be taken to avoid thinking that all work with groups can or should be group counseling. It is doubtful if a group larger than twenty can be made a genuine counseling situation even if the leader's skill is very great. Certainly an address, with discussion following, never makes a counseling situation. The pastor will perhaps do best to say nothing about group counseling but to select some group such as the older young people and lead a specified series of meetings on a subject like marriage. The group counseling will come if he succeeds in getting enough reciprocity into his content and methods of procedure.

Non-Ministerial Counselors in the Church. It is of great importance for church school teachers, church secretaries, church "visitors," church social workers, and others who work with individuals in the church with a more or less conscious awareness of their responsibility to help other people, to have all the insights they can about personality development and the relation of religion to it. To make or try to make self-conscious "counselors" out of this group is quite another thing.

Most people who participate in such activities within the church, including ministers, have a deep desire to help other people. More frequently than we like to think this desire itself is not as single-minded a motive as it appears to be. To make the process of helping other people become more conscious without an accompanying understanding of oneself and one's limitations is merely to give blanket approval to all desires to help, healthy or otherwise. This tends to make for busy-bodying around the local church.

Any education which will make the lay worker realize that "counseling" for him lies in "person-mindedness," and in securing all the insight of which he is capable into why human beings are as they are, is valuable. But his knowledge is applied not on a pseudo-professional basis which apes the superficial circumstances of counseling by the minister, but in terms of the natural contacts which he has in his work. The teacher of six-year-olds will not "interview" her charges, nor have the mother of a child "interview" her in the worker's office. She will do as she has always done superficially; but the "counseling" for her is in using her new insights for understanding both the child and the relationship of his parents to him.

Of course the situation is different if the minister has associated with him some one like a psychiatrist to whom, they mutually understand, certain types of situations may be referred. The psychiatrist will talk with the parishioner either in his office or in the church office, but he will not have changed his own "procedure." And this will not constitute a "church clinic." The more personal the minister's relationship with the psychotherapist, the more useful and successful the therapist's work will be.[14]

It is possible for a few large city churches to have a member on their staff who has had special training in interview-counseling. This is a good thing, but even this should not relieve other ministers of the church from counseling obligations. It is usually unwise to designate such an individual as "counseling minister" because that tends to keep from him many people who most need his help. The suggestions above would be equally applicable here.

It is unwise for the minister to have and to announce that there are lay counselors who do part of his counseling for him. In a very real sense, only he can do pastoral counseling. If he knows persons in the church who, by reason of training or general ability, are equipped to help with certain kinds of problems, he is perfectly justified in putting parishioners into their hands. But if they are not professional people, this should not be done on a professional basis. And the parishioner should not get the idea that this is "pastoral counseling." Naturally great care should be exercised in any such procedure, and the minister should keep a careful check on anything of this sort. But he should definitely not think of it as "pastoral counseling" or publicize it as such. Indeed, he defeats the strength of all pastoral counseling if he publicizes it at all. The people who can be really helpful in such situations are not the type who need publicity to spur them on.

Some ministers have tried to use theological students as pastoral counselors to supplement their own efforts. The difficulties with this are the same as those with assistant ministers of the church but are accentuated. They may be permitted to do counseling to the extent that their ability and training indicate. But their "rôle" is still different from that of the pastor in the eyes of the people. They do not have the authority, status, or experience which the people attribute to the pastor, rightly or wrongly. Students are really, therefore, closer to the category of lay workers than to that of ministers. Their best counseling in fact will come as they proceed with assigned duties but with new insights into personality and its development.

It is probably true, as some have said, that people do not often come to a pastor just because he is a pastor. They must know something about him, and, above all, have confidence in him. Such confidence cannot be built in a day. Relatively long pastorates tend to make the minister more useful to his people in this way. It might also be pointed out parenthetically that the church which has assistant ministers should see that they are given every opportunity to develop the pastoral "rôle" in the eyes of the people. If it is difficult for the pastor to make the proper contacts in his calling and counseling, it is much more difficult for the assistant who may not be given any of the "prestige-making" duties within the church.

Many have said that a little knowledge in this field is a dangerous thing. One astute minister has said that a little knowledge is not a dangerous thing if one knows how little it is.[15] This should be the basic guiding principle of all counselors, ministers and laymen alike. Counseling should not be used as a backdoor to professional standing, to ministerial standing by the layman, or to psychiatric standing by the minister. But even a little knowledge, if it is used more to understand than anything else, is of great value. The counselor is wise to do in all situations a little less than he believes his understanding makes him capable of doing. For one deals here, not with machines, but with the lives of other people who are children of God.

CHAPTER IX

PASTORAL WORK AND COMMUNITY RESOURCES

There are two aspects of the relation of pastoral work to community resources. One is utilizing whatever resources are available. The other is helping to create resources which do not exist. The second task is no less important a part of the minister's or church's function than the first, but confusion may result if the attempt is made to consider them together. We shall consider here the methods of utilizing existing sources of help, recognizing that these resources are nowhere as adequate as they should be, and that in some areas there are almost none upon which the minister may depend.

A distinction must be drawn also between the use by the minister or church of character-building agencies as against therapeutic or rehabilitative agencies. Co-operation with the Boy Scouts, Girl Scouts, recreational and educational agencies of various kinds, and other character-building agencies is an important function of the church. But these can be separated, for purposes of discussion, from agencies which are designed mainly to help individuals out of particular kinds of difficulty.

In dealing with individual or family problems the minister makes use of resources within the parish, within the denomination, and within the Protestant fold generally. But to greater or less degree he also uses general community resources. Only rarely are the community resources available as a supplement

206

to pastoral work considered together in their entirety. Getting increased perspective on community resources as a whole from the pastoral point of view is the justification for this chapter. Suggestions will be made wherever possible about each of the following points: how to get in touch with the resource, how to discover and evaluate its ability to render service, how to make referrals to it, and what it should expect of the pastor in return for its co-operation.

Personal Resources

Under this heading come contacts with professional individuals, persons who work for themselves rather than as representatives of an agency or institution.

Physicians. The minister should begin with those physicians who are members of his parish. He should utilize his status as their pastor and friend to establish a relationship out of which may come mutual referrals on a professional basis. He should interpret to the physicians his own rôle as counselor and guide, and discuss the relation of this function to theirs. He may get in touch with physicians not members of his parish in similar ways. The point is that he should know them personally and should establish such relations that when a referral is needed it may be made on a personal basis.

He will have to use his best judgment in deciding whether a physician is competent in the ordinary medical sense. Probably more physicians are competent in this restricted sense than are the members of any other professional group; so he should have little trouble. His judgment about the physician's understanding of the psychological factors in medicine will more frequently be discouraging. But some co-operation is possible even with physicians who are ignorant of psychological and spiritual factors in medicine.

Referrals to physicians should be made personally. The pastor should be able to say to the parishioner, "I should like you to talk to my friend Dr. Smith about this." Most consultees will already have personal physicians, and the minister should be able to consult with them on a professional basis. The minister may sometimes feel that a supplementary physician would be helpful to the patient; and so long as he goes about this tactfully, and on the basis of larger human and spiritual considerations, he may be helpful in such situations.

In return for such co-operation, the physician should expect understanding, inter-professional contacts being held confidential, and a due humility about the minister's own ability to help. He should also expect some sympathy with his own financial problem, his services being compensated on a fee basis, and a recognition that fees should be charged if the patient can afford them. He is hardly within his rights, however, if he expects the minister to agree that the "fee for service" system of payment for medical care is necessarily the best of all possible systems in all situations. Inter-professional co-operation should not be dependent upon agreement on matters of medical economics, though in practice such differences of conviction have often impeded co-operation. Whatever their convictions along this line, physicians and ministers should continue to work together.

Physicians and clergymen have a great deal in common. Physicians naturally resent excessive claims on the part of the clergy for the therapeutic influences of religion; let ministers avoid this. Clergy of course dislike an attitude in physicians which acts as if psychological and spiritual influences had nothing to do with health and illness; let physicians learn more about psychosomatic medicine. Discussion groups of physicians and clergy, looking toward their better co-operation in the community, have been started in some places, and hold great promise for the future. Each group may thereby become a bit less defensive about the resources which his particular outlook emphasizes, and even more concerned about the total welfare of the individual in need.[1]

Psychiatrists. The same procedures would hold in reference to psychiatrists as to other physicians, at least to those psychiatrists who are in private practice. They are hardly ever to be found in private practice outside the largest cities. The minister should always know about, and if possible know personally, the psychiatrists who are nearest to him, even if there are none in his immediate locality.[2] Personal acquaintance is even more important here than in the case of other physicians, because laymen so often think that going to a psychiatrist is tantamount to admitting that one is "crazy." If the minister knows the psychiatrist personally, much of the difficulty of referral may thereby be overcome.

Some ministers have established such close relationship with psychiatrists that the latter may almost be considered as part-time members of the church staff. This is highly desirable, but care should be taken against thinking of this arrangement as a "church clinic." This should be largely a means of supplementing pastoral service, and should not attempt to duplicate or displace community guidance clinics.

Psychologists. There are a few "consulting psychologists" who do psychological re-education with patients whose problems lie mainly in the psychological area. Psychiatrists, recognizing the importance of general medical knowledge as one of the bases of psychological therapy, usually consider such practitioners officially as quacks. Some of them are, and many of them have had inadequate training along psychological lines. But there are some who are competent, who never consider cases which have not been diagnosed as within their therapeutic area by a physician or psychiatrist; and where this is true, there would seem to be no reason why they should not be used as resources by the minister.

There are a few psychologists (or psychological agencies) which profess to give guidance on personality problems by the use of psychological tests. Some of these specialize, as in the case of vocational problems. The minister is warned to be suspicious, not of the individuals or agencies, but of what he may reasonably expect to find out as a result of such testing. Effective testing with such means as the Rohrschach test is exceedingly valuable.[3] But tests which give the patient long series of questions to answer are only very approximate in the accuracy of their results about any particular individual. They may be good supplements; but in themselves their value is limited.

Lawyers. Many types of problems will arise in the pastoral ministry in which the advice of the lawyer is needed. His function is not so obviously related to healing as is that of the physician, nor has he been a giver of service in the same sense as the physician has. But there is evidence of a growing spirit of service within the profession, and some signs that clinical education may one day be a part of legal training as it is now of medicine and as it is slowly becoming of theology. The minister should know lawyers personally as he knows physicians, and he should know what he can justifiably expect a lawyer to tell him and what he cannot. An understanding lawyer may be a gem in the minister's pastoral crown.

Laymen. Every church possesses laymen or laywomen who are competent in helping with certain kinds of problems. This may be because of some professional occupation, or it may be simply because of their personality and general ability. In some circumstances a banker, an insurance man, an industrialist, a labor leader, an engineer, or many others may be just the persons to call on for assistance. Unfortunately the attempts by some laymen, who are more enthusiastic than competent, to be given such responsibility prevents the pastor from making full use of other competent laymen. It sometimes seems criminal to see so many competent laymen in a church doing nothing to help on problems where they would be competent. Such laymen may usually be put to work without being given the spiritual equivalent of uniforms and titles.

A Case-Worker Adviser. Almon R. Pepper suggests that the best community resource a pastor can have is a trained case worker willing to act as his confidential adviser.[4] This suggestion may be heartily seconded. Such a case worker knows all the resources of the community and how they can be utilized to help an individual or family. She also knows more than most ministers about when a particular type of problem ought to be referred to some resource or agency. If a minister is fortunate enough to have such a confidential adviser, she could give him quickly all the specific information about resources available in their locality which are discussed in the following pages only in general. Other case workers may serve as resources to the pastor through their connection with agencies. But there are probably few sounder moves which he can make than creating a confidential relationship with a selected case worker as he would with a psychiatrist or physician. It is for this reason that we consider such a relationship in the personal category.

A few of the councils of churches in larger communities have secured full-time executives for their departments of social welfare or social service. Although these persons are trained case workers in most instances, their job is one of co-ordination and aid to churches rather than of carrying out firsthand case work. They are ideally suited, both by experience and position, to be the case-worker adviser to the minister. They know the community resources intimately, and they see them from the point of view of the church. The minister who can find such a person in his local council of churches is very fortunate.

The patterning of private social agencies varies widely in different communities. But there are certain essential agency functions which, however inadequately, are fulfilled somehow in every community.

Family and Child Welfare Agencies. These agencies are equipped to do case work, which means that their workers are different from the general public's conception of the "ordinary social worker." They are trained in social diagnosis and social treatment. They are competent to help even in many of the most complicated and delicate types of family maladjustments. These family case-work agencies usually do little or no relief work. They should be used by the community, and by the minister, to help with difficult family situations of many kinds; yet their ability to be of service is dependent to a large extent upon the community's understanding of their function and its willingness to utilize what they offer. Sometimes churches, unaware of the service offered by the family and child welfare agencies, will expend valuable staff time in case work which the existing agencies could do better.

The pastor should know the heads, and usually some of the case workers, in the family and child welfare agencies. The services which the good case worker can perform, for the rich as well as the poor, are so little known to the layman that there must be constant interpretation if the community is to receive full value from the agencies. In referring people to these agencies, the minister who knows the workers personally and can explain the agency's function cogently is the one who can make the referral useful. Referral incidentally should not connote getting rid of the problem, but rather getting expert help on it. Putting a family situation in the hands of the family welfare agency should not mean that the pastor loses all interest in or responsibility for it.

How can the minister discover whether his local agencies are competent? This is one place where his confidential case-work adviser may be of great value. Unless he has had unusual training or experience in connection with case-work, the pastor's own judgment at this point may not be much better than that of a layman. But his case-work adviser will know; and if she is a confidential adviser, she will tell him. It is not so much a matter of judging the agency as wholly effective or ineffective, as it is of evaluating the kinds of problems which this agency is equipped to handle well and those which it has handled poorly. Failing such a confidential adviser, the local council of social agencies may be found very useful in evaluating the local agencies on the basis of what problems they have handled best. If there is a social welfare executive in the local council of churches, he is, of course, the ideal person to consult.

These agencies, which are usually private and ordinarily receive most of their support from the community chest, may reasonably expect to get certain information which is not confidential from the minister on an interprofessional basis. They may expect understanding of what they can do as well as of their limitations. They may expect the church to be their boosters and interpreters in the community. They may expect prompt attention when they in turn make a referral to the minister.

Public Schools and Visiting Teachers. Public schools generally are still not idyllic centers of instruction to meet the individual needs of every child, but they have improved markedly in recent years in the intelligence brought to bear on the problems of individuals. Even where the minister may have to make all his own interpretations, he may frequently secure useful facts about a child from the school teacher or administrator when this would be difficult to get from the family. Sometimes he may be able to put in a word of information or interpretation at the school which will result in a needed change of attitude toward the child on the school's part. Many ministers find a school executive their most understanding counselor and resource.

Where there are special counselors in the schools or so-called visiting teachers (who have also had social case-work training), the minister will be particularly fortunate. He should by all means know personally any of these people in his community or district. The fact that visiting teachers are already being used in rural school systems indicates that they are far more than a luxury and that they will increasingly be available as aides to the minister.[5]

School people are not generally so accustomed to dealing with individual problems on a professional basis as are physicians and social workers, but this situation is changing. Some judgment must be made about their interest and competence before exchange of information or judgment can ordinarily go as far as it does with other groups. Special guidance workers are generally familiar with interprofessional contacts, unless they are interested only in so-called "objective" test methods, in which case they are not guidance people in this sense at all.

General and Specialized Hospitals. These should be a great resource of the minister, as has been amply indicated in previous chapters. Here only a few basic points need to be emphasized. The minister should try to know personally the administrator, some physicians, and some other workers in the hospital.

Hospitals in America were originally places where the sick poor were kept in charge of matrons. Their functions have changed very greatly. Not only are they the centers for the treatment of bed-patients of all economic classes, but they are the centers of preventive medicine, medical education and medical research. The number of out-patients they treat is usually far larger than the number of patients who are put to bed. Physicians increasingly do a larger proportion of their work at hospitals, and this trend is likely to be increased in the future. The point is that hospitals offer more types of service than is ordinarily recognized. The minister will do well to learn, from a hospital executive or from his social work adviser, what some of the services are which might not be immediately apparent to him.

Ordinarily it is the physician who refers patients to a hospital but this may sometimes be in order for the pastor, especially when he is collaborating with the physician. Hospitals are increasingly, and sometimes with justice, getting the reputation of being huge and impersonal places; and it is therefore even more important that the minister's referrals be as personal as possible. If the hospital has a chaplain, the pastor may secure his services in helping the patient through the hospital. Putting the patient in touch with a physician or nurse or social worker, especially in the larger hospitals, is of great value to the patient, and makes the hospital an entirely different kind of resource for the pastor.

His case-work adviser is the one who can inform him best of the types of care and service offered by different hospitals. It is important that he have some expert judgment at this point; for the judgment of the general public is not always correct in evaluating a hospital's capacity for service. Naturally the pastor will make his own judgments as to the relative humaneness and attention to the patient's personality shown at different hospitals. He will learn such things as the rates charged, where free care can be secured, and the like. For the extent of the services offered by a modern hospital is so great that many of them may be relatively unused if such persons as the minister do not learn what they are and under what conditions they are available.

In return for its co-operation, the hospital may expect such things of the pastor as will be described in the following chapters. These include an understanding of its complex character and problems, a willingness to co-operate in the exchange of non-confidential information about patients, in addition to certain conditions relating to the pastor's own calling at the hospital.

There are many specialized hospitals, rendering distinctive types of service, which the pastor should know about as resources. He should be especially familiar with rest and convalescent homes because their standards of service vary so much more widely than do those in acute hospitals. They are also a particular concern because so much of the useful ministry of the church is related to persons who have recovered from serious illness in the acute sense but who still need much care and attention. Medicine is now paying more attention to these persons, and rest and convalescent institutions should improve considerably in quality of service rendered. They will probably be more of a resource, therefore, for the pastor in the future than they have been in the past.

Guidance Clinics. These are all too often a rarity except in the largest cities and even here there are still too few of them.[6] The pastor should know that a good clinic is conducted by a psychiatrist, a psychologist, a psychiatric social worker, and others, with a consulting general physician. Some of these clinics operate independently under general community auspices, but the tendency in more recent years has been to have them in connection with general hospitals, mental hospitals, public schools, courts, or other similar agencies. With the first flush of the clinic movement past, it has been increasingly difficult to get the small funds needed to establish adequate guidance clinic service, either for children or adults. Some states, however, have begun .to establish clinics, often traveling clinics, manned by qualified workers on the staffs of mental hospitals. Because this clinic movement shows so many different administrative patterns, ministers have not been sufficiently aware of its resources. Any guidance clinic conducted by reputable personnel should receive closest attention from the minister, regardless of what its administrative auspices may happen to be. Even a traveling clinic, meeting once a month, if manned by good personnel, may be a life saver for a minister in a smaller community.

It is important that the pastor know the personnel, especially the director, who is usually a psychiatrist. These clinics are rarely able to do real preventive work, but their "early detection" of potential disorders often has significant preventive influence. The personnel who work with them are likely to be those who see the preventive potentialities in this work and will therefore be most sensitive to the opportunities which the minister himself has for truly preventive work. If referrals can be made by the minister to someone whom he knows at the clinic rather than merely to "the clinic," many will go who would otherwise merely turn up their noses. In return, guidance-clinic people may indeed expect the minister to be a quiet but effective press agent for them in the parish and community. The contacts should be similar to those with the psychiatrist in private practice.

Courts and Jails. All too often the concern of criminal courts for the offense rather than the offender will seem to the minister to make them a liability rather than an asset. But there has been a real growth of juvenile courts, of older boys courts, and of other types of courts in which special attention is paid to the offender as well as to the law. A few of these courts have trained social workers, usually probation officers, attached to them; and where this is the case, they are a great resource for the minister. It is ministers of churches where the parishioners are in the lowest income groups who will have most contact with the criminal courts; but every minister will have some. The picture of these courts as resources to help the minister solve individual problems is not as yet very inviting from the point of view of quantity but there are signs that more intelligent handling of offenders, and not merely of offenses, will become the rule in the future.

There are other types of courts which may also be considered as pastoral resources. This is particularly true of family relations courts. Family recourse to the courts used to portend, in most cases, dissolution of the family ties. Family relations courts, manned by progressive judges, aided by social workers, are now instrumental in remaking many families. The pastor's case-work adviser will let him know what may reasonably be expected from the family court of his area, if there is one.

There are other types of courts which may be considered resources in some communities. The courts where commitments to state hospitals are ordered, for example, may be a resource. If the pastor is concerned with a commitment, and knows the judge and commitment procedures, he will be able to give reassurance either to the patient or the family much more effectively.

Although county jails have been, and too often still are, among the most backward social institutions in this country, the increasing number of them which have moved in a progressive direction may well be genuine resources for the pastor. If someone he knows has gone through the courts and received a sentence, the information and interpretation which the pastor can bring to the proper authorities should be of great value in making the inmate's sentence rehabilitative in effect. The pastor can do much himself for persons in jails, either those who have been sentenced or those awaiting trial; and that work, too, will be aided if he has used the jail itself as a resource in his pastoral work.

Public Health Agencies and Visiting Nurses. Where the function of public health agencies is confined to testing water, overseeing sanitation, and the like, they will hardly be of much help to the minister in dealing with the problems of individuals. But public health is rapidly becoming concerned with other types of health problems. Its first agent has usually been the visiting nurse who, if qualified, has had some social work as well as nurse's training. Public health is now taking an interest even in mental hygiene; and there is no doubt that the next few years will see a great increase not only in the quantity but also in the scope of public health work.[7]

Other Community Agencies. Although most agencies could be classified under the broad headings which have been used, there will invariably be some with more specialized functions in larger communities, and even some which might not easily fit into our categories. The minister should be as familiar with them as possible. For it is a rule with all resources that the more intimately they are known in fair weather, the more use they will be when it rains.

STATE AND FEDERAL AGENCIES

The increased responsibility, assumed in recent years by the state and federal governments, for the economic, social, and mental problems of individuals suggests the growing resources in these agencies for the minister confronted with problems of individuals. In addition to the better known services, there are many others with which the minister should be familiar.

Social Security and Relief. The pastor should know the forms of social security and something of the conditions for individuals' qualifying under them, if he is to be able to give proper pastoral guidance. In addition to the old age and survivors' benefits, there are provisions for aid to the blind, aid to dependent children, unemployment compensation, and others. Some of the forms of social security legislation antedate the federal act, as for example the workmen's compensation laws in most states, but the federal laws cover such a wide area that the pastor will do well to familiarize himself with their provisions. Excellent explanatory material is available from the Federal Social Security Board. Naturally it is not the business of the minister to offer legal advice about eligibility under any of the statutes; but there are people who are eligible for some assistance and do not know it, and others who complain because they are without some benefit to which they have no rightful claim. It is well to emphasize that all governmental agencies, and especially this group, operate under many limitations of a legal nature which are usually unknown to the public. It is essential that the pastor know these limitations. In so doing he will not only be able to aid in the interpretation of the agency to the community but will also be able to utilize its resources more intelligently in his pastoral work.

The relief picture has changed rapidly, but a better core of relief administration wisdom has been accumulated than most persons realize. The minister should certainly know personally the relief administrator of his area and some of the workers. He may realize, too, the difference between home relief, for which the recipient does not perform specific services, and work relief, for which he does. Where official matters are concerned, the pastor should deal with the local administrator; but on other matters he may often find the workers helpful if he indicates his understanding of their job. The personnel standards for relief workers still seem low; but when viewed in the light of the rapid growth of this administration, their improvement seems almost miraculous.

Mental Hospitals. Enough has been said in previous chapters to suggest the great importance of the mental hospital as a pastoral resource. For the modern mental hospital is not merely a place for the care and treatment of psychosis. It may also operate a guidance clinic, do mental hygiene education, and carry out similar important functions with its trained personnel. The mental hospital is not a last resort; it is often the best place to go for diagnosis. The minister should know it, know its administrator and some of its psychiatrists, and be an interpreter of its functions to the community.

Various Rehabilitation Agencies. There are an increasing number of these under state and federal auspices, ranging from state homes for blind or crippled to agencies like the Civilian Conservation Corps, the Resettlement Administration, the Rural Electrification Administration, the Farm Security Administration, or the child labor provisions of the Wages and Hours Law. While this latter type of agency (and a large number of them are either under the U. S. Department of Agriculture, or were inspired by it) is primarily concerned with groups, in many sections the minister's pastoral problems can only be solved by getting help to several individuals in the same boat. The function of the state agencies (which may give funds for home care as well as provide institutional care) which deal with the blind, etc., is more obviously related to the minister's pastoral work in trying to meet the problems of individuals.

State Clinics and General Hospitals. Some states operate general hospitals and clinics; and these are mentioned here because of their importance as a resource where they are available. State general hospitals usually offer a high type of service especially because of their frequent connection with medical schools. A "teaching" hospital is usually most alive to new discoveries.

Special Government Institutions. There are now splendid hospitals for treatment of narcotic drug addicts, operated by the U. S. Public Health Service. There are special hospitals run by the Veterans' Administration. And there are many other types of institutions for special purposes run by state and local governments. The minister will not make frequent contact with any of these; but he should know they exist, what they do, and how well they do it. For when he does meet a problem which requires highly specialized treatment, as in the case of drug addiction, he may otherwise be ignorant that an agency exists for this purpose. He should know, for instance, that the narcotic farms are hospitals and not prisons and that a person may commit himself voluntarily there for treatment.

War-Time Agencies

The war has created the need for many new services to individuals, and various agencies have been created, or had their functions expanded, to meet these needs. From the point of view of our consideration here, the Red Cross is among the most important. It has been charged with the responsibility of keeping in touch with the families of men in service who may need help of any kind. The Red Cross, in turn, looks often to ministers for help; but the services it can now perform are manifold and are therefore special new resources for the pastor.

Chaplains in service may be considered a tremendous resource for the pastor. So well is their status as ministers of religion protected that they are able to devote a very large proportion of their time to work with individuals. The chaplain deals with the men in service; the parish minister, with their families.

To know that it is a large part of the chaplain's job to work with individuals puts a real resource in the minister's hands.

Most of the special agencies which have been set up by the churches themselves are organizational or group-work agencies. Yet through some of them new means are offered for giving aid to individuals. This is true of both denominational and inter-denominational agencies, concerned with aliens and prisoners of war, work in camp and defense communities, and others. It is becoming increasingly true of the United Service Organizations and of several governmental agencies, including the Defense Health and Welfare Services of the Federal Security Administration.

These and other war-time agencies have become well known. They are mentioned here, however, because they offer resources for pastoral aid in addition to their better-known functions.

CONCLUSION

This is by no means an exhaustive survey of agencies.[8] But it is important to consider the broad scope of the agencies functionally, from the point of view of the minister's making use of whatever resources are available in his work with individuals. Seen from this point of view, it is a rare community which does not have access to most of these services, even though many of them may be poor. It is so commonly assumed by ministers that resources are to be found only in the largest cities that this kind of functional analysis is important.

We have concentrated our discussion on those agencies which deal obviously with the problems of individuals, emphasizing those most closely related to health. It should be remembered, however, that group work agencies may be among the pastor's most useful resources in his pastoral work with individuals. There are several reasons why this is true. Not all pastoral problems, perhaps indeed a minority of them, can best be approached directly. Especially those in which socialization, or social achievement, is necessary are best approached by the indirect route. Group work agencies are recognizing increasingly their power to help individuals, and group work itself is becoming a recognized branch of social work. Furthermore, the minister who knows the group work resources of his community can help to get people into the groups where they will be helped, even though the leaders of these groups may be unaware of what they are doing for the individual. It is needless to add that what applies to the general group agencies of the community applies with double force to the groups within the parish itself.

No analysis should attempt to gloss over the inadequacies of established agencies and institutions, especially in town and country areas, to meet obvious needs of individuals. The minister has a tremendous function, as community and church leader, to attempt to have such resources improved and extended. This discussion assumes that everything he or his parish does by way of using current resources will be a first step in showing the values that would accrue from helping to make more resources available.

Church social workers point out that almost all parishes engage in a wide variety of social work activities in unorganized fashion. The activities may be good; but there is rarely an integrating agency within the parish to link them together as, for example, the finance committee links all activity concerned with finance. The pastor might well start such a committee on the basis of preparing a list of the local resources available, utilizing the services of a case work adviser as special expert, if there is one available. The information would in itself be valuable both to the minister and to the laymen; and it would aid in clarifying the kinds of social services which most need support and backing from the church. This kind of parish organization has been carried out in some places and has proved successful. If carried out widely enough, it would be significant not only for the pastoral services of the church, with which we have been concerned here, but also for the whole social program of the church.

CHAPTER X

MINISTERING TO THE SICK

"The minister goes to the sickroom because he is the duly recognized representative of Him who said, 'For I was hungered, and ye gave me meat: I was thirsty, and ye gave me drink: I was naked and ye clothed me: I was sick and ye visited me: I was in prison and ye came unto me.' . . . To be sick is to be a stranger, naked, stripped of vigor, weakened by lack of determination, feverish by helplessness, bared by broken confidence; a stranger among strange people, even one's clothes changed for a queer abbreviated gown. To be sick is to pass through strange places of the spirit: the night before an operation, with its haunting dreads and imaginings, the taking of an anesthetic, the struggle with post-operative discomforts. To be sick is to face the uncertainty of diagnosis, the loneliness of convalescence, the difficulties of facing life as a cripple or an invalid. These are new paths of our spirit: 'A stranger and ye took me in.' To be sick is to be in prison, imprisoned in one bed, one room, ward, building; imprisoned within one's helplessness and one's handicaps, chained to the threat of death. The minister goes to the sickroom by authority of the needs of the patient, needs which will not be met otherwise. By right of the heritage which is his he must go to the sickroom, and by right of the needs of the spirit, he may be trusted by doctor and patient, after he has trained himself. By virtue of the special methods and of the de-

226

votion which are his heritage he may minister to the sick to their advantage, to the advantage of the doctors and nurses who care for the sick, and to the advantage of his own spiritual welfare." [1]

Thus Richard C. Cabot and Russell L. Dicks describe why the religious worker must minister to the sick, the basic attitudes he must hold in this ministry, and the reasons why it must be done well. This chapter will lean heavily on their book, which is the best available on this aspect of our subject.

A previous chapter has presented something of the significance of emotional factors in the development of illness. To present these in such a way that they make an impact on the reader demands a work of art more than a mere description. Yet unless there is comprehension of the emotions which the patient feels, as well as those which he may not "feel" but which have nevertheless influenced him, the minister will overlook what may be a great aid in his work with the sick as well as a great incentive.

Sick people in increasing numbers are taken care of in hospitals. While this usually improves the quality of the treatment and care, it accentuates the emotional concomitants of illness for the patient. Consider but a few of them. Usually there is a strangeness, not only in the face of the perhaps unnecessarily white and bleak look of hospital rooms and wards, but also in the face of hospital customs and routines. Why, for example, the patient asks himself, should he be awakened at some unearthly hour in the morning when he has lain sleepless much of the night, merely to have his face washed and his temperature taken? The hour is strange; the fact that it is so taken for granted in the hospital only makes it seem stranger. Incidentally, no one ever seems to have found a logical answer to this question, if considered solely from the point of view of the patient's welfare. The patient, quite naturally, finds it difficult to see the matter from any other point of view half so important.

The hospital patient experiences isolation and emotional tension in the night when he cannot sleep or in the early morning hours when he is awake and before anything around him seems to happen. He has fear, not knowing what will be done to him. The aggressive patient may get over this by referring to "medical arrogance," but most sufferers merely lie in fear of whatever they do not know. There is usually anxiety about the job outside, whether it will be waiting or whether he will be able to fill it— and about the patient's family. All kinds of emotions which have the general characteristic of isolation and strangeness are natural at this time and in this situation.

Otis R. Rice reports that fear of the "next pain impulse" is one of the most disintegrative and disturbing of all the emotional concomitants of illness.[2] For in many illnesses pain is not constant but intermittent, and the fear of expectation may exceed the feeling during the pain impulses themselves.

Whatever emotions have been hovering about before illness, so to speak, generally come into prominence during it. If there has been anxiety, it may be accentuated. If there has been hostility, it may be brought into the open. If there has been guilt, it may come out. And persistently may come the question, though often unexpressed: What have I done to deserve this?

It is only fair to note that the experience of being cared for in a hospital brings a semblance of emotional peace to some people—and indeed hospitals could hardly justify their existence unless they brought some peace to most patients. But it is obvious that the emotional problem of the patient whose chief feeling is to enjoy being taken care of is different from that of the patient whose dominant feeling-tone is anxiety, hostility or loneliness.

He who ministers in a hospital must be aware of the existence of emotional overtones if his work is to be helpful. There is probably no aspect of the pastoral ministry where inattention can cause so much destruction. The need is enormous, and such emotional concomitants of illness as we have suggested serve to indicate how much greater it is than is commonly realized. Even though the physician, the nurse, the social worker and others do their best, there is still the basic emotional and spiritual problem which in many cases only the minister himself can reach and help.

There can be no question but that the religious worker should *work* with the sick, and Cabot and Dicks rightly suggest that this is different from *visiting* the sick, which implies casual, unplanned social calling far removed from the kind of work they and we advocate. Religious work with the sick ought to be on as high a plane of planning, diagnosis, record-taking, and general skill as that of physicians, nurses and social workers. This may be plain enough for the minister, but it may well be asked: how much does this apply to the layman who also visits the ill —his relative or friends? The answer is that hardly one of the basic principles which should be kept in mind in work with the sick may go unheeded by the layman, though naturally some things will be different since they are dependent upon the pastor's professional status.

General Principles of Work with the Sick. One should know why he is there. This should involve not only the recognition of Jesus' command to minister to the sick, nor merely friendship or acquaintance with a particular patient, but also the kind of self-understanding discussed in previous sections. There are a few, both ministers and laymen, who unfortunately have a somewhat morbid interest in illness, and they therefore visit the sick with results that all too often do as much harm as good. One's motives in religious work with the sick basically should be as objective as those of the physician; whatever depth of sympathy one may feel, and of course he must have it, will then be subordinated to the needs of the patient.

One should start with the patient. Dicks has stated this well. "The minister cannot swiftly create religion and morals in people who have neglected them all their lives. He cannot expect a man to be ready for prayer and meditation if he has scorned these forces up to the minute when sickness seized him. The minister has to take sick people where he finds them and work up the ladder rung by rung." [3] There are many implications of this principle, of which we may suggest only a few. One may not use methods of spiritual ministry, such as prayer, with a patient who is not ready for them. One must make a careful "spiritual diagnosis" as to where the patient really is. Communion, given thoughtlessly to the person who interprets it as a last rite, may be dangerous. "Attacking" methods of attempting to produce change in personality are most out of place in work with the sick.

The emotion and attitude of the patient must be accepted before one can proceed. It does no good and sometimes much harm to tell the patient that everything is going to be all right, if he feels despondent about his condition. That merely cuts the minister off from any real chance to help. The basic attitude may not be evident at first; much of it will be in that "unconscious" area which cannot be comprehended without deductions from little signs that are perceptible. But unless one accepts the basic attitude of the patient as a fact, it will be impossible to establish contact.

A contact must be made, or rapport must be established, before help can be given. With some patients the minister's status or rôle will help at this point and, with others, it will be a detriment. There are as yet no formulae for establishing rapport, other than those based on discovery of and sympathy with the real needs of the patient, but established it must be if anything further is to be done.

Work with the sick, even more than other counseling activities, must avoid falling into stereotypes, and yet must be an authentic expression of the personality of him who ministers. There is no use in the ebullient extrovert's attempting to masquerade as a mouse because someone tells him that quietness is demanded in the sickroom. Yet, on the other hand, to bounce from room to room is hardly appropriate when the patient in one room is lonely and the patient in the next is anxious. Such a minister can retain his personal integrity and identity without bouncing. He can be quiet without putting on a mask. He can be joyful without pulling out all the plugs. And he can adapt himself somewhat to the needs of each patient without losing himself. The same might be said of other stereotypes sometimes seen in the sickroom: the watch-fob player, the ain't-it-awful visitor, the caller who impersonates a ray of sunshine, the one who is morbidly interested in every physical detail of the illness, or the one who can not keep still. Stereotypes of any kind do not work.

Work with the sick must usually be brief. A judgment about the length of time one should stay with the patient should always be made in view of his condition, but rarely should it be more than fifteen minutes; and sometimes a two-minute call is better. There are, needless to say, many exceptions.

One should have a purpose in mind before making any call on any patient. This purpose may change during the call itself; but without it, made consciously in advance, the work is likely to be opportunistic. The purpose at a particular time may be merely to gather certain bits of information, or to cement the contact in certain respects; but if it is merely to "do everything possible for the patient," it is too general to be of any value.

One should be comfortable himself in the sick-room and have an eye to little things which will not make the patient uncomfortable. One should sit or stand where he is comfortable and where the patient can see him without straining. Illness and lying in bed in a strange place may have made the patient unusually sensitive to little things. By thinking generally of making the patient comfortable and recognizing that one's own discomfort probably will be sensed by the patient, one will usually do the right thing.

Work with the sick should never be a matter of swapping stories about illnesses. There are rare occasions when spiritual strength can be communicated to the patient by telling him how someone else met a situation, but these occur less frequently than most pastors and laymen think. Unless just the right moment has arrived, telling such a story is like giving advice. If the patient makes a renewed effort and fails, he is inclined to think that "only great men" can do this. If he tries and succeeds, he is likely to attribute his improvement to factors which in reality may have little to do with it. In any case, telling a story to match any story the patient tells about his illness is poor therapy.

Complaints or expressions of lack of confidence in physician or in the hospital on the patient's part may be heard but not argued. Frequently complaints arise from lack of understanding and where a word of explanation is obviously appropriate, it may be given. But lack of confidence in physicians can usually be overcome only by physicians. A word to the doctor will often do the trick, and physicians usually appreciate such hints.

Many more such principles could be given but these are as important as any. Little has been said thus far about the distinctive resources which the religious worker has or how they may be used, or of the specific methods which he will use in his work. These will come later.

Spiritual Diagnosis. Three elements are involved in the "spiritual diagnosis" which is necessary before any "spiritual treatment" can be applied intelligently. These might be called the personality diagnosis, the situational diagnosis, and the spiritual resources diagnosis.

Personality diagnosis refers, of course, to anything which will present background material for understanding the personality of the individual as a whole. Suppose that we are dealing with a man who is in the hospital for treatment of a heart condition, who is expected by the physicians to get well but who must take things much easier than he did before. He has been a domestic tyrant, bossing his wife and children around, getting red in the face when his slightest whim is disregarded. In the hospital he is deprived of every defense of this type. The personality diagnosis is the discovery of the patterns which he has used to get what he wanted, the understanding of those factors in his background which led him to be a little dictator in his own home.

But the *situational diagnosis* is equally important. He is no longer a tyrant. All the authority of modern medicine tells him that he cannot get red in the face and issue orders to his wife while she is visiting him, nor is the prohibition off when he deals with her *in absentia*. The situation has changed completely the defenses which he may use; indeed, it is better to say that some basic strategies of his approach to life have suddenly been taken from him. What his reaction to the loss of these strategies is would be our situational diagnosis. He may splutter helplessly, which indicates that no change is being made. He may suddenly appear docile, which may indicate that this is what he wanted to be all the time or may mean that he is merely appearing to be at the other extreme in order to avoid any real change. Or he may get some insight and thereby lose some of his need to be a tyrant. Our judgment as to what is really going on is important if we are to be of help.

The *spiritual resources diagnosis* can become effective only when some attention has first been given to the other types. To return to our heart patient, it is obvious that he must make a change in his basic outlook as well as in his activities. When he leaves the hospital, a little change in his domestic environment may be possible; but if this change is merely a request that his wife never "cross" him, an impossible situation is bound to be set up for her. Plainly, some change in our patient is required.

We recognize, however, two elements about the strategy which the patient has used. It has been useful to him, however much we may believe it to be a poor approach. It has had its strategic value, lending him some confidence in himself at times when he would have been spiritually deflated if he had not had it. Second, we recognize that it is not effective to take his strategy from him. There must be a substitute, or there must be insight which will make unnecessary the use of any such unfortunate strategy. On what resources may he call during the transitional period when the strategy is being given up and when there is no perfect assurance that it is being replaced?

This question lies not merely in the realm of values but in that of personal valuation. Does the patient have an emotionally rooted faith of any kind which will give him something to lean on while the difficult transition is being made? If Christianity has permeated him below the level of the cerebrum, he has at least something. What the religious worker offers is, of course, something of this sort. But there must be some degree of this inner stability or steadfastness, whatever we may want to call it, which will enable one to undergo a change in personality strategies without feeling that the whole world is crumbling to bits and that therefore one can only fight and resist change.

Like the physician, the religious worker does not cure. He can only hope to aid in setting free the healing forces. Walter B. Cannon has spoken of these forces as *The Wisdom of the Body* and John M. Fletcher has argued for a corresponding "wisdom of the mind." [4] Richard C. Cabot calls this the *vis medicatrix Dei,* which is behind all healing.[5] But however difficult it may seem to make an estimate as to the hold of the patient on this power, it is nevertheless necessary.

No formulae have as yet been discovered to enable a person to make such estimates. When more religious workers report more precisely on their contacts with patients, we shall undoubtedly receive more clues about types of responses, and shall therefore have more adequate means than are available at present.[6] The subjective element in such judgments at present seems overwhelmingly large. But the fact is that every religious worker makes such estimates anyhow; what we advocate is doing it with a greater awareness of the implications, so that accuracy and refinement will increasingly be possible. For if we are to start with the patient, we must know as fully as we can, from every relevant point of view, where he is now.

The Religious Worker's Resources in Work with the Sick. Not all the resources of the religious worker in ministering to the sick are distinctive resources. That is, not all of them are his peculiar possession. Understanding how to treat the patient as a person is a resource he may share with physician, nurse, or anyone else. The use of listening or quietness are both resources which may be used by others. It might be true to say that whoever uses these is a religious worker; but we are thinking more practically of the person who comes to the sick room armed with no technical knowledge of medicine, psychiatry, nursing, or social work. This point needs emphasis; for many religious workers are inclined to believe that unless the resources they use are distinctive, it is a waste of their time to visit the ill. This point of view is fallacious. The fever thermometer is not a distinctive resource of the physician, but he would have a hard time getting on without it. A physician or nurse may help to bring courage and confidence into a sick room as well as a religious worker, but there are a large number of reasons why help brought by the minister may be as important or sometimes more important than by the doctor. Concentration on resources merely because they are distinctive is to put something else above the welfare of the patient.

The first resource of the religious worker is what he represents. One aspect of this is covered in the statement opening this chapter. Another aspect is the "rôle" of the religious leader in the eyes of the community and therefore of the patient. Whether he likes it or not, the minister is thought of in certain ways merely because he *is* a minister or religious leader. In reference to morality, he is often thought of as the "professional good man" of the community. This may mean, for example, that a patient will find it more difficult to tell him of some immoral or supposedly immoral act than to tell it to a physician or social worker who would not be expected to judge adversely. But it also means that if something is confessed, and the person is not judged harshly for it (that is, if the personal bonds are not broken by the fact), the chance of the patient's accepting God's forgiveness are much greater than they would have been if confession had been to someone else. This suggests the need for humanization of the religious worker. If he simply falls into the mold and accepts his rôle as professional upholder of the community conscience, then no confessions will be made to him, for he has insulated himself. But if his personality is one to attract confidence, he will find his rôle a resource and not a handicap. This has nothing to do with his being a jolly good fellow or with his approving acts of which he does not really approve. But it does mean that, in his own deepest feelings, he puts the person above the act and recognizes that where confession is made there has been enough pointless self-condemnation already without his adding fuel to the flames. His rôle may be a great resource.

The personal contacts he has had with the patient before illness are also a resource and are so obvious that they need only be mentioned. A third resource, and the most basic, the worker's personality, is so plainly of central importance that it too need only be noted. The minister or other religious worker, furthermore, when he calls on the sick, represents the resources of the Christian religion. To enumerate these is in a sense to enumerate the benefits of Christianity itself, but not altogether. For work with the sick places some resources in the foreground and lets others temporarily languish.

In representing the resources of Christianity to the patient, the minister acts on behalf of a concerned community. This community is first local but it goes on to transcend the barriers of space and even of time. We often think of this mainly as friendliness when the focal point is the interest of the local church community, and so it is. But this friendliness is a concern with great therapeutic implications. Cabot and Dicks have given a picture of the minister's function in combating loneliness which shows the power of this resource. "The clergyman can perhaps help more than others because he studies more accurately the nature of the patient's loneliness. As an outsider he may be quicker than others to catch its flavor, and so by giving companionship and affection he may effectively palliate the symptom. But, as with fears, it is always quite possible that behind the obvious signs of loneliness there is a deeper loneliness, a sense that no human being can ever understand what he cares for most, that his real home is not on this earth at all; in short, the religious loneliness which has been the beginning of religious faith in many of us. To be ready to recognize this, to see slight dawning symptoms of it, and to be ready to respond the instant he does see them, is another of the clergyman's best opportunities." [7]

The religious worker represents too the resources of prayer and spiritual meditation. "The use of prayer in the sickroom by a second person, the minister, is a method whereby the patient may be brought into touch with God. The minister plays a secondary part; he is the sufferer's representative; he fastens his mind on those whom he would bring together: patient and God. Prayer under such conditions is a learning-teaching process. The patient is the learner, the minister teacher, God and the ways of God the subject matter." [8] All prayer is not equally appropriate, and it is hardly necessary to say that there is a time to pray and a time not to pray. Cabot and Dicks say that "prayer should be used for a definite need seen in the light of our understanding of the patient's spiritual development." [9] When a patient calls for a minister, he usually hopes that the minister will pray with him. When the minister comes to him through some other channel, the situation may be different; and whether prayer is to be used will depend on the minister's judgment as to whether it will help. Cabot and Dicks give some excellent illustrations of the kind of prayers which are usually most helpful in the sickroom.[10] They are more specific and shorter than most prayers. They do not beg the question of illness in any way, but face it frankly. Above all, they fit the patient's condition and his state of spiritual development. Of course, the patient may be taught to pray, or to pray more relevantly and helpfully for himself, but the best way to do this is to pray with him until he begins to comprehend what courage, confidence and peace true prayer can bring.

There are great resources in meditation upon passages of Scripture or other great affirmations. The mystical resources in religion are nowhere of greater proved value than for the sick. The body cannot rest or relax unless the mind and spirit also rest, and that rest can come only through quietness and confidence. There are great passages of Scripture which, judiciously used, may be of untold value to patients.[11] One factor enters here, however, which is more important than is generally recognized. The person's level of intelligence and sophistication will have some influence upon the way he can meditate. For some, a repetition of "In quietness and confidence shall be our strength" will actually help to bring great strength. For others, the mode of meditation will be more abstract. Some will be more poetic than others; metaphors and images will flash across their minds, while others may find these unsubstantial. Some will make much use of words; others will find words have little to do with their meditations.

There is an understandable but an unfortunate confusion about the relation of these various modes of meditation to the act of meditation itself. Especially for ministry to the sick, this points to the need for adequate diagnosis of the patient's spiritual development. It is merely tossing crumbs to a hungry lion to suggest to one type of person that he repeat to himself or with the minister a single verse of Scripture. It is sacrilege with another to use many words or with another to use a silence which the patient comprehends only as embarrassing. But the resources of prayer and meditation, and use of the Scriptures, with the sick are deeper than we know.

Dicks and Cabot point out that the minister should have the equivalent of the physician's kit-bag. We may merely mention the resources which they feel should be contained in this bag. There should be the equivalent of the Roman Catholic priest's sacramental materials. Most ministers will actually have material with them to give communion, but even those who rarely or never give private communion will want its mental equivalent. There should also be the minister's note-book, which is a real resource. There will be little articles to give or to loan, something to refresh the patient or start a new train of thought. The pastor will also carry stories with him, to be used at appropriate times and places. "Carefully selected books are great instruments to release the spirit, to stir the imagination, and to give one perspective upon one's illness." [12] Literature should be carefully prescribed in view of the spiritual diagnosis, and not given haphazardly. The weight and size of type in books should be considered. The status of a patient's illness is important; books valuable during convalescence from an operation might be entirely inappropriate before. Devotional books may be of great value but should also be carefully selected. The kit-bag may also include suggestions for a hobby for the patient. One patient is cited who was encouraged to keep a record of great music he heard by radio.[13] Modeling in clay, sewing, letter-writing, use of games are all suggested as things which may be encouraged under proper circumstances by what is contained in the minister's kit-bag.

Listening is a great resource of the religious worker. It serves "two important ends. It helps the patient to 'express' and it helps the minister to understand." [14] We may "listen to the point and we listen round it." [15] Thus listening as a resource does not mean dragging things out of a patient by the scruff of the neck, or refusing to talk. It may be an active process, in which case it becomes directed listening instead of passive listening. "Directed listening is teaching at its best." [16] Passive listening takes the worker wherever the patient may happen to go. Both methods are appropriate in different circumstances. It should be noted that directed listening is not merely a prelude to reassurance by the worker. In general, it should bring its own reassurance to the patient. There is a great gulf fixed between affirmation by the patient and reassurance by the worker. Occasionally reassurance helps, but it is the reassurance which follows from obvious signs of interest, friendliness, and concern rather than reassuring words. For the patient to become reassured, or to begin to affirm more actively, is something else; and many things may help to bring this about. Perhaps a combination of passive and directed listening is the goal to be achieved in most of our work with the sick.

Quietness, too, is a resource. It might be called that response of the personality when it first feels, then consciously recognizes, how the healing forces which God has put into life are operating to cure ills of one's body, mind, and spirit. It may come through a sudden recognition of the great carefulness that is implied in a modern hospital laboratory examination. It may come through a recognition that others care as evidenced in the calls of friends. It may come through the work of the minister. It cannot be coerced. Dicks writes: "The only rule I know for determining the use of this method in work with the sick is some such general statement as this: be prepared with all patients at all times to be quiet, but do not work too hard at it and do not be surprised when you fail in its use." [17] Incidentally, it is well to remember that quietness and confidence are closely related. Confidence is scarcely present if the minister is embarrassed, ill at ease, wishing he were somewhere else, tripping over a rug, or aware only of the strange aspects of the sick-room situation.

Keeping records, or note-writing, is wisely considered a resource of the religious worker by Cabot and Dicks, as well as an obligation. The most obvious reason for keeping records is to extend one's memory. It also serves to check one's work. No religious worker who has ever kept careful notes upon his work with the sick has failed to comment on how much insight the actual writing of the notes gave him. Notes may also serve as a "release from strain" on the worker's part, relieving one's mind of carrying details, and actually being creative in large measure. "Doubtless it will be said that the minister has no time to keep notes. That sounds familiar. Lazy doctors say the same thing; but competent doctors, no matter how busy, keep notes because they know that they cannot otherwise do good work. Are ministers busier than doctors?" [18]

There should be distinctions in keeping records. The beginner in the record business should write fuller notes than he will write after he becomes more adept. The patient who is seen many times should have more written about him than the person who is seen only once or twice. Even the writing of simple facts by the use of symbols may be of value. But some record should be made of all such contacts, and it should be lengthier and more significant where the work is more intensive. A distinction may and should be made between "confidential" and other material. Sometimes non-confidential material may be of great value to other workers in the hospital; and it is becoming increasingly evident that a brief note on the patient's hospital record by the minister after a call will be considered as necessary in the future as such a note is now by the physician.

The question may well be asked: are these principles and resources applicable to the sick person at home as well as in the hospital? The answer is yes. If the patient is in the hospital, his schedule is more strict; he probably feels more strange; and it is easier for the religious worker to confer with other workers like the physician and nurse. He may find it more difficult to see the patient alone at home than in the hospital; but there are times when his most effective pastoral calls can be made with other members of the family present. But the principles and resources are essentially the same.

Dividing One's Time. How shall one divide his time in reference to work with the sick? This problem may seem more pressing to the religious worker who spends his full time in dealing with the sick, but it is no less important to the pastor or other religious worker who spends only a fraction of his time in such ministry. Unless some plan is formed, he will minister only by importunity or by crisis; and those patients who talk most, or who are closest to death, will get most of his attention.

Undoubtedly the religious worker has certain "routine" obligations to the sick, and these cannot be scheduled with much accuracy. Patients who are approaching death and who want their minister must of course be seen. Patients approaching an operation should also be seen—always assuming that there is a willingness on the part of the patient to have the minister come to him, which does not often or usually imply a request. Dicks and Cabot have written helpfully about ministry to the dying and ministry in connection with surgical operations.[19]

But shall the minister come only when the patient is critically ill, bodily speaking? Are we to say only that there must be *more* time given by ministers to work with the sick, when this is often an impossibility in view of other obligations? The minister should have a plan whereby whatever time he has available for work with the sick may be utilized most profitably. Certainly his first obligations are ones of crisis. But there are spiritual crises as well as physical ones; and if he fails to allot time to them, he is misunderstanding the purpose of religious ministry to the sick.

Many ministers work with the sick only when there is a physiological crisis and spend the rest of the time, set aside for work with the sick, merely visiting "those who are not critically ill."

This indicates poor planning and is one of the reasons why religious ministry to the sick has acquired such a poor reputation in the minds of many other health workers.

Dicks estimates that the nearly full-time religious worker in a hospital cannot deal intensively with more than thirty patients at one time. This probably suggests that the minister who can give but a fraction of his time to work with the sick can minister effectively to not more than five or ten patients at a time. Of course he may say hello as he goes through a ward, or stop a half-minute by the side of a bed to tell a story to a patient; and these activities may be valuable. But they are not "work with the sick." They illustrate casual friendliness, not "the art of ministering to the sick."

Psychological and spiritual crises present the religious worker's greatest opportunity. The patient with heart disease who was compelled to change not only his mode of activities but his strategy as domestic tyrant was at a critical period where religious ministry might be most useful. If the minister, however, were unable to achieve rapport with him, he might waste precious hours in attempting to help without having the preconditions of giving help. In general, the minister seems most capable of giving help at those times of crisis where life readjustment of some kind has to be considered. Dicks cites heart patients who must change their activities and outlook, colostomy patients who must face the prospect of having their bowel outlet moved, with all the social discomfort that may imply, amputation patients who must readjust to loss of arm or leg, and others. Where the illness affects the whole outlook (and therefore the values) most deeply, there religious ministry is likely to be of most help.

Usually the minister will choose for intensive work those patients who most need his help in this spiritual sense. But he should have at least three categories or levels of work in his own mind and should make a decision as to which applies to any particular patient. These are: intensive work, occasional work, and casual calling. Seeing a patient twice a week is or should be intensive work. Seeing a patient three times during a long illness is occasional work. Seeing a patient once, or greeting him casually many times, is casual calling, unless of course the single contact be unusual in what it accomplished. If it does not need to be followed up, however, it is seldom intensive work. The minister should distinguish, too, between acute crises and adjustment crises. The patient who may die or the patient who faces a surgical operation represent acute crises. The patient who faces the prospect of a long convalescence, or readjustment to a heart condition, represents an adjustment crisis. The minister has a function with both, but the obviously critical nature of the former should not be permitted to cloud the equally critical nature of the latter.

Each worker will be able to make some judgment on the amount of time he can afford to spend with the sick and can prepare a rational plan for utilizing this to best advantage. Cabot wrote, "The habit of making no preparation for a visit is popular because it saves trouble. Original sin makes us hide our laziness behind reverence for a spontaneity which rarely comes off." [20]

How to Find One's Patients. The religious worker is ineffective in his ministry to the sick in almost direct proportion to the degree to which his is a "lone-wolf" service. The physician is in charge of the patient, but he knows well how ineffective his service would be without that of the nurse, the social worker, the laboratory technician, and the other specialists of various kinds. The minister or religious worker is one of these specialists, and he needs to work with them as much as they need to work with one another. However much he may be "set apart," ecclesiastically speaking, no one who ministers to the sick in any way whatsoever can be set apart from his fellow-workers in a practical sense.

The implications of this are only now being realized. The hospital and the physician are becoming concerned because they are realizing the tremendous influence for good or ill which the religious worker may have on the health of the patient. Religious workers are realizing its importance because they see that they can be most useful only by dealing with the right people at the right time with a proper understanding of the background. They are particularly concerned to find the people who most need them and they see that in many cases they cannot do this themselves. The physician does not and cannot sit up all night with every patient, waiting to find whether he is needed; the nurse does this for him. The minister cannot enter a hospital and metaphorically sit up all night with every patient until he finds which need him most. He needs help.

His first and most important sources of help are the physicians themselves. It is amazing how physicians, even those not personally interested in religion, awaken to the possibilities of a religious ministry, based upon some adequate notion of spiritual diagnosis and acting in co-operation with the whole corps of health workers. They rightly distrust good intentions alone, and they have all had experience with pastoral calls which raised patients' blood pressure with no corresponding compensation. What is needed is to clarify to them what religious ministry may mean when carried on co-operatively, intelligently, with full attention to the needs of the patient as a whole person.

Physicians must have confidence in a particular minister before they are likely to suggest that he go see Mr. So-and-So. Dicks estimates that it takes approximately two years of work by a good religious worker to bring members of a hospital staff to this point. A part-time worker might require an even longer period. But a minister should eventually be getting from physicians many of his best leads about the patients who need him. He should follow through with the physicians and keep them posted on the state of the patient's outlook. Physicians, it is hardly necessary to add, usually need education and a new attitude about working with ministers.

Nurses may be a tremendous help to the religious worker. They see the patient much more than the physician does; and if they can acquire an understanding of what the minister can do to help their patients, they will be of as much help as physicians. Because their status in the hospital is not as high as that of the physician and because they are more likely to see the good as well as the bad results of the pastor's ministry, they are likely to be reached more easily than the physician. But no effort on the part of the religious worker to have patients referred to him by nurses should obscure the necessity of establishing working relationships with doctors.[21]

Social workers will be the group with whom it is easiest to establish contact because the area with which they deal is more obviously close to that of the religious worker. They are likely to feel that the minister has plenty of pills but does not know when to use the right one. Social workers will become ardent boosters of religious ministry if they are convinced that spiritual diagnosis always precedes spiritual treatment.

The hospital admission slips may tell the religious worker a good deal. He can usually arrange to have certain kinds of patients, or crisis situations with patients, reported to him in a routine way, and that is good. But this should not be a substitute for finding out which patients need him from doctors, nurses, and others. If he learns that a patient has been admitted with the probability of a serious operation within two days, the chances are that a brief call to see whether the patient needs his help will be indicated.

There will always be a few patients who ask to see a minister. About these there can be no question how to make contact. But since the religious worker is not usually associated with hospitals or sickness, many patients will appreciate seeing a minister who would not think of asking for him.

Friends or relatives in the parish may inform the minister of someone's illness. But even in the case of the parish minister, he should not depend solely on parish information for his leads. He needs help from those at the hospital in finding those who need him. For even though he may concentrate his attention on patients who are members of his parish, he can scarcely wish to make this limitation exclusive.

Naturally his own observation of patients' needs in the hospital will tell him about some patients. But if the minister depends upon this alone, he will waste much valuable time talking to patients who do not really need him and let others languish without the care they need.

The theme is co-operation. Whether the minister likes it or not, the burden of proof that he is willing, and knows how, to co-operate, at present generally rests with him. This is equally true of the deaconess or other non-ordained religious worker. This does not imply the need to be defensive, but it does suggest that one should not speak of the "anti-religious trends of doctors and nurses" until he has made an honest effort to show that he believes in co-operative and not in lone-wolf work.

How to Improve One's Ministry to the Sick. Ministry to the sick is one form of ministry to individuals, or counseling ministry. The basic steps taken to improve it must therefore be those taken to improve the counseling ministry generally. These should include increased self-understanding, knowledge of the nature of health and illness, and the like. Ministry to the sick requires also some specialized knowledge, both of illness, of methods used to treat it, and of religious resources in connection with it.

A period of supervised clinical training is strongly recommended for those who can take it. Reading such books as Dicks and Cabot's *The Art of Ministering to the Sick,* attending good courses and conferences—these things will help. But the fact is that most religious workers are now doing ministry to the sick and wonder whether they can improve on the job. If careful records were kept on ministry to a few patients, and some person especially expert were consulted even by mail, much could be accomplished. It sounds brash to suggest improving ministry to the sick by correspondence courses. The note-writing itself would be of great value but the comments of someone else would, of course, be of greater value if they came in the course of a personal interview. But any objective comments would be worth something.

Even more significant is the possibility of having a small group of religious workers engage in private and confidential discussion of their cases on the basis of notes. It is not altogether clear why ministers shy away from this practice, usually on the ground of being too busy; but perhaps this will not be true as more ministers in a local area see the necessity for learning by observation and by examination of that observation. This is not a general pooling of ignorance, especially if someone who is admittedly more expert can be brought in now and then.

The time must come when adequate clinical training under supervision will be considered a requisite for religious ministry to the sick just as internship is considered a requisite of the physician. Just as this applies to the physician who spends only a small part of his time in the hospital as well as to the one who spends much time, so it must apply to religious workers who spend most of their time in the parish as well as to those who specialize in ministry to the sick as chaplains. After all, medical internships are less than a century old; and they have not been universal in any sense for more than twenty or thirty years. So there are grounds for hope.

The Layman Calls on the Sick. It was mentioned earlier that most of the principles which are relevant to the minister's work with the sick are also important for the layman. The layman has two functions in connection with the sick. He is a kind of spiritual first-aid worker, and he is a friend. First-aid is important in case of accidents; and there is a basic knowledge of it which anyone will find useful. But no one confuses the knowledge and skill of a person trained in first-aid with those of the physician. It is not merely that the first-aid worker operates until the physician arrives or that he deals with less serious things. The physician has a broader perspective and *knows why* he is doing something even when the action he is performing could be carried out equally well by the first-aid worker. It is the perspective, the breadth of knowledge, seeing this incident in context, which gives the physician his rightful skill and standing. First-aid operates until the physician arrives. First-aid may continue to deal with conditions which are minor but the first-aid worker is not qualified to say whether they will stay minor.

So the layman is a spiritual first-aid worker in ministry to the sick. He is on hand until the clergyman arrives. He may have just the right attitude, do just the same thing that a minister would do. But unless he has had special training (in which case he is not quite a layman), he does not *know why* he is doing it. And this is as important in spiritual as in physical therapy. Whatever he can learn is very much to the good, but he should not think of himself as a special minister to the sick on a professional basis if he has not so qualified himself. Yet his first-aid work can be vastly improved, and can be exceedingly useful.

His second function is as a friend. This means, first, that it is seldom appropriate for a layman to consider himself as the proper religious visitor over a period of time to a patient unless he has known the patient beforehand or developed an unusual contact early in the patient's illness. Of course he should check with the patient's minister if the layman's ministry is at all extended. But more positive things should be said. Sick people are lonely, fearful, discouraged, anxious. The layman should leave it to the professional to figure out the whys and wherefores and to institute self-conscious treatment to alleviate these conditions. The layman should have a better understanding of them than he now has; but his ministry will be effective if he has knowledge of a few basic principles and then proceeds to act as a friend.

The prejudices which most hospitals have against lay visitors representing churches are similar to the prejudices against the clergy—mainly the belief that they do not take the patient and what the hospital is doing for him sufficiently into account. There is sometimes another objection to laymen, the belief that few people visit the sick (except their personal friends) who do not have somewhat morbid motives for doing it. This presents a challenge, especially to younger churchmen and church women. Under the organization of an intelligent pastor, laymen and laywomen could be taught to make some ministry to the sick one of their chief contributions to the cause of Christ. Some day there may be records to show whether this will work.

But every layman who visits even a close personal friend in sickness should know something about the principles of ministering to the sick.[22] As Cabot and Dicks suggest, it is more than knowledge; it is also an art. Which does not say that there are not things to be learned about it, however fine one's personality or however deep one's Christian experience may be. Ministry to the sick offers its greatest challenge to the clergyman, but the layworker should have an increasing knowledge of its principles.

CHAPTER XI

THE CHURCH IN RELATION TO HOSPITALS AND OTHER INSTITUTIONS

So far as the church is concerned, the great need in modern hospitals is for more effective religious ministry. The church has two kinds of relationship to hospitals and similar institutions, which we may call administrative and pastoral. Because of the tremendous increase in the numbers of these institutions, run by government or other non-church groups, many have concluded that the church's own hospitals are slipping. As a matter of fact, there are probably more church hospitals, and more beds in them, than there have been at any previous time.

There are at least four hundred and fifty hospitals in the United States under Protestant church auspices. And there are many more institutions for the care of children, of old people, and of other groups. Increasingly these institutions have become "church-inspired" or "church-related" rather than "church-administered," particularly the hospitals. Official church bodies have less authority over them than they once had. Superintendents of Protestant hospitals are increasingly Christian physicians rather than Christian ministers. These are just a few signs which suggest the administrative trends. The church is still strong in the hospital field, but the kinds of ties which once bound hospitals to official church bodies have been slipping.

Protestant Hospitals. For our purposes, the main conclusion to be drawn from these trends is this: churches now have an obligation to provide for pastoral ministry in their institutions in a way which they did not have even fifty years ago. In the case of hospitals, with which we are chiefly concerned, it seemed sufficient a half-century ago to have an administrator who, because he was a ministerial representative of the church, could both administer and be the center of religious influence at the same time. Doubtless this was more possible then than now. At any rate, it is rarely possible now. Running a hospital is a highly complex administrative and business affair these days. The increase in medical knowledge, the development of therapeutic equipment, the growth of specialized professions such as social case work, occupational therapy, or laboratory technics, together with specialization in the fields of medicine and nursing, have added to the complexity of the job. The tremendous increase in costs of medical treatment has brought new financial problems, and administrators have had to tackle them. Sometimes they have had to raise new funds, or to work out methods for use of public funds, or to devise other means, but all of it has meant that administration is a more complicated and technical process than it once was.

It is not strange then that the administrator (or his aides) are no longer able to do pastoral work, even in the sense in which they did it fifty years ago. Yet during this same period it has become emphatically clear that distinctively religious ministry to the sick, alongside the ministry of the physician, nurse and others, is integrally necessary to the welfare of the patient. What has been done to meet this situation? For church hospitals, above all others, should have been conscious of the need.

A recent study of religious work in Protestant hospitals by the American Protestant Hospital Association shows that five methods are in use to provide religious ministry. Fifteen per cent of the hospitals have a superintendent who is also the religious worker. Eight per cent have full-time chaplains. Twenty-two per cent have part-time chaplains—the chaplain being an ordained minister officially designated as pastor of the hospital. Eleven per cent have directors of religious work, that is, non-ordained persons who are placed officially in charge of religious ministry. Thus fifty-six per cent of all Protestant hospitals designate some worker to be officially in charge of religious ministry. This seldom means a monopoly on carrying out such ministry; for the pastors of patients are encouraged to come to the hospital. As a matter of fact, a larger proportion of ministers visit hospitals which have a religious officer than those which do not. This leaves forty-four per cent of Protestant hospitals which have no religious officer at all, and depend entirely upon clergymen who choose to call. The complete results of this study have been published by the Association.[1]

There is much that clergymen from the neighborhood can do in a hospital, and in many hospitals that ministry has been of a high order, even sometimes to patients who are not members of a minister's congregation. But this service has been wholly unorganized in most places, and nowhere as yet is it comparable in organizational efficiency to that of "visiting physicians."

This problem has been complicated by the fact that denominational hospitals have in almost every case ceased to be denominational in the sense of treating only or mainly persons from the denomination. This means that any group of visiting clergy must represent many communions; and to most hospitals this new problem in organization has seemed almost insuperable. A few have turned to church federations and ministers' associations for help; and this highly progressive move has done much to prevent duplication, conflict, or complete absence of service in particular hospitals or wards. But so far these efforts have seldom gone beyond the clearing house stage, preventing gross competition or duplication of effort.

In spite of the proportion of Protestant hospitals, fifty-six per cent of which have a regularly assigned religious officer, the standard of ministry is generally conceded by the hospitals to be far below what it should be. The superintendents who act also as chaplains, even in small hospitals, must neglect one job or the other. The directors of religious work, usually deaconesses, are given such status that they find it difficult to do significant religious work. Among the chaplains only a handful have been especially trained for their work. What is done by clergy who "visit" the hospital, either to call upon their own parishioners or to see other patients also, is seldom thought of as having an integral relationship to the other services of the hospital. Quantitatively, the situation is better than in public and non-sectarian hospitals; but there seems to be little difference on a qualitative basis.

Responsible religious work by trained chaplains has increasingly been considered desirable by Protestant hospitals. In the past five years quite a number have established chaplaincies which did not have them before, and several others have taken progressive steps to improve their chaplaincy service. In such institutions chaplains have been encouraged not only to minister themselves to patients, but also to take steps leading to co-ordination of the services of visiting ministers. They have begun to educate other hospital personnel about the rôle of pastoral ministry in the hospital, and to co-ordinate the religious with the other services.

A great step forward was taken in 1940 with the acceptance by the American Protestant Hospital Association (founded in 1920) of an excellent statement of standards for religious work in hospitals. Because these standards state so well the kind of religious work which should be done in a hospital, they are summarized here.[2]

1. The chaplain shall be responsible to the administrator of the hospital. What the religious worker does relates to the health of the patient, and the hospital has therefore a legitimate concern with what is done. The religious worker should co-operate in a positive way with the other services of the hospital.

2. The chaplain shall co-operate with the other personnel of the hospital. The chaplain must be the kind of person who can enjoy the confidence of other hospital workers. While respecting confidential information, he can nevertheless work on the team which the physician leads.

3. The chaplain shall have a rational plan for selecting his patients. The plan should be rational as over against the practice of merely making rounds of all patients. He should work to the end of having physicians recommend that he see certain patients. He will see the patients who request his services. He will find some patients from a study of admission records. He will have some patients referred to him by the patient's clergyman, by nurses, by social workers, or in other ways. In hospitals having no religious worker there should be a rational plan for notifying and informing the local pastors of patients who need their help.

4. The chaplain shall keep records. He should keep his own records to help his memory and serve as a check on his work, writing extensively and confidentially about some patients, at least briefly about all. He may also find it desirable in the future to insert notes in the patient's regular hospital record.

5. The chaplain should see that worship is provided of a kind appropriate to the hospital and to the background and condition of the patients. Worship in a convalescent hospital will be different from that in an acute hospital. The type of worship will take the condition of the patients, as well as their religious background, into account.

6. The chaplain shall have special training for his work. In addition to the educational qualifications of college and theological school training, the chaplain should have supervised clinical

training. Selected Protestant hospitals should prepare themselves
to give such training.

7. The chaplain should be selected, wherever possible, by some
   kind of joint action of the hospital and the proper church
   authorities, to the end that the best qualified person be secured.
8. The function of the chaplain as spiritual leader of the hospital
   should not be forgotten, even though it is difficult to describe or
   to circumscribe. What he does to bring the far view is of great
   importance to the entire life of the hospital.

The fact that this document, which loses clarity in summariza-
tion, has been officially adopted by the association representing
church hospitals gives great promise of gradual but continuing
emergence of these principles in practice. It is not merely, however, a statement of the ideals to which religious work in hospitals should some day be brought. It is also a statement of certain standards which should be considered necessary as a minimum if there is to be any kind of effective religious ministry in
operation.

The central problem with chaplaincies in church hospitals is to
get trained men. But in order to do this, chaplains can no longer
be considered either by the hospital or by the church as "step-
cousins" operating on the periphery of health. Good chaplaincy
service cannot be secured without giving adequate status and
salary to the chaplain. One church hospital has recently taken a
tremendous step forward in this connection. It has dropped the
word "Chaplain" and has appointed a "Director of Religious
Work." His salary is somewhere near what his caliber would
command in the parish ministry. His status is in line with that
of the Chief of Medical Service and with that of the Assistant
Director of the hospital. Thus he—and the ministry of religion
through him and through all the religious work of the hospital,
by visiting ministers and by such workers as nurses—is accorded

an integral place in the hospital family. This hospital recognizes that a "religious atmosphere" is no more an accident than is an efficient "medical atmosphere," that certain steps must be taken in order to produce it. The atmosphere in this hospital has changed, for employees as well as for patients.

Church hospitals have now set standards which, if increasingly followed, will produce the kind of ministry needed. May the process be accelerated. But let it be noted that these steps can scarcely be taken without the full understanding and co-operation of both ministers and laymen. Hospital boards of trustees are struggling with difficult problems of administration and finance. Many of them would welcome the services of a trained chaplain or director of religious work if they knew how to finance him. And many would be inspired to find ways to finance him if the demand from the church were sufficiently great. This is not merely a problem for the overloaded boards of hospitals. It is a concern of the whole church.

Religious Work in Public and Non-Sectarian Hospitals. The standards of the work itself are the same in these institutions as for work in church hospitals. But certain problems of administration arise in reference to religious work in public or non-sectarian hospitals which do not occur, at least to such an extent, in denominational hospitals.

Such hospitals have usually felt in the past that they could not employ chaplains, for this would imply their recognizing the denomination to which the chaplain belonged as over against others. This situation, however, has changed in two important ways. First, the ecumenical movement of the churches has made it plain that they agree far more than they disagree and has followed this through by the creation of councils of churches designed not as "super-churches" but as agencies for carrying out those functions which the denominations can do better in common than separately. Institutional ministry was one of the first fields in which the need for such co-operation became obvious. Second, the actual nature of ministration to the sick is now seen to depend more upon the specific needs of the patient than upon denominational "correctness." Some denominations still feel that only their duly ordained clergy can administer the sacraments to a patient of their communion; but ministry to the sick is vastly more than this. If such ministry is what we have described it to be, it is quite possible for any ecumenically-minded minister to carry out complete and full ministry to most Protestant patients, except in some cases the sacramental ministry, without there being the slightest suspicion of proselytizing. Hospitals are just beginning to recognize this new spirit in Protestantism.

Religious ministry to public institutions was originally developed by denominations. It was the so-called "liturgical" churches, chiefly Episcopal and Lutheran, which developed a ministry most closely in accord with the principles on which we are now generally agreed. The Lutheran Inner Mission societies and the Episcopal City Mission societies paid full salaries to chaplains who gave their whole time to pastoral work in institutions. It is estimated that in 1940 there were fifty-two full-time, paid chaplains working for the Episcopal group, and thirty-one part-time ones. There were approximately fifty Lutherans who gave full time to such work. Support for these institutional workers comes from various sources: national denomination, diocese or synod, or funds secured by local societies. Other churches have a few such workers, but only a fraction of the total of these two groups. We are arbitrarily excluding from consideration the projects of certain mission societies which were purely evangelistic at their start, and some of which have now added social services (as for example the Salvation Army). Only occasionally have these touched hospitals and similar institutions; and when they have, their service has rarely been pastoral in any significant sense.

These two groups of Episcopal and Lutheran workers have not increased significantly in number during the past twenty years, but the quality of their work is undergoing constant improvement. Their tendency is to accept the standards now generally agreed on for good religious ministry in institutions and increasingly to secure workers who can put them into operation. The Episcopal church has had the most "responsible" attitude about such work in the sense that it has realized that the institutions themselves are necessarily concerned with the quality of work done. Lutherans have tended more to look on themselves as "outsiders," but in recent years have increasingly accepted the concept of responsibility to the institution as well as to the patient.

This "denominational visitor" method of handling the problem has much to commend it, but it does not *necessarily* relate itself integrally to the service given by the whole institution. It may do so, as a goodly number of these workers have demonstrated; but whether or not it does so depends on the attitude of the chaplain and of the denominational administrators. Where the institution does not pay the bill, it can call on such workers only as it could call on volunteers, unless the workers accord such rights to the institution.

These "denominational visitors" have been under tremendous handicaps. Many of them have been ordered by their church groups to cover a large number of institutions. One worker is on record within the past five years who was supposed to cover more than fifty hospitals and other institutions! The Episcopalians have been at the front in reducing the number of institutions visited to a place where at least some work could be done beyond mere "visiting." But the service of such voluntary church groups alone cannot be considered a satisfactory solution to the problem as a whole, even if the number of workers should be expanded enormously; and even a comparatively small increase seems unlikely for some years to come.

Public and non-sectarian hospitals tend to be larger than denominational hospitals; and this fact has created a problem for many of them in regard to religious service. Even if neighborhood ministers, or "visiting missionaries," or other workers visited the institutions, there have rarely been enough to go round, and their work has often overlapped and been unco-ordinated. Some institutions therefore have hired full-time or part-time chaplains to be paid for out of institutional funds. These have usually been hired in three groups: Protestant, Roman Catholic and Jewish, provided there was a significant enough number of any group present to make selection of a representative advisable. The Roman Catholic church has been the largest booster of pastoral service on this basis; and it is directly due to its efforts that public funds have been given for chaplaincy service in many public hospitals.

Such a system has many advantages for the institution. It guarantees that men will be on call and therefore available in emergency. It enables the hospital to keep out religious enthusiasts, who might have a pernicious influence upon health, by explaining that pastoral service is already provided for. It provides machinery for informing appropriate religious leaders outside the hospital when they are needed at the hospital. It allays the fears of many patients who might otherwise interpret the strangeness of hospital surroundings as fearsome and therefore godless. And today hospitals are beginning to recognize that the greatest advantage of all is the contribution religious ministry makes to the actual health and welfare of the patients.

When public hospitals began to install chaplains, they had no problems about securing Roman Catholic chaplains; a central authority was ready not only to co-operate, but to name the person whose services could be secured. The problem of securing Jewish chaplains was usually not easy; but there were so few Jewish centers that this really was of small magnitude. But hospitals recognized no central authority in Protestantism and were puzzled. The Protestants sometimes could not or would not designate anyone to represent them (but only some segment of them); and consequently any choice by the hospital would be criticized. In this situation a good deal of political maneuvering took place, and its influence has by no means disappeared at present. But it is increasingly difficult to place men in chaplaincies who are obviously unfitted or unprepared.

The growth of inter-church agencies has been a boon to hospitals wishing good chaplaincy service. For where the inter-church body is strong, the hospital can deal with all major denominations through it, and conflict is at a minimum. Most church federations will have to become stronger before they can act authoritatively at this point; but the trend must be in that direction if public-supported chaplaincy is to be continued at all.

The problem has been complicated by the fact that even in the few places where public funds have been used for chaplains they have been insufficient to provide a worker even with a minimum salary. This has meant that the salary has had to be supplemented by some mission body, or that chaplaincy work has been relegated to a part-time position. For anything like an adequate religious ministry in public hospitals, the only alternative to increased public support is a tremendous increase in support by the churches. It is doubtful if even partially adequate religious ministry in public hospitals, and only in the larger ones at that, could be provided by the Protestant churches at less than twenty-five times their present rate of expenditure. To consider this practically impossible for some years to come is only realistic.

An important issue is involved in the use of public funds for religious service. Some are content to say: no service on behalf of the churches unless the churches pay for it. Enforcing such a position would leave most of our hospitals (and other public institutions) almost entirely unserviced. Others say the public institutions have a right to hire chaplains, but these should not be considered representatives of the church. This would be to remove the strongest resource the chaplain possesses. Provided the relationship of the churches to chaplains is intimate and authoritative, there seems no reason why public-supported chaplaincies should be questioned by church people. This would assume also that chaplains were selected and nominated by the churches, that the churches themselves protected their rights as religious representatives, and backed them up in time of difficulty. Another way to see it is this: these chaplains do have an official relationship to their own denomination; is the service to be merely denominational, or is it to be on behalf of the Protestant group as a whole? We are concerned with the complicated issues involved in this problem, but our major concern is to see adequate service rendered. We deplore the tendency of those groups which merely stand on the sidelines and criticize.

The statement of standards referred to above suggests how public-supported religious workers should be chosen to represent the Protestant group. There should be nomination by an authoritative body representing the Protestant churches, who have agreed as to their candidate, to the public authority. If the public authority ignores this and gets some unrecommended Protestant, then of course the chaplaincy service cannot represent the churches. Provided Protestantism is united at this point, the public authority can no more risk church disfavor in the Protestant case than it could in the Roman Catholic.

It is essential to point out that any committee representing the Protestant churches on such matters should be competent as well as representative. It should contain specialists and experts who know what is involved in institutional work, and who also know something of the qualities needed to make a chaplain effective.

The lead taken by the American Protestant Hospital Association in the matter of standards, and that taken by certain public and private non-sectarian hospitals in the matter of supervised clinical training, suggests that church opinion may sometimes lag behind institutional opinion on these matters. Even a denominational hospital may sometimes be ready to go ahead when the church group is not. In such cases we can urge the hospital to try to convince the church groups before going ahead too far. After all, the hospital would have the weight of expert opinion on its side and could secure help in the educational process. Sometimes it is the church groups who are ahead of the hospital. In these cases it is clear that education comes first.[3]

In the case of non-sectarian private hospitals, the principles involved should be not unlike those applicable to public institutions. Clearance on chaplaincy service, if paid for by the hospital, ought ideally to be through the inter-church organization. But inter-church organizations must support the minimum standards of chaplaincy service; and non-sectarian hospitals are even more justified than public hospitals in ignoring a church council which considers *only* representation and not also quality of service rendered. There are increasing signs that more of the non-sectarian, private hospitals recognize the need for securing adequate religious ministry. Protestants on Community Chest committees have usually been tongue-tied at the point of religious ministry; it is high time they put some oil in their mouths.

Religious Ministry in other Public Institutions. Prisons have more often had full-time religious workers than hospitals, because it was more obvious that a "visiting" type of service would endanger the purposes of the institution. Many more of these men, for similar reasons, have been supported from public funds than in the case of hospital chaplains. It is estimated that there are sixty-five Protestant chaplains on full-time service in state and federal penal and correctional institutions this year in the United States, with about eighty-five doing part-time work.[4] A statement of standards which should govern such work has been issued by the Commission on Prison Chaplains.[5] There are, however, at least a hundred state or federal institutions in which the only religious service is that performed by visiting clergy. Unlike hospitals, this service is not usually to individuals but is only the conduct of public worship. No figures are available on the kind of religious ministry being carried out in city and county institutions; but with a very few exceptions, perhaps a dozen institutions in all, it seems likely that these institutions do not have chaplains.

Prison chaplains generally maintain connections with their own denominations, but they have only rarely had a significant relationship to other denominations as well, though they ministered to inmates coming from many communions. The first complete move in this direction was made by the Federal Bureau of Prisons in collaboration with the Commission on Prison Chaplains of the Federal Council of Churches. This Commission selects and nominates all candidates for full-time Protestant chaplaincies in federal penal and correctional institutions. One of the qualifications established for candidates is that they have an approved course of supervised clinical training. This training program has been carried out by the Council for Clinical Training. Training centers have now been established in several of the federal institutions in order to give the training a direct relationship to the kind of work the chaplain himself will do.

This Commission of course co-operates with appropriate denominational authorities. The U. S. Department of Justice has been pleased with this plan, for it is thereby enabled to deal with a single agency on behalf of Protestantism. It is also pleased because the training and caliber of men has been high. No other complete system of chaplaincies has as yet been so fully established along these lines, though the New York City plan approaches it. Chaplains' salaries are paid by the government, but the work of the Commission is paid for by the churches.[6]

A few state and city jurisdictions have either adopted some features of this plan or have worked them out independently, and there is evidence that there will increasingly be more moves in this direction. State and city councils of churches are now interested; for they see in such plans a solution to a problem which has always plagued them. State and city officials are interested; for they long to deal with a unified authority and not have to pit opposing Protestant forces against one another.

Reference has been made in another chapter to mental hospitals. There are nearly a half-million people in these at any one time in the United States, most of them in public hospitals. Religious ministry to them has been more inadequate than that to any other institutional group with the possible exception of the mentally defective. A half-dozen hospitals have secured trained and full-time Protestant chaplains; but this has been due to the vision of a few hospital administrators and to the work of the Council for Clinical Training, and especially to Anton T. Boisen. It was in 1924 that Boisen became chaplain of Worcester State Hospital in Massachusetts; and rapidly he and the Council for Clinical Training proved how necessary a full-time and skilled religious worker was in such institutions. Yet despite this work, there are still only a handful of hospitals which have such chaplains. Due credit must be given the hospitals for providing services of public worship, which are very important in a mental hospital; and this practice has been almost universal. But it is still a far cry from the responsible kind of full-time ministry which Boisen and the Council for Clinical Training have shown is possible and necessary. No public mental hospital system has as yet accepted the policy of having full-time, trained chaplains in all its institutions. Yet the average size of these institutions, in terms of daily population, is between five and ten times as great as that of general hospitals.

Undoubtedly one of the reasons why public authority has seldom been willing to pay for chaplaincy service in mental hospitals has been the comparative lack of interest in the problem on the part of the Roman Catholics. They seem less susceptible than Protestants to the more dynamic point of view which refuses to draw a sharp dividing line between mental illness and mental health, or between the "rational" and the "irrational." Most of our conclusions about chaplaincy work would, so far as they go, be acceptable to Roman Catholics; but it is uncertain whether in the future they will see equal reason, as we do, for effective religious ministry in mental hospitals. Full-time chaplains would seem even more important to us here in that there is less chance—on account of the great size of most such institutions, and the unfamiliarity with the special problem on the part of most clergy—of other religious ministry being brought to their patients.

There is neither time nor need to consider all the other types of public institutions which should have the ministry of religion. There are institutions for developmental deficients, commonly but often incorrectly called "mental defectives" or "feeble-minded." There are at least a hundred thousand persons in such institutions; and the number will probably increase, as it is estimated that another half-million could profit by either temporary or permanent institutional care. Specialists in this field report that a surprisingly large number of them could profit from effective religious ministry.

There are tuberculosis hospitals, convalescent hospitals or homes, and many other types of homes or hospitals for meeting various kinds of problems requiring institutional care. There are the semi-institutions, so much needed, which have just begun to be developed, an example of which is Camp LaGuardia, maintained by the City of New York for temporary care and rehabilitation of men who are down and out but who are not criminals or sick in the ordinary sense. There are many other types, and the church should be increasingly sensitive to the needs in these institutions.

Conclusion. There are three basic problems in reference to full-time Protestant workers in institutions. The first is the quality of the work which the chaplain carries on. The second is the personal qualifications and training of the chaplains. The third is the methods of appointment and payment of chaplains. All three have been discussed here, and suggestions have been made not only as to what constitutes standard procedure, but also as to how to take steps to bring about the desired service. With the proper standards of training, appointment and the work in operation, we have indicated that in our judgment far more full-time chaplains are needed in general hospitals, mental hospitals, special hospitals such as those for convalescence and tuberculosis, penal and correctional institutions, and others than the Protestant churches have realized.

We have also indicated that we are strongly in favor of those "visiting" chaplaincy services which are thoroughly responsible, and which fulfill the standards of training and work. High praise should go to the two groups which have contributed most in this direction: Episcopal and Lutheran. This service, like the more "official" chaplaincy, should increasingly be on behalf of the whole Protestant body; and it is most encouraging to see these responsible visiting services co-operating through the local inter-church agencies.

Ministers of local churches do not have their function of work in neighboring institutions threatened by the full-time worker. In fact, their function takes on added importance as a full-time religious worker in the institution is able to help them use their limited time to greatest advantage. We recommend the experimental setting up of staffs of visiting clergy somewhat after the medical fashion; or at least bringing in the neighboring clergy to make it clear how the coming of a full-time worker may help to co-ordinate the services they render rather than replace them.

Full-time workers should be available, generally speaking, in any institution where there are two to four hundred Protestant patients or inmates at any one time. In the case of general hospitals, where the turnover is very great, this figure should be about one hundred. In smaller institutions, the future should see the establishment of responsible part-time chaplains, who not only do work with patients themselves but who also aid in co-ordinating the services of neighborhood clergy.

It should be noted again that the services of religious workers in institutions, while their main function is ministry to the individual patient, are by no means so limited. The statements of standards suggest that there are significant functions in connection with worship, with religious education, and the like which parallel most aspects of the program that would be found in any parish. Of great importance is the religious worker's function in reference to other personnel of the hospital. He should, by formal and informal means alike, constantly interpret the relations of religious ministry to the other ministries of the institution. Every Christian health worker, whether physician, nurse, or social worker should know something about the relations between religion and health.

Finally, the problem of religious ministry in institutions is not one for the chaplain alone to solve, or for the minister alone to consider. We believe that lay church visitors have a real place, under professional guidance, in some types of institutions, especially the general or chronic hospital. But more important, the kind of religious ministry which is needed in all these institutions can be brought into being only in so far as it is demanded by the layman.

NOTES

CHAPTER I

1. Clifford Beers, *A Mind that Found Itself*, N. Y., Doubleday, Doran, 1908, 25th anniversary edition, 1937.
   This volume is the basic autobiographical charter of the mental hygiene movement.
2. See *The Mental Hygiene Movement* from the Philanthropic Standpoint. By the Department of Philanthropic Information, Central Hanover Bank and Trust Company, New York City, 1939. Available from the National Committee for Mental Hygiene, 1790 Broadway, New York City.
   This gives an excellent concise account of the formation of the mental hygiene movement, with an analysis of the movement's current status and needs.
3. Milton E. Kirkpatrick, Director of the Division of Community Clinics, National Committee for Mental Hygiene, in a personal letter.
4. See E. K. Wickman, *Teachers and Behavior Problems*, The Commonwealth Fund, 1938.
   This pamphlet is discussed further in chapter five.
5. Agnes E. Benedict, *Children at the Crossroads*, N. Y., The Commonwealth Fund, 1930.
   This is an excellent description of actual work done by visiting teachers.
6. See G. Canby Robinson, *The Patient as a Person*, N. Y., The Commonwealth Fund, 1939.
   This is a valuable research study on the social components of illness. Further reference to it will be found in chapter four.
7. See W. Carson Ryan, *Mental Health through Education*, N. Y., The Commonwealth Fund, 1938.
   A description of specific educational situations throughout the country where mental hygiene principles are being used in education.
8. See George K. Pratt, *Your Mind and You*, N. Y., Funk and Wagnalls, 1937 (revised edition).
   An effective popular treatise on mental hygiene.
9. These resources are considered in some detail in chapter nine.
10. The relation of religious education to mental hygiene is considered at greater length in chapter five.

11. See for example Margaret Mead, *Sex and Temperament in Three Primitive Societies*, N. Y., William Morrow, 1935. Or see Ruth Benedict, *Patterns of Culture*, Boston, Houghton Mifflin, 1934.

Studies of primitive tribes, easily readable, showing what a variety of cultural patterns can be built on the basis of the same "human nature."

12. Reported to me by Milton E. Kirkpatrick.

13. Frankwood E. Williams, *Adolescence: Studies in Mental Hygiene*, N. Y., Farrar & Rinehart, 1930.

A book which has been accused of bias but which nevertheless suggests some significant implications of the newer elements of mental hygiene knowledge.

14. Lawrence K. Frank, "The Fundamental Needs of the Child" in *Mental Hygiene*, July, 1938. Reprints available from the New York State Committee on Mental Hygiene, 105 East 22nd Street, New York City.

One of the most penetrating articles on mental hygiene ever written.

15. *Ibid.*, p. 364.

16. See Milton E. Kirkpatrick, "Mental Hygiene and Religion," *Mental Hygiene*, June, 1940.

An excellent brief statement by a psychiatrist.

Carroll A. Wise, "The Clergy and Community Education for Mental Hygiene," *Mental Hygiene*, January, 1941.

By a clergyman who has done much of it.

Smiley Blanton and Norman Vincent Peale, *Faith Is the Answer*, Nashville, Abingdon-Cokesbury, 1940.

The sections by Dr. Blanton show some of the implications of modern mental hygiene content for the church.

CHAPTER II

1. Earl D. Bond, M.D., Quoted in "Aims, Commission on Religion and Health, Federal Council of Churches."

2. J. A. Hadfield, M. D., "The Psychology of Power" in *The Spirit*, ed. by B. H. Streeter, The Macmillan Co., 1919, p. 110. Quoted by George A. Buttrick in *Prayer*, Abingdon-Cokesbury, 1942, p. 50.

3. *Ibid.*, p. 51.

4. See chapter four.

5. G. Canby Robinson, *The Patient as a Person*, N. Y., The Commonwealth Fund, 1939, p. 10.

6. See for instance Charles T. Holman, *The Religion of a Healthy Mind*, N. Y., Round Table Press, 1940.

This volume deals well both with religions which are healthful and unhealthful, and with interpretations of religion which are healthy and unhealthy.

7. See Carroll A. Wise, *Religion in Illness and Health*, N. Y., Harper and Bros., 1942.

This is the best volume now available on this point. This is one of the most helpful books available on several aspects of the field relating religion to health, including psychosomatics and religion, religious symbolism and health, and healthy or unhealthy interpretations of religion. It would be quoted more extensively in this volume if it had appeared before work on this was completed.

8. See also chapter seven.
9. See Erich Fromm, "Selfishness and Self-Love," *Psychiatry,* November, 1939.
10. A. N. Whitehead, *Religion in the Making*, N. Y., The Macmillan Co., 1926.
11. Luke 11:24-26.
12. See for example Ruth Benedict, *Patterns of Culture,* Boston, Houghton Mifflin Co., 1934.
13. Chapter four.
14. George A. Buttrick, *op. cit.*, p. 117.
15. John W. Suter, Jr., "Prayer and Health," a pamphlet to be published by the Commission on Religion and Health, Federal Council of Churches.
16. Karen Horney, M.D., *Self-Analysis,* N. Y., W. W. Norton & Co., 1942, pp. 8-9.
17. See for example Edmund Jacobson, *You Must Relax,* N. Y., McGraw-Hill, 1934.
18. John W. Suter, Jr., *op. cit.*

CHAPTER III

1. Mark 3:14-15.
2. *A Survey of Medical Missions in India,* Prepared by the Committee on Survey, Efficiency, and Co-operation of the Christian Medical Association of India in conjunction with the National Christian Council of India, Burma and Ceylon. Poona, 1928.
3. K. S. Latourette, *A History of the Expansion of Christianity,* V. 2 *The Thousand Years of Uncertainty,* Harper and Bros., 1938, p. 363.
4. *Ibid.,* p. 364.
5. *Ibid.*
6. *Ibid.,* p. 365.
7. *Ibid.,* p. 364.
8. Albert Deutsch, *The Mentally Ill in America,* N. Y., Doubleday, Doran, 1937.
9. *The Ministry of Healing in India,* Handbook of the Christian Medical Association of India, Mysore, 1932, p. 5.
10. *A Survey of Medical Missions in India* (See note 2).
11. *The Ministry of Healing in India* (See note 9), p. 25.
12. Harold Balme, *China and Modern Medicine,* London, 1921.
13. John Lowe, *Medical Missions,* Revell, 1896, p. 204.
14. Balme, *op. cit.,* p. 55.

15. *Ibid.*, p. 56.
16. Edward H. Hume, *Occasional Leaflet,* Organ of the Council on Medical Missions, Chinese Medical Association. V. 6, Nov., 1938. "Christian Medicine in China Tomorrow," p. 30.
17. *Ibid.*, p. 25.
18. *Ecumenical Missionary Conference, N. Y., 1900,* Report of the Ecumenical Conference on Foreign Missions, held in Carnegie Hall and Neighboring Churches, V. 2, p. 195.
19. Hume, *op. cit.*, p. 31.
20. Albert Schweitzer, *Out of My Life and Thought,* N. Y., Henry Holt, 1933, pp. 168-169.
21. Paul W. Harrison, *Doctor in Arabia,* N. Y., John Day, 1940, p. 275.
22. Edward H. Hume, *The Chinese Way in Medicine,* Baltimore, Johns Hopkins Press, 1940.
23. *Ecumenical Missionary Conference 1900,* p. 197.
24. Hume, *The Chinese Way in Medicine,* p. 61.
25. See chapter four.
26. *The World Mission of the Church,* Findings and Recommendations of the International Missionary Council, Tambaram, Madras, India, N. Y., I. M. C., 1939, p. 81.
27. Henry P. Van Dusen, *For the Healing of the Nations,* Scribner, 1940, p. 59.
28. Former Ambassador Hu Shih in "Have a Heart for China," Bulletin of the Church Committee for China Relief, November, 1941.
29. *The World Mission of the Church* (See note 26), p. 80.
30. Russell L. Dicks, *Who is My Patient: a Religious Manual for Nurses,* Macmillan, 1941.
31. See chapter ten.
32. Hume, *Occasional Leaflet, loc. cit.*, p. 38.
33. *Ibid.*, p. 46.
34. *Re-Thinking Missions,* by the Laymen's Commission of Appraisal, W. E. Hocking, Ed., N. Y., Harper and Bros., 1932, p. 201.
35. Harrison, *op. cit.*, p. 272.
36. Figures were estimated by the Christian Medical Council for Overseas Work, in autumn 1941.
37. Dermott Monahan, "The Relationship of Religion and Health," *Journal of the Christian Medical Association of India, Burma and Ceylon,* Sept., 1940.
38. Hume, *Occasional Leaflet, loc. cit.*, p. 28.
39. George W. Gray, *The Advancing Front of Medicine,* N. Y., Farrar and Rinehart, 1941, pp. 7-8.
40. Hume, *Occasional Leaflet, loc. cit.*, p. 29.
41. *Journal of the Christian Medical Association of India, Burma and Ceylon,* Jan., 1938, p. 29.
42. *Ibid.*, p. 31.
43. Edward M. Dodd, *How Far to the Nearest Doctor?* N. Y., Friendship Press, 1933, p. 163.
44. Robert L. Calhoun, *God and the Common Life,* Scribner, 1935.

CHAPTER IV

1. Flanders Dunbar, *Emotions and Bodily Changes: A Survey of Literature on Psychosomatic Interrelationships, 1910-1933,* N. Y., Columbia University Press, 1938, 2nd edition, p. 70. Quotations have been reprinted by permission of Columbia Univ. Press.
   This is the most comprehensive volume in the field today. It is necessarily too technical to be easily understood by others than medical workers, but presents a wealth of information for the student. It is generally considered authoritative in medical circles, and has been drawn on largely in preparation of this chapter.
2. F. Mohr, "Die Wechselwirkung körperlicher und seelischer Faktoren im Krankheitsgeschehen," *Klinische Wochenschrift,* Vol. 6, 1927, pp. 772-6.
3. See Carroll A. Wise, *Religion in Illness and Health,* N. Y., Harper and Bros., 1942.
   This book now contains the best and most complete description in print for the non-medical reader of the facts about psychosomatic interrelationships. Had it been available prior to the writing of this chapter, it would have been quoted extensively. The reader is urged to consult it as giving a more comprehensive picture than our single chapter can profess to do.
4. George W. Gray, "Anxiety and Illness," *Harper's Magazine,* May, 1939, p. 605.
   Gray is an excellent lay writer on the emotional aspects of illness, and on other medical and scientific subjects, and is quoted especially because of his clarity in presenting the essential point to non-medical readers.
5. Walter B. Cannon, *Bodily Changes in Pain, Hunger, Fear and Rage,* Appleton-Century Co., 1936, 2nd edition, pp. 256-257.
6. Dunbar, *op. cit., p.* 58.
7. *Ibid.,* Introduction to 2nd edition, p. xx.
8. H. E. Ruggles, "Emotional Influence upon the Gastro-Intestinal Tract," *California and Western Medical Journal,* Vol. 29, 1928, pp. 222-3.
9. Dunbar, *op. cit.,* p. 270. The man was Flemming.
10. L. Alkan, *Anatomische Organkrankheiten aus seelischer Ursache,* Stuttgart, 1930.
11. Nolan D. C. Lewis, "Psychological Factors in Hyperthyroidism," *Medical Journal and Record,* Vol. 122, 1925.
12. Anita M. Mühl, "Problems in General Medicine from the Emotional Standpoint," *Psychoanalytic Review,* Vol. 16, 1929, p. 392.
13. Dunbar, *op. cit.,* p. 391.
14. John H. Stokes and Donald M. Pillsbury, "Theoretical and Practical Considerations of a Gastrointestinal Mechanism," *Archives of Dermatology and Syphilology,* Vol. 22, 1930, pp. 962-993.
15. Gray, *op. cit.,* p. 611.

16. *Ibid.*, p. 608.
17. Dunbar, *op. cit.*, p. 135.
18. Harry L. Segal, H. F. Binswanger and S. Strouse, "The Effect of Emotion on Basal Metabolism," *Archives of Internal Medicine*, Vol. 41, 1928.
19. Dunbar, *op. cit.*, Introduction to 2nd edition, p. xxx.
20. Glenn Clark, *How to Find Health through Prayer*, N. Y., Harper & Bros., 1941, p. 38.
21. Walter B. Cannon, "The Role of Emotion in Disease," *Annals of Internal Medicine*, Vol. 9, No. 11, 1936, p. 1458.
22. Gray, *op. cit.*, p. 614.
23. Dunbar, *op. cit.*, Introduction to 2nd edition, p. xxii.
24. In conversation.
25. See Walter B. Cannon, " 'Voodoo' Death," *American Anthropologist*, April-June, 1942.

> Cannon has called this phenomenon "Voodoo" Death. In this paper he indicates that, however rare in occurrence, the phenomenon is possible, and he suggests the physiological processes which would account for it. It is not something which disregards the body, so to speak; but even in these extreme instances it is something for which modern physiology and psychology can suggest a process explanation.

26. See Smiley Blanton, "Analytical Study of a Cure at Lourdes," *The Psychoanalytic Quarterly*, V. 9, 1940, pp. 348-362.
27. *Ibid.*, p. 359.
28. G. Canby Robinson, *The Patient as a Person*, N. Y., The Commonwealth Fund, 1939, p. 3.
29. The Henry Ford Hospital, Detroit. Reported in verbal communication by Frank J. Sladen, M.D., Chief of Medical Service. He reports that the study is to be published.
30. Robinson, *op. cit.*, pp. 3-4.
31. *Ibid.*, p. 4.
32. It is to be noted, however, that the study by Dunbar which has been drawn on so extensively in this chapter was initiated by the Joint Committee on Religion and Medicine of the New York Academy of Medicine and the Federal Council of the Churches of Christ in America. This Joint Committee operated from 1923 to 1936. See "History of the Joint Committee. . . ." by Ethel P. S. Hoyt and Helen Van Voast, 1936.

CHAPTER V

1. Proverbs 23:7.
2. With apologies to Dr. Maude Royden. In selecting fictitious names, she reports that long ago she stopped referring to "Mrs. Jones" or "Mrs. Brown." There was always a Mrs. Jones or Mrs. Brown present; whereas Mrs. Juggins is usually safe!

3. Dr. Fritz Künkel, the noted psychiatrist, now of Los Angeles, reports in personal correspondence that he believes the minister is by far the most important contact with people who are going through the normal problems of growth, but which do not seem normal when one is going through them. It is the type of symptom which emerges which suggests whether or not a physician will see them; whereas Dr. Künkel suggests that the minister can always see them. He believes that it is in this area, rather than that of defined illnesses, where the minister's greatest opportunity lies.
4. Richard H. Edwards, *A Person-Minded Ministry,* Abingdon-Cokesbury, 1940.
5. Richard C. Cabot, *What Men Live By,* Boston, Houghton Mifflin, 1914, pp. 267-268. This tendency is well described and analyzed here.

CHAPTER VI

1. See for example W. C. Bower, *Character Through Creative Experience,* University of Chicago Press, 1930; Walter S. Athearn, *The Minister and the Teacher,* Century, 1932; George H. Betts, *Teaching Religion Today,* Abingdon, 1934; Stewart G. Cole, *Character and Christian Education,* Cokesbury, 1936; Harrison S. Elliott, *Can Religious Education Be Christian?* Macmillan, 1940; George A. Coe, *What is Christian Education?* Scribner, 1929; Theodore G. Soares, *Religious Education,* Univ. of Chicago Press, 1938; and Paul H. Vieth, *Objectives of Religious Education,* Harper, 1930.
2. Harrison S. Elliott, *Can Religious Education Be Christian?* Macmillan, 1940. This is the best volume we have relating the thoroughly progressive and thoroughly Christian point of view in religious education to modern theological thought generally. It is well written and shows far-reaching insight into the implications for religious education of mental health and hygiene.
3. E. K. Wickman, *Teachers and Behavior Problems,* N. Y., The Commonwealth Fund, 1938. This is a digest of the full study published some years previously and entitled *Children's Behavior and Teachers' Attitudes.*
4. *Ibid.,* p. 3.
5. J. J. Van Boskirk, with the aid of Charles T. Holman, "Religious Leaders' Attitudes and Children's Behavior Problems." This is an unpublished paper generously made available to the author.
6. Lawrence K. Frank, "The Fundamental Needs of the Child" in *Mental Hygiene,* July, 1938. Reprinted and available from New York State Committee for Mental Hygiene, 105 East 22nd Street, New York City. This is a noteworthy brief account of the basic knowledge which is available on child psychology and the mental hygiene of childhood. A similar article by the same author on "The Reorientation of Education to the Promotion of Mental Hygiene" in *Mental Hygiene* magazine for October, 1939, is also available in reprint from the same source.

7. *Ibid.*, p. 356.
8. *Ibid.*, p. 362.
9. *Ibid.*, p. 364.
10. *Ibid.*, p. 374.
11. *Ibid.*, p. 375.
12. *Ibid.*, p. 377.
13. Elliott, *op. cit.*, p. 286.

CHAPTER VII

1. Anton T. Boisen in a lecture.
2. See for example John S. Bonnell, *Pastoral Psychiatry,* Harper, 1938.
   The author does not believe this, but his title has suggested it to a number of his readers.
3. Thomas M. French in a lecture.
4. See William Healy's epoch-making early work, *Mental Conflicts and Misconduct,* Boston, Little, Brown, 1917, for the early intimations of this; and Franz Alexander and Hugo Staub, *The Criminal, the Judge and the Public,* Macmillan, 1931, for the conclusions of psychoanalytic investigators.
5. See *Mental Health,* Science Press, Lancaster, Pa., 1939, published by the National Committee for Mental Hygiene. It is the most comprehensive statement about mental health and illness now available. It is a report of the symposium on this subject held in 1938 in co-operation with the American Association for the Advancement of Science.
6. Perhaps the best psychiatric textbook is D. K. Henderson and R. D. Gillespie, *A Text-Book of Psychiatry,* for students and practitioners, Oxford University Press, 1927, and later. Other good ones are William A. White, *Outlines of Psychiatry* and the more popular *Lectures in Psychiatry,* Washington, Nervous and Mental Disease Publishing Company. That by Edward A. Strecker and Franklin G. Ebaugh, *Practical Clinical Psychiatry,* for students and practitioners, Philadelphia, Blakiston, is also good. All have gone through more than one edition. Carroll A. Wise's *Religion in Illness and Health* covers this ground sufficiently for the non-technical reader.
7. Bernard Hart, *The Psychology of Insanity,* Macmillan, 1912, and later. This book has merit in removing the mystery of terminology.
8. This general approach has been best developed by Anton T. Boisen in *The Exploration of the Inner World,* Willett Clark, 1936.
9. This has been described most cogently in Karen Horney's *The Neurotic Personality of our Time,* Norton, 1936.
10. See the suggestive discussion along this line by Harry Bone in *Christianity and Mental Hygiene,* published in 1939 by the Commission on Religion and Health, Federal Council of Churches.
11. Perhaps the best single volume on the relation of personality to cultural patterns is James S. Plant, *Personality and the Cultural Pattern,* N. Y., The Commonwealth Fund, 1937.

12. The most suggestive writing on this point has been by Erich Fromm in an article entitled "Selfishness and Self-Love" in *Psychiatry* for November, 1939. See also his *Escape from Freedom*, Farrar & Rinehart, 1941.

13. An especially illuminating book is Clara Bassett's *Mental Hygiene in the Community*, N. Y., The Macmillan Co., 1936.

14. For evaluation of figures, see book described in note 5 above.

15. *Ibid.* See also "Religious Work with the Mentally Defective" in *Information Service*, June 27, 1942. This is published by the Federal Council of Churches.

16. A "Research Council on Problems of Alcohol" was recently formed under the auspices of the American Association for the Advancement of Science. It publishes the *Quarterly Journal of Studies on Alcohol*. For a summary of the material on alcohol addiction, see "Alcohol Addiction—A Problem for the Church," *Information Service*, April 25, 1942.

17. See Albert Deutsch, *The Mentally Ill in America*, Doubleday, Doran, 1937. This is a remarkable study of the history of treatment of the mentally ill and some related groups in this country.

18. See chapter nine for an elaboration of community resources.

19. See volume mentioned in note 5 above.

20. See *Hymns of Hope and Courage*, edited by Anton T. Boisen and Cecil M. Smith, N. Y., A. S. Barnes & Co., 1942. A hymnal especially designed to meet the needs of the suffering, including mental hospital patients. See also "Improving Protestant Worship in Mental Hospitals," by Seward Hiltner, *Mental Hygiene*, Oct., 1942.

21. For what the chaplain may do in the mental hospital see "Mental Hygiene and the Church" by Carroll A. Wise in the volume described in note 5 above.

22. See Anton T. Boisen, *The Exploration of the Inner World*, Willett Clark, 1936. The real significance of this point was discovered, and is here elaborated by, Dr. Boisen.

22a. Edith M. Stern, *Mental Illness: A Guide for the Family*, N. Y., The Commonwealth Fund, 1942.

23. The point emphasized by Anton T. Boisen.

24. See T. H. Hughes, *The Psychology of Preaching and Pastoral Work*, N. Y., The Macmillan Co., 1941.

25. Grace Stuart, *The Achievement of Personality*, The Macmillan Company, 1938, is especially good at this point.

CHAPTER VIII

1. See John T. McNeill and Helen M. Gamer, *Medieval Handbooks of Penance*, N. Y., Columbia University Press, 1938.

2. Rollo May, *The Art of Counseling*, N. Y., Abingdon-Cokesbury Press, 1939. This volume is especially good at this point.

3. Good introductory treatises on the principles of counseling are by May (note 2 above); *Solving Personal Problems* by H. S. and G. L. Elliott, Holt, 1936; and *The Cure of Souls* by Charles T. Holman, University of Chicago Press, 1932.

4. The suggestion for these distinctions came from Samuel W. Hartwell, M.D., in verbal communication and in *Fifty-Five Bad Boys*, Knopf, 1931.

5. This case, as with others in the volume not quoted from published sources has been so disguised in all details as to be unrecognizable and unidentifiable, and is in part a "composite" case. All names are of course fictitious.

6. Luke 8:39.

7. A bibliography is published by the Commission on Religion and Health, 297 Fourth Avenue, New York City. A bibliography on marriage and family life is published by the Commission on Marriage and the Home, at the same address. A bibliography of pamphlet literature on mental hygiene is published by the National Committee for Mental Hygiene, 1790 Broadway, New York City.

8. For information about supervised clinical training write to:
   Council for Clinical Training, 2 East 103 Street, New York City;
   Theological Schools' Committee on Clinical Training, 99 Brattle Street, Cambridge, Mass.;
   Graduate School of Applied Religion, 634 Oak Street, Cincinnati, Ohio;
   Or, for general information, to Commission on Religion and Health, 297 Fourth Avenue, New York City.

9. Information about various courses and conferences may be obtained from the Commission on Religion and Health, 297 Fourth Avenue, New York City. See the Commission's pamphlet, "Religion and Health in the Local Community," for description of various programs carried on in several communities.

10. Information about psychotherapists in most sections of the country is available from the Commission on Religion and Health.

11. Suggestions about such courses, or special leadership for them, may be received from the Commission on Religion and Health, if the request is accompanied by a description of the situation and needs to be met.

12. Russell L. Dicks has made these helpful distinctions between general and specific crisis situations in verbal communication.

13. Regina W. Wieman has devoted attention to methods and conditions of group counseling, and has given some helpful suggestions in *The Modern Family and the Church*, N. Y., Harper and Bros., 1937.

14. A good illustration of such a relationship was that of Norman Vincent Peale and Smiley Blanton, M.D., at the Marble Collegiate Church, New York City. See their *Faith Is the Answer*, N. Y., Abingdon-Cokesbury Press, 1940.

15. George A. Buttrick in an address.

CHAPTER IX

1. For information on what several local communities have done to promote closer relationships between physicians and ministers, see "Religion and Health in the Local Community," Commission on Religion and Health, 297 Fourth Avenue, New York. See also "Report of the Clergy-Physician Relationship in Protestant Hospitals," by the American Protestant Hospital Association, 1942.
2. Information about psychiatrists available in any locality may be secured from the state or local mental hygiene society, or from the National Committee for Mental Hygiene, 1790 Broadway, New York. The Commission on Religion and Health of the Federal Council will give guidance to ministers at this point.
3. The Rohrschach test (and certain similar tests) differs from those personality tests (like the Bernreuter) which ask the person to answer such questions as "Do you ever cross the street to avoid meeting some one you know?" These latter tests sometimes suggest the "right" answers, often raise emotion during the answering of questions. Such tests as the Rohrschach can be administered only by experts. They involve the interpretation by the person of things which touch deeper areas of the personality and for which "right" answers are not the point. They are proving increasingly valuable in the hands of experts, but long and special training is required to prepare oneself to give them.
4. Almon R. Pepper in verbal communication.
5. See Agnes E. Benedict, *Children at the Crossroads,* N. Y., The Commonwealth Fund, 1930.
6. Information about guidance clinics in all localities may be secured from the Division of Community Clinics, National Committee for Mental Hygiene, 1790 Broadway, New York.
7. The U. S. Public Health Service publishes a valuable list of publications on health, including titles from all government agencies dealing with health.
8. *The Social Work Yearbook* is published by the Russell Sage Foundation, 122 East 22nd Street, New York. The Department of Research and Education of the Federal Council of Churches publishes an annual "Directory of National Social Agencies."

CHAPTER X

1. Richard C. Cabot, M.D., and Russell L. Dicks, *The Art of Ministering to the Sick,* N. Y., The Macmillan Co., 1936, pp. 12-13.
2. Otis R. Rice in verbal communication.

3. Cabot and Dicks, *op. cit.*, p. 178.
4. Walter B. Cannon, M.D., *The Wisdom of the Body*, N. Y., W. W. Norton, 1932, and John M. Fletcher, "The Wisdom of the Mind," *Sigma Xi Quarterly*.
5. Cabot and Dicks, *op. cit.*
6. Russell L. Dicks, *And Ye Visited Me*, N. Y., Harper and Bros., 1939.
7. Cabot and Dicks, *op. cit.*, pp. 61-62.
8. *Ibid.*, p. 215.
9. *Ibid.*, p. 218.
10. *Ibid.*, pp. 222-233. See also Russell L. Dicks, *Meditations for the Sick*, Willett Clark & Co., 1937.
11. For examples see Dicks and Cabot, *op. cit.*, pp. 236-241.
12. *Ibid.*, pp. 162-163.
13. *Ibid.*, p. 168.
14. *Ibid.*, p. 190.
15. *Ibid.*, p. 194.
16. *Ibid.*, p. 197.
17. *Ibid.*, p. 207.
18. *Ibid.*, p. 260.
19. *Ibid.*, pp. 283-328.
20. *Ibid.*, p. 162.
21. See Russell L. Dicks, *Who Is My Patient: A Religious Manual for Nurses*, N. Y., The Macmillan Co., 1941.
22. See Russell L. Dicks, *When You Call on the Sick*, N. Y., Harper and Bros., 1938.

CHAPTER XI

1. "Study of Religious Work in the Protestant Hospitals," American Protestant Hospital Association, 1941.
2. "Standards for the Work of the Chaplain in the General Hospital," American Protestant Hospital Association, 1940. Reprinted from *Hospitals*, November, 1940.
3. For information in reference to supervised clinical training, consult note 8 in chapter eight.
4. "Chaplains in Penal Institutions," *Information Service*, Federal Council of Churches, December 27, 1941.
5. "Standards for the Work of the Protestant Chaplain in the Penal Institution," *The Prison World*, June, 1940. By the Commission on Prison Chaplains, Federal Council of Churches.
6. For a description of the prison chaplain's functions, see "The Function of the Prison Chaplain," excerpted from the U. S. Prison Service Study Course, 1941, by the Commission on Prison Chaplains.

ACKNOWLEDGMENTS

Sincere thanks are due to the several persons who gave comments on the manuscript, in whole or in part. Their helpful suggestions and criticisms, in a considerable number of cases, resulted in changes greatly improving the manuscript. I am deeply grateful to them.

Roswell P. Barnes, Federal Council of Churches, New York

Smiley Blanton, M.D., Psychiatrist, Nashville

Harry Bone, Consulting Psychologist, New York

Russell L. Dicks, Highland Park Methodist Church, Dallas

Harrison S. Elliott, Union Theological Seminary, New York

John L. Fortson, Federal Council of Churches, New York

Charles T. Holman, The Divinity School, University of Chicago

Mrs. John Sherman Hoyt, Darien, Conn., Founder of the Commission on Religion and Health, Federal Council of Churches

Edward H. Hume, M.D., Director, Christian Medical Council for Overseas Work; and Vice-Chairman, Commission on Religion and Health

Milton E. Kirkpatrick, M.D., National Committee for Mental Hygiene, New York

Arthur Cushman McGiffert, Jr., Pacific School of Religion, Berkeley

John A. MacSporran, Clifton Springs Sanitarium, Clifton Springs, N. Y.

Rollo R. May, Author and Lecturer, New York

Marian McBee, New York City Committee for Mental Hygiene

John L. Mixon, Church Federation of Los Angeles

Norman Vincent Peale, Marble Collegiate Church, New York

Almon R. Pepper, National Council of the Protestant Episcopal Church, New York

J. Arnold Purdie, New York Protestant Episcopal City Mission Society

Otis R. Rice, St. Luke's Hospital, New York
Howard Chandler Robbins, Chairman, Commission on Religion and Health, New York
G. Canby Robinson, M.D., The Johns Hopkins Hospital, Baltimore
Frank J. Sladen, M.D., The Henry Ford Hospital, Detroit
John W. Suter, Jr., Church of the Epiphany, New York
J. J. Van Boskirk, University of Chicago
E. K. Wickman, The Commonwealth Fund, New York
Carroll A. Wise, Worcester State Hospital, Mass.

The author gratefully acknowledges the use of material cited from various works and indicated in the notes. Special acknowledgment for the use of quotations is due to the following.

Abingdon-Cokesbury Press, publishers of *Prayer* by George A. Buttrick.

Columbia University Press, publishers of *Emotions and Bodily Changes* by Flanders Dunbar.

The Commonwealth Fund, publishers of *The Patient as a Person* by G. Canby Robinson and *Teachers and Behavior Problems* by E. K. Wickman.

The John Day Company, publishers of *Doctor in Arabia* by Paul W. Harrison.

Harper and Brothers, publishers of *A History of the Expansion of Christianity* by K. S. Latourette, *How to Find Health through Prayer* by Glenn Clark, *Re-Thinking Missions* by the Laymen's Commission of Appraisal and edited by W. E. Hocking, and of *Harper's Magazine*.

Henry Holt and Company, publishers of *Out of My Life and Thought* by Albert Schweitzer.

Edward H. Hume, author of articles published in the Far East, from which quotations were used.

Milton E. Kirkpatrick, for verbal communications used.

Fritz Künkel, for communication used from personal letters.

The Macmillan Company, publishers of *The Art of Ministering to the Sick* by Richard C. Cabot and Russell L. Dicks, *The Spirit* edited by B. H. Streeter, and *Can Religious Education be Christian* by Harrison S. Elliott.

The Missionary Education Movement, publishers of *How Far to the Nearest Doctor* by E. M. Dodd.

The National Committee for Mental Hygiene, publishers of *Mental Hygiene* magazine. Permission was given to use paragraphs without quotation marks from an article by the author which appeared in *Mental Hygiene* in June, 1940.

W. W. Norton and Company, publishers of *Self-Analysis* by Karen Horney.

Otis R. Rice, for verbal communications used.

Charles Scribner's Sons and Company, publishers of *For the Healing of the Nations* by Henry P. Van Dusen.

Frank J. Sladen, for verbal communications used.

John W. Suter, Jr., author of "Prayer and Health" to be published by the Federal Council of Churches.

J. J. Van Boskirk and Charles T. Holman, authors of the unpublished study on attitudes of church school teachers.

The author wishes it were possible to express appreciation to all those who have played a special part in guiding his thought and work. Where guidance and help have been given so generously and by so many, that task is an impossibility. For personal influences lay the foundation of ideas and experiences which may emerge only much later. My list would therefore start, in love and gratitude, with my parents, Clement S. Hiltner and Charlotte Porter Hiltner. But in a more strictly professional sense, I want to express my sincere thanks to a few who have played an especially important part in the development and guidance of my interests in this field, as my teachers or counselors: Edwin E. Aubrey, Roswell P. Barnes, Donald C. Beatty, Anton T. Boisen, Harry Bone, Harold Leonard Bowman, Samuel McCrea Cavert, H. Paul Douglass, Lewis B. Hill, Charles T. Holman, Edward H. Hume, Arthur Cushman McGiffert, Jr., Otis R. Rice, Howard Chandler Robbins, Herbert W. Rogers, Norris L. Tibbetts, Henry P. Van Dusen, and Carroll A. Wise.

INDEX

Affirmations, and psychosomatics, 87; religious, 91; types of, 110f
Agriculture, Department of, as resource, 221
Alcoholics, Anonymous, 147
Alcoholism, 139
American Board of Commissioners for Foreign Missions, 46, 47
American Protestant Hospital Association, 254, 256, 265; religious work by, 255f
American Red Cross, as resource, 222
Anger, function of, 16, 77f. See also Emotion
Anxiety, 17, 71, 140ff
Asthma, 74

Balme, Harold, 55
Beers, Clifford, 3, 4
Behavior, healthy and unhealthy, 139ff
Behavior problems, church teachers' view of, 120f; desirable point of view of, 122ff; mental hygicnists' view of, 117f; teachers' view of, 116ff
Bernard, Claude, 59
Bibliographies, 197, 281
Blanton, Smiley, 81
Boisen, Anton T., 267, 268, 279
Bond, Earl D., 22
Bone, Harry, 279
Boy Scouts, 10, 206
"Bums," 146
Buttrick, George A., 23, 36

Cabot, Richard C., 227, 229, 235, 237, 238, 239, 241, 243, 249, 251
Calhoun, Robert L., 61

Cannon, Walter B., 68, 77, 235, 277
Carey, William, 46
Case, discussion of use of, 198, 249; method, explanation of use, 182f; worker adviser, 211
Chaplains, Army and Navy, 222f; denominational workers as, 260ff; in federal prisons, 266f; in mental hospitals, 267f; in Protestant hospitals, 254f; standards of work by, 257f; in state and city prisons, 266, training of, 258f. See also Religious worker
Chaplaincies, interdenominational problems of, 263ff; interfaith problems of, 262f. See also Chaplains
Character, meaning of, 10; strength of, 13f
Child, control of emotion by, 125; fundamental needs of, 124f; judgment of conduct of, 125f; religious education of, 126ff; welfare agencies, 212f
Christianity, see Religion, Spiritual resources, Worship, Prayer, Religious worker
Christian Medical Association of India, 42, 59
Christian Medical Council for Overseas Work, 58
Christian Science, reasons for rise of, 96f; future of, 97f
Church, administration and mental hygiene, 165; counseling in, 167ff; as fellowship, 34f; history of healing work by, 42ff; and hospitals, 253ff; and mental hygiene, 21, 165f; and mental illnesses, 133ff; religious edu-